W9-AFE-447
A12900 417784

Library of Shakespearean Biography and Criticism

I. PRIMARY REFERENCE WORKS ON SHAKESPEARE

II. CRITICISM AND INTERPRETATION

A. Textual Treatises, Commentaries

B. Treatment of Specal Subjects

C. Dramatic and Literary Art in Shakespeare

III. SHAKESPEARE AND HIS TIME

A. General Treatises. Biography

B. The Age of Shakespeare

C. Authorship

Library of Shakespearean Biography and Criticism

Series I

A SHAKESPEARE HANDBOOK

*Marshall's Copy of
The Droeshout Engraving*

Library of Shakespearean Biography and Criticism

A Shakespeare Handbook

By

RAYMOND MACDONALD ALDEN

Revised and enlarged by

OSCAR JAMES CAMPBELL

BOOKS FOR LIBRARIES PRESS
FREEPORT, NEW YORK

First Published 1932
Reprinted 1970

STANDARD BOOK NUMBER:
8369-5248-0

LIBRARY OF CONGRESS CATALOG CARD NUMBER:
75-109639

PRINTED IN THE UNITED STATES OF AMERICA

PREFACE

THE purpose of this book is to place in the hands of students of collegiate grade, and of other mature but not learned readers, the materials needed for the study of the principal works of Shakespeare, with the exception of interpretive notes on particular passages in the several plays. Just what degree of completeness or thoroughness should be attempted in such a manual, is a question which admits of no little difference of opinion. The editor can only say that his decisions have been based on his experience as teacher of college undergraduates, in classes where it was proposed, not to make Shakespeare a means to historical or linguistic learning, but to insist on the use of an amount of such learning sufficient to the understanding of Shakespeare's text. In order to limit the size of the book to the practical objects contemplated, the materials presented, so far as they concern particular plays, are confined to the nineteen dramas believed to be of chief interest to those for whom the handbook was made; namely: *A Midsummer Night's Dream*, *Romeo and Juliet*, *The Merchant of Venice*, *Richard the Second*, the two parts of *Henry the Fourth*, *Henry the Fifth*, *Much Ado about Nothing*, *As You Like It*, *Twelfth Night*, *Julius Caesar*, *Hamlet*, *Othello*, *King Lear*, *Macbeth*, *Antony and Cleopatra*, *Coriolanus*, *The Winter's Tale*, *The Tempest*.

Two divisions of this material perhaps call for some further remark. The first is the linguistic, represented by the grammatical and glossarial sections of the book. That Shakespeare did not write modern English, and that the language has changed greatly since his time, are troublesome facts which most of us (no doubt wisely) forget so far as possible, but which we have to confront when we come to make a serious effort to understand what he said. The cultivated English-speaking reader, especially if he is so fortunate as to know well his English Bible, makes his way through the Shakespeare text with a fair degree of facility, very much as a tourist possessed of the usual elementary school French makes his way among the sign-boards and newspapers of Paris, possessing himself of the gist of the thing, and passing lightly over many words and phrases, some of which he knows that he does not understand, others of which convey a meaning to him, but a wrong one. It is a cause for thankfulness that the general reader can do as much as this, and not find the Shakespeare text as forbidding as the greater lapse of years has rendered the text of Chaucer. But to the English student the very fact that the thing can be done with a fair degree of superficial ease is perplexing and misleading. At the other end of the series is the advanced student, the true scholar, who insists on knowing the language of the chief classic of his race as the competent scholar in French learns the French language; but such persons must remain few. There is surely a place for a third, an intermediate, group, representing an understanding of Elizabethan English comparable to that which is attempted in good college courses in French and German literature; it is recognized that time forbids a really scientific knowledge of the language in question, but that it is possible to learn to read it with a fair degree of rapidity and at the same time with an accurate understanding of what the author meant to say. This is what the present writer attempts with students of Shakespeare who go beyond the general elementary course in the rapid reading of a large number of the plays, and who, by taking a somewhat more advanced course in the subject, raise the presumption that they really wish to know how to read the Shakespeare text not only with the spirit but with the understanding. It is for such students, whether in college or out of it, that the linguistic materials in the present handbook reduced, as they are, to very modest proportions, are designed. To speak more particularly of the glossary, it is planned to include only those words which should be mastered by one who intends to go on reading Shakespeare, prepared to recognize the principal peculiarities of his vocabulary, as distinguished from those words which occur only once, twice, or occasionally, and will ordinarily be learned only in connection with the particular passages in which they stand.

The other section which calls for some remark is that to which by far the greater portion of the book has been devoted, the source material of the principal plays. There are those to whom the study of such material seems a matter of dry-as-dust learning, fit only for the scholar whose conscience imposes it upon his task. And we should all, no doubt, admit, that for the very young or very elementary student of Shakespeare it is only the absolute values, so to say, which should be emphasized: the child may freely enjoy *The Merchant of Venice* on the supposition that Shakespeare wrote the story for the first time, and when he is a little older his first enjoyment of *Hamlet* should not be confused by the consideration of the fact that it is not the original version of the play. But when he comes to a more mature and serious attitude, the intelligent reading of either of the plays mentioned is utterly impossible, unless with reference to their historic relations to the materials of earlier romance. Indeed, when we have once become aware of the method which Shakespeare usually followed in the making of a play, — creating atmosphere and characters to fit a tale already taken freely from outside his own mind or experience, — we realize that almost every question which is raised by the more intensive examination of the drama is to be answered first of all (not necessarily with finality) by a consideration of the sources. And as for dryness! if there be any more fascinating process of literary study than that which enables us to see Shakespeare at work in the transformation of his materials, noting precisely what he rejected, what he retained unchanged, and what he altered to serve his fresh purposes, one hesitates to say what it is. But for the student who is devoting a comparatively modest amount of time and energy to the subject, the process is difficult; the materials are sometimes bulky, not within easy reach, and in indigestible form. In consequence, he commonly takes the word of his editor for it, that Shakespeare followed Holinshed, Plutarch, or Lodge, in the play under consideration, "but transformed the comparatively crude materials of the original by his own incomparable genius," — etc., etc.; he will glibly repeat these allegations, if you question him, usually with no knowledge, in the least degree adequate to the occasion, of the real character of Shakespeare's source or the changes with which he made use of it. It is for just this reason, then, that so large a space has been devoted to the source materials included in this handbook. In some cases (perhaps, indeed, in most cases) they remain inadequate to a full understanding of the dramatist's art; but it is hoped that, so far as they go, they may enable the reader of any of the plays concerned, without the expenditure of an unreasonable amount of time or energy, to see what it was that Shakespeare was about. In the experience of the editor, even a moderate degree of such knowledge has exercised a positively transfiguring power upon the student's understanding of the play.

It remains only to acknowledge indebtedness to certain works, aside from the standard authorities so obviously drawn upon, which have proved particularly useful in the making of this book: the introductions to the several plays in Dr. Neilson's Cambridge Edition of Shakespeare; the First Part of Professor A. H. Tolman's handbooks called *Questions on Shakespeare;* and Neilson and Thorndike's *The Facts about Shakespeare.* For the text of Plutarch's *Lives,* that in *Shakespeare's Plutarch,* edited by Tucker Brooke (1909) has been followed; the Holinshed text is taken from the original (edition of 1587). All quotations from Shakespeare follow the text and line numbering of Neilson's edition.

R. M. A.

PREFACE TO REVISED EDITION

THE revision of Professor Alden's *Shakespeare Handbook* has been undertaken in order to add chapters on certain subjects now considered essential to such a volume and to incorporate some of the important results of recent scholarship into his admirable chapters. The bibliography also has been brought up to date. The distinguishing feature of the original work was the publication of the most significant material from the most important of the sources of the plays. These passages remain invaluable for the still popular genetic study of Shakespeare's work. The source material is of slight importance to the young student if he is allowed to regard it as a kind of isolated historical curiosity. He should rather be encouraged to see in it the original incentive to the imaginative transformations which can be discovered in the finished dramas. Such a study does not explain the inscrutable ways of genius, but it does illuminate them. The new material in this revised edition is designed to throw further light on Shakespeare's work as an Elizabethan playwright by presenting those facts of his age and those conditions prevailing in the theatre and in the drama that were responsible for certain distinctive features of his work.

To the original acknowledgment of indebtedness I must add my own sense of deep obligation to the great works of Sir Edmund K. Chambers, *The Elizabethan Drama* and *William Shakespeare*.

O. J. C.

Ann Arbor, Mich.

CONTENTS

Contents

INTRODUCTORY NOTE

THE manuscript of this book was all but complete when the illness, which was to bring to him so untimely a death, overtook the late author; and it has therefore been left to his friends to see his book through the press, carrying out as nearly as possible his plans for it. In designing *A Shakespeare Handbook,* Dr. Alden had clearly in mind a collection into convenient form of that general and accepted material and information concerning the great dramatist which should be in the hands of everyone as a necessary preliminary to the understanding of Shakespeare and his work. For this purpose is included a summary of the known facts of Shakespeare's life, the canon of his plays and their chronology, that the student may have before him the extent of his authorship and the order of the plays, so far as possible, in their probable writing. The book concludes with an epitome of Elizabethan grammar, a brief account of the versification of the time, a bibliography for general guidance and a glossary of the more usual words employed in the more important plays which are given specific consideration in this volume. A feature, which can not, I venture to think, but commend itself to both teacher and student, is the reprinting at some length of the actual source material of several of the most important of Shakespeare's plays. It is not that this material might not be sought and found in libraries, but that there is an obvious advantage in having it so easily accessible that the student may see for himself, by minute and accurate comparison, how closely and honestly the great dramatist followed his immediate models and learn that his originality lies in things more deep and subtle than the invention of a story or even the initial conception of a personage. Dr. Alden in modest appreciation of his task in collecting and ordering material generally known and accepted, has called himself editor, not author. But it might be a nice question to determine — were this the place for it — to what degree the creative impulse enters into the arrangement of anything into an orderly and useful integrity.

Of our late friend Professor Raymond MacDonald Alden, it is difficult for those of us who knew him to speak calmly even now, though months have passed to lighten our grief since he left us. The writer of this prefatory note first knew him in 1892, when he entered one of the upper classes in the College of the University of Pennsylvania. Young Alden came to us from the south, from Rollins College, Florida, and Columbian, now George Washington, University, Washington, a tall, handsome, rosy-cheeked boy, of winning and almost diffident manner, and he made his way in our regard, in our affections, from the first. It is always a difficult matter to migrate from one college to another. The surroundings are different and the associations all to make over again. It is creditable to maintain standing, in such an experiment, in a new curriculum and under strange conditions. Young Alden not only maintained an excellent standing from the first, but in his new classes was soon pushing the best of his classmates for leadership. "Pushing" hardly seems the right word; for seldom have I known a young man who was less aggressive, more truly gentle, more prone in all that he did to be found ready than to the display of readiness. Singularly gentle indeed was Alden, quiet, even somewhat deliberate of speech, not because he was not quick of wit but because the conscientiousness which was at the basis of his serious nature stood aloof from the mere banter of idle words. I shall give a false impression if I convey that Alden was in any wise Puritanic or superior, much less dull or slow; it was simply that his direct and capable mind brushed aside the irrelevancies, with which we are many of us accustomed to fringe and fritter away our conversation, and kept forthright to the topic in hand. It was this that made him the splendid scholar he soon became: conscientiousness, directness, swiftness of thought, deliberation in speech.

At graduation, Alden was at the head of his class. I do not remember whether it was the salutatory or the valedictory that was his; but I do recall that it stood out as a very remarkable address for so young a man to make, and that there was pride that he was among us. Alden left us for Harvard where he advanced to an M.A. and assisted for a time in the Department of English. But he returned to a fellowship at Pennsylvania, taking his degree of Doctor of Philosophy in the Graduate School in 1898. It was my privilege to advise him as to his thesis, *The Rise of Formal Satire in England,* 1899; and I recall how easily, how independently and thoroughly he accomplished that piece of scholarly research. In it are discoverable already the distinguishing qualities of Alden's scholarship, its completeness, its clarity, its freedom from bias and its directness. Of course, we wanted such a young man in the Department of English, for he was after our own hearts. Alden became an instructor with us, and left only to accept an assistant Professorship of English in Leland Stanford University, California, where he remained, except for a short period, 1911–1914, as Professor in the University of Illinois, Professor of English Literature up to the time of his death. Alden was for all too short a time a teacher among us, and I recall my pang at having to let him go, knowing as I did, how soon his promise was sure to reach fulfillment.

The scholarly and literary work of Raymond MacDonald Alden comprises many subjects and is varied in kind. He began authorship with a sensible little book on *The Art of Debate*, in which he was no little skilled himself, having acquitted himself admirably in student debating. And he proceeded to clarify the difficult subject of *English Verse*, in an equally clear and well written book. Meanwhile at Leland Stanford his interest in Elizabethan drama had staged successfully by his students *The Knight of the Burning Pestle* and begotten a suggestive little pamphlet *On Seeing an Elizabethan Play*. Alden was always a fervent lover of poetry, and in 1909 appeared his *Introduction to Poetry*, once more a tried subject seen anew and freshly to the clarification of our knowledge of it. Nor did he leave untried original authorship in which, could the busy life of a college professor have allowed it, he might have achieved a high place in prose and verse as well. To one who would know the ripeness of Alden's scholarship I should advise the two, each in its kind, most readable volumes, *Tennyson, How to Know Him* and the *Shakespeare*, and especially his Variorum edition of the *Sonnets of Shakespeare*, a work of great difficulty in the accomplishment and an enduring monument to his judgment, his industry and his restraint. Alden's later scholarship was falling more and more within the powerful orbit of Shakespeare. In the guidance of such a scholar as he whom we have lost was always certainty of foothold, the sustaining grasp of a firm but a human hand, an outlook over broad landscape.

As one who still moves onward in the path that stretches from sun to sun, it seems strange, untoward, desolating, to think of this choice scholar, this true man, this beloved friend and brother, as having " gone home and ta'en his wages." When promise unfulfilled dies, our imagination can work to the creation of almost a consolation in a sad romantic story. When those, who have reaped and garnered full harvests, leave us, it is as a good book, read and closed with acquiescence that all is completed. It is when the harvester, full in the swing of his scythe, waist high in his golden treasure, is reaped by a mightier harvester than he, that we stand perplexed and abashed.

I have touched upon but some of the many activities of Raymond MacDonald Alden, those which I happen as one of his teachers, to have known best. His other activities were many, those of the Drama League of America for example, of which he was Director for many years, and those in societies such as The Modern Language Association of America, the American Philological Society and the like. His counsel was ever wise and his services ungrudging. Capable of an extraordinary amount of work himself, largely because of the orderly way in which he did it, he was considerate of less strength than his own and governed by a reasonableness of spirit, willing to weigh things in which he knew he could not concur. In the death of Raymond MacDonald Alden the scholarly world has lost a scholar of commanding rank, and we who knew and loved him, a man whose like we shall not hope to look upon again.

FELIX E. SCHELLING

ENGLAND IN SHAKESPEARE'S DAY

THE reign of Queen Elizabeth (1558–1603) was one of the most glorious in all English history. The Civil Wars of the Roses had been forgotten and the devastation which they had caused fully repaired. The House of Tudor was firmly established upon the throne. Its monarchs had given up the old ambition to make England a Continental power. Instead they had turned their attention to consolidating their kingdom at home, to achieving national unity and to awakening patriotic spirit. In 1588 the fleet of England routed and destroyed the great Spanish Armada. This victory awakened in the country a vigorous new nationalism. Englishmen suddenly realized that Spain, the political giant of the sixteenth century, was not invincible and that their country had become a great world power. The subsequent peace ushered in a period of enormous commercial expansion and economic prosperity.

The Italian Renaissance, the result of the recovery of the literature of Greece and Rome and the reawakening of its spirit, had exerted some influence in England as early as the reign of Henry the Seventh (1485–1509), but only after the accession of Elizabeth did it there come to full flower. Its first and most important effect was to give the individual a sense of emancipation. During the Middle Ages he had regarded himself as a unit in the feudal system or as a member of a trade-guild. Now these social bonds were loosened and opportunities for individual experience seemed unlimited. Therefore his ambitions and aspirations soared accordingly. England had at last become definitely a Protestant country, but the national church, being a compromise, did not seriously complicate thought or hamper action. It was in the secular world that the Elizabethan sought his achievements, to be won largely by his individual efforts. The chances for the self-made man were greater in Shakespeare's England than they have been in any subsequent time, except the era of the Industrial Revolution of the nineteenth century.

The boundaries of the world had also become greatly extended. On the Thames at Deptford, just below London, lay *The Golden Hind,* the ship in which Sir Francis Drake had recently circumnavigated the globe. It was regarded as one of the chief sights of the city, a resort to which people went on holidays to eat and drink. The exploits of daring sea-rovers, particularly as read in *The Voyages* of Richard Hakluyt (1582, 1587, 1589) furnished familiar matter for wonder and patriotic admiration. Before Shakespeare's death the first English colony was established in America and England's thoughts became imperial. The exhilaration produced by all these events expressed itself most naturally in poetry. In drama only the vulgar and the comic events of life were expressed in prose. Even histories like Daniel's *Civil Wars between Lancaster and York* (1595, 1599, 1609) and Drayton's *Polyolbion* (1617), a description or a kind of guide-book to England, were written in verse.

Of this national unity and glory, Queen Elizabeth became the symbol and the emotional center. She is now too often regarded as having been merely a vain woman with an insatiable appetite for adulation that often became ridiculous. We know that she affected youth and beauty long after both had departed and expected her courtiers to pay on all occasions exaggerated tribute to these vanished charms. She frequently chose her political favorites from among the gentlemen at her court with the most obvious personal attractions and the greatest skill in flattery. Two of the most famous were the Earl of Leicester and the Earl of Essex, to the latter of whom she became devoted in the last years of her life, with tragic results for him.

Such a picture of the Queen ignores the sources of her power and their significance for the nation. She did sincerely love her people and used all the resources of her keen mind to promote their welfare. Whatever were the actual reasons for her never marrying, she made her subjects believe that she remained celibate so that she might devote all of her energy to their government. Sir Walter Raleigh wrote of her, " She led a life of unbroken loneliness in the single-minded pursuit of her duty to her people." She encouraged them to make a kind of religion of her virginity. This announced consecration to their interests inspired in them an ardent, unquestioning devotion. They apparently realized that the supreme political need of the country was a sovereign strong enough to destroy forces of anarchy at home and to resist foreign aggression. The most famous of the stories illustrating the idolatry of Englishmen for their Queen is that told of the Puritan John Stubbs. For writing a book against a proposed marriage of Elizabeth with the French Duke of Alençon, he was sentenced to have his right hand cut off. The cruel sentence was executed, but the moment the offending member was severed, Stubbs seized his hat in his left hand, and waving it above his head, shouted, " God save the Queen."

Elizabeth loved all forms of magnificence and display. She delighted in travelling about England with a huge retinue, stopping to visit at the country houses of her noblemen, who feasted her, fêted her and provided lavish entertainment to occupy almost every hour of the time spent at a castle, — occasionally as long as three weeks. These " Progresses " gave her great pleasure. She loved to be the center of gorgeous ceremonials; she basked in these magnificent evidences of her popularity. Pageantry of all sorts delighted her, as did the drama. She often ordered her Master of Revels to summon a company of actors to present at Court such plays in their repertory as this officer of her household thought suitable.

The Queen was also a woman of many intellectual accomplishments. She could make speeches in Greek and Latin, or carry on an extended conversation in Italian with Scaramelli, the Venetian ambassador; yet she had not so fully overlaid her bluff English nature with Italian culture as to keep her from eager enjoyment of so savage a sport as bear-baiting. She would often have the animals brought to Whitehall so that she and her ladies in waiting could witness the sport from a balcony. She was capable of giving her temper full sway to the point of fetching an offending waiting-woman a blow in the face. On occasions she indulged in coarse jokes and in good, round, mouth-filling oaths. Underneath her Renaissance magnificence and intellectual subtlety lay an only partially concealed substratum of plain, primitive feeling. Of these two elements most Englishmen of Shakespeare's day were compounded.

England in Elizabeth's reign was still largely an agricultural country, supporting not more than five million inhabitants. The growing of crops was still the principal industry, but it was yielding in importance to cattle-raising. The roads were poor and in remote places, instead of being fifty feet wide as the law required, had become mere tracks not more than twelve feet wide. Travellers commonly rode horseback, and if they needed to make speed, "rode post." That is, at intervals of ten miles along the roads frequented by the Queen's couriers were inns at which government horses could be procured by one who had influence to obtain the necessary authority. Poor men, such as scholars and laborers, walked. Many of the companies of actors, when touring the provinces, packed their properties in a wagon or on pack-horses and themselves trudged behind on foot. Carts, lumbering two-wheeled vehicles, were gradually superseding the pack-horse. Coaches, first introduced into England in 1564 by a Dutchman, became the desired conveyances for ladies and gentlemen. They were designed more for ostentation than for comfort. They were drawn by four or six horses and the sides were open, exposing the travellers to the eyes of the curious and envious. But they were not provided with springs or even with leather straps upon which to swing the coach body. Only cushions protected the afflicted passenger from the terrible jolting, inevitable even on the highways. The roads were also infested with highwaymen; it was estimated that there were ten thousand outlaws in the kingdom. Certain places not far from London, such as the famous Gadshill or Shooters Hill on Blackheath, were as notorious and terrifying as the most remote and deserted stretches of road.

Though the forests were being rapidly cut down, the houses continued to be built of timbers. But during the last years of the sixteenth century, England was rapidly transformed from an agrarian civilization to a commercial and industrial one. Manufactures were developed and foreign trade was enormously extended. Wealth grew apace and the dwellings began to show greater convenience and comfort. Chimneys first came into general use, so that the family, as it sat in the hall, was no longer stifled by the smoke wandering about in its search for egress through a hole in the roof. The walls were hung with painted cloths, tapestry or even paintings. Newly invented second stories were reached by fine broad stairways. Glass began to be used in windows, which were no longer mere narrow slits in the wall from which defending archers could shoot. They were broad surfaces for the admission of light and air into the house. The simple rushes spread upon the floor made way for carpets. Straw pallets covered only with a sheet and a good round log on which to lay the head were replaced by beds and pillows. Wooden spoons and trenchers disappeared and pewter and silver implements took their place. Finally, the Elizabethan gentleman somewhat reluctantly gave up the homely privilege of conveying his meat to his mouth in his hand and adopted the new-fangled fork imported from Italy.

The new prosperity showed itself in other ways. Dress became elaborate and ornate. Large sums of money were spent on silk-embroidered waistcoats, on garters and rosettes for shoes, which were themselves made of various colored leather, often embroidered with gold and silver. The gallant's hats were splendid creations of silk, velvet and taffeta, and often ornamented with great bunches of feathers. Ruffs began their flamboyant career as simple linen collars worn round the neck. They became gradually larger and larger and more and more weighted with pleats and embroidery, until after the introduction of the use of starch into England, the ruffs were made to stand erect and to floriate until they became a foot deep. Then as Sir Walter Raleigh says, " A man's head looked like a head on a platter."

Food and drink were lavishly provided by the gentry. Dinner in the country was served at eleven o'clock, and the diners often sat at the table until two or three in the afternoon. The principal article of diet, except in the winter, was fresh meat. The tables groaned with huge platters of beef, mutton, lamb, veal, pork, and every kind of fowl, both wild and domestic. The Elizabethan had no means of preserving his meat, so that during the winter he lived on salt meat and salt herring, supplemented, on occasion, by fresh fish, venison, and poultry. Vegetables were used largely only to garnish the meats. Potatoes were as yet a rarity and usually served as a kind of pickle. In the home of the humble, bread was the staple of diet and was more often made of barley and rye than of wheat.

The amount of half-spoiled or salt meat which the contemporary of Shakespeare consumed made liberal drinking with his meals a necessity. Over one hundred varieties of wine could be purchased in Elizabethan England, and sometimes between forty and fifty were served at the great Corporation banquets in London. The favorite drink of many besides Sir John Falstaff was sack, a sweet wine which came from Spain or the Canary Islands. It was served in a cup nearly half-filled with sugar. The popular drink with the people was ale brewed from malt. This brewing was as common a domestic occupation as the baking of bread. Even for a small household, the good wife might brew as much as two hundred gallons of ale a year. Tea and coffee being yet unknown in England, ale was served even at breakfast, and given to young children instead of water and milk, both of which drinks were very sparingly consumed. Drunkenness, however, was frowned upon and regarded as a swinish characteristic of Dutchmen or Danes. Whiskey was drunk in Scotland and brandy on the Continent, but neither of these distilled drinks was commonly used in England. Drink in Shakespeare's day was dedicated to mirth only.

Elizabethan England expressed its merry spirit in other ways than in its delight in consuming food and drink. The games and pastimes of the people, though often betraying the brutality and naïvete of vigorous boys, were the various expression of an irrepressible joy in living. The feasts, festivals, and folk-celebrations were innumerable. These, as well as the more solemn occasions of funerals or weddings, were accompanied by loud and incessant ringing of the bells of the village church. Often two or three lusty fellows would keep the bell jangling for hours at a time for no other reason than to indulge their taste for joyous noise. Bonfires were built on all occasions and sometimes the amazing new fireworks were shot off on the village green. Dancing took place there nearly every Sunday in fine weather. The dances of the folk were gay and vigorous. The favorites were violent dances such as jigs, horn-pipes, the " hay " or reel and the popular Morris. At Court, naturally, the steps were more stately and decorous, but the gaillard, so popular with Queen Elizabeth in her youth, was full of capers. It ended with two or three mighty springs into the air, such as Sir Toby Belch urged the foolish Sir Andrew Aguecheek to practice. Every gentleman was supposed to dance, to sing well enough to bear his part in a song, to play it at sight on the viol, and to play also upon the lute. Indeed, musical ability was so widespread that lutes were supplied in barber-shops, with which the customer could while away the time until his turn came. Most noblemen maintained in their houses some musicians to teach this essential art of a gentleman. Judging by the numerous accurate references to music in Shakespeare's works, we may say that he himself possessed some technical knowledge of the art.

The brutal amusements of cock-fighting, bull-baiting, and bear-baiting were popular with all classes of people. The first of the three was least in favor and the cockpits were resorts of the rabble. Bear-baiting, on the other hand, had a kind of official sanction. Almost every village owned its local bear, often a deeply scarred hero of many contests. On the day set for the sport, he was led to a ring, around which were benches for the spectators of local importance. In the center the bear was fastened by a rope long enough to give him plenty of freedom of action. Then four or five short-nosed mastiffs were turned into the enclosure. They soon sprang to the attack and created a great uproar of snarling, growling, and howling as the pack rolled with the bear in a bloody mass. At the end of the first round, the beast usually emerged covered with blood and saliva, but having squeezed the life out of some of his attackers and brought others near to death by blows from his paw. Then fresh dogs were turned in and the attacks continued until the bear was so near complete exhaustion that another onslaught might have been fatal to him. From bull-baiting, the spectators could derive the unusual thrills of seeing the dogs trampled to death or tossed high into the air on the horns of the infuriated beast. Other sports like hunting of the deer or hare with packs of dogs, selected partly for the musical harmony of their voices, or hawking, in which tame hawks brought down large birds from the upper air at the feet of their keepers, were less deliberately cruel.

Some of the manly sports were brutal and dangerous. Duelling with the newly introduced rapier and dagger was no sport for the inexpert. Wrestling was very violent in Elizabethan times, controlled as it was by no rules, and often led to fatal results, — witness the wrestling match with which *As You Like It* begins. Indeed if the fallen contestant refused to yield, his victorious opponent might jump upon his chest and crush in his ribs. Bowling was universally admired. Every gentleman's house possessed a bowling green and public alleys were maintained by most villages. Tennis was a fashionable game played upon covered courts. The ball was driven not over a net, but over a taut rope with a racket or sometimes with the bare hand. Contestants were not limited to two or four, but sometimes as many as five played on one side of the net. In winter chess, draughts (checkers), and tables (backgammon) were popular diversions, and cards and dice maintained their usual popularity with persons who craved the excitement of gambling. Everywhere the new custom of taking the smoke of tobacco, introduced into England in 1565 by Sir John Hawkins, gained popularity. Its devotees believed that when drawn into the nose or the stomach, it had excellent medicinable properties. Even the women began to smoke their pipes around the family hearth, and in London pipes and tobacco could be obtained in many inns and apothecary shops.

To London, the center of English life as never before, we must now turn. At the close of the sixteenth century it was a city of 200,000 inhabitants, nearly half of whom had overflowed into the suburbs beyond the gates. It possessed in the Tower, the citadel which always guarded the mediæval city and in old St. Paul's, the cathedral which dominated its religious and intellectual life. In Shakespeare's day this church had become a kind of club, the fashionable resort and market of London. The middle aisle was the gathering place of gallants, who went there to exhibit their elegance, to display their wit, and to learn the latest news and gossip. To the church also apprentices went in search of masters. Merchants offered many kinds of commodities for sale, such as ale, beer, fish, bread, and other foods. The tombs and even the baptismal font had been converted into counters, over which the money of the traders was paid. St. Paul's Churchyard, surrounded by a high wall, was the center of the book-trade of the City. No more striking proof of the pagan and commercial spirit of Elizabethan London can be imagined than this desecration of a mediæval cathedral.

The city proper lay on the north side of the Thames and formed within its walls a parallelogram about two miles long and half a mile wide. The river itself was the central highway of the place. Westward along its bank the great palaces stretched to the separate city of Westminster. These houses were all provided with stairs which led down to boat-landings. The Queen, the Lord-Mayor, the Archbishop, and other dignitaries possessed magnificent official barges. Innumerable small boats were offered for hire at the foot of the various public stairs, and their owners, the watermen, made an hubbub with their incessant cries of "Westward Ho," or "Eastward Ho." London Bridge, which spanned the river, was one of the wonders of the city. Over it one crossed to the town of Southwark and the Bankside, where some of the most famous Elizabethan theatres were situated, and thence to the great highway leading to the south and the sea coast.

The water used in the city came from the river, and was either fetched by hand or brought by conduits to numerous public spouts. From these, water-bearers, called "cobs," drew off the water into large wooden tankards, each holding about three gallons, and peddled it about town. The sewers of the city were open and, sanitation of all sorts was exceedingly primitive.

Within the walls, the religious houses, dismantled in the reign of Henry the Eighth, still occupied large areas of land. Some of these had become ruins and had been cleared away; some had been transformed into palaces of courtiers; some had been made into schools; Old Greyfriars, for example, had become Christ's Hospital School; and two of the old monasteries, Blackfriars and Whitefriars, eventually were converted into theatres.

The streets of the city were generally narrow, crooked, and filthy. They were lined with open shops from which the shopkeepers shouted incessantly, "What do you lack?" The streets echoed with other noises,—the musical cries of hawkers, the songs of ballad-mongers, the beating of the clappers in the hands of beggars, and the rattling of coaches. These new coaches had become a necessity to those who wished to protect their gorgeous clothes from the foulness of the streets, and increased so rapidly that in 1601 a law was passed limiting their use. Beyond the walls were meadows and green fields, which served as public parks. The immediate suburbs, however, possessed an unenviable reputation. There were congregated the houses of ill-fame and other low resorts.

Crime was rampant in this city, the new commercial prosperity of which had attracted to it not only every sort of pleasure-seeker and adventurer, but also rogues, sharpers, and thieves to prey upon them. The number of felonies for which death was the penalty was very large. The chief place of execution was Tyburn, and there were six prisons in London, to say nothing of those across the river in Southwark. The typical Londoner was habitually dirty and used scents more commonly than soap and water. Instead of frequently changing the rushes on the floor of the rooms of his house and clearing away the rubbish, he was apt to perfume them with vinegar, juniper or rosemary, odors which were considered disinfectant as well as grateful to the nostrils. No wonder that disease ran rampant in the midst of this filth. The plague was endemic in the city and broke out with unusual violence in the years 1593 and 1603. During the first of these attacks, 15,000 persons died in London and its suburbs. Smallpox took an almost equally large toll. Medical treatment was crude and frequently involved with superstition. For example, a favorite remedy for the first symptom of the plague, the appearance of swellings or carbuncles on the body, was the application of a newly-killed fowl from which all the tail-feathers had been carefully removed. Bleeding was a sovereign prescription for every ailment, and the first ministration of a doctor was to open one of his patients' veins and drain him of some supposedly superfluous blood.

The presence of the Court so near to the city exerted a strong influence on the life and thoughts of the people. The courtiers themselves, their retainers and hangers-on formed a large part of the population. The absolutism of the Queen was resisted by the government of the city in the hands of the trade-guilds. On no subject were there more clashes between the Court and the Corporation than on the questions of plays, actors, and theatres. The city objected to the stage, not so much on strict moral grounds, as for reasons of public safety. The Corporation believed that the plague was spread by the nondescript crowds who gathered to see the plays, that the theatres, being huge wooden structures, formed a dangerous fire hazard, and that the crowds gathered by the play might be easily led to riot and sedition. To avoid these objections, the theatres were commonly built outside the jurisdiction of the city. However, it was only the interest and protection of the Court and the Queen's repeated employment of the actors to entertain her that prevented measures so severe as to threaten the Elizabethan drama with extinction.

It may seem strange that some of the very greatest works of English literature should have come from a civilization as turbulent, as extravagant, and as brutal as the description above has suggested. But with the stir of this life went an unequalled boldness and eagerness of spirit. The range of the Elizabethan mind was so great that it had room for tastes which seem to us incompatible. Along with delight in bloodshed, violence, and horror, went a ranging intellectual curiosity, generous idealism, and an eager and discriminating response to beauty in all its forms. These were the intellectual ingredients of the Italian Renaissance of a hundred years before, a movement which flared into a brief and glorious second life in the England and London of Queen Elizabeth's day. Whatever Shakespeare's personal tastes and prejudices were, his imagination was fired by almost every phase of the varied and contradictory life of this English Renaissance, and he translated it into enduring beauty and splendor.

LIFE OF SHAKESPEARE

WILLIAM SHAKESPEARE was born at Stratford-on-Avon, Warwickshire, in April 1564 (baptized April 26th), the son of John and Mary Arden Shakespeare. His father was a well-known merchant of the town, — seemingly a glover or tanner, and dealer in skins and wool, — who at various times won local honors in the offices of burgess, constable, chamberlain, alderman, and bailiff. Presumably the boy attended the free "grammar school" of Stratford, where the course of study was based primarily on the Latin language and literature; generally speaking, in such schools of the period, the curriculum included readings in Sallust, Cicero, Terence, Ovid, Horace, and Virgil. There is a tradition that William Shakespeare was withdrawn from school when comparatively young, because of his father's impaired financial condition, and this may be thought to be supported by evidence that, about 1577 and in the years following, John Shakespeare was in pecuniary difficulties.

On November 28, 1582, Shakespeare was licensed to marry Anne Hathaway of Shottery, a neighboring hamlet. A daughter, Susanna, was born in the following May, and twins, Hamnet and Judith, in February 1585. Beyond this we know almost nothing of the family history, save that the boy Hamnet died in 1596, while the daughters married and (with their mother) survived the poet. There have been many conjectures of unhappiness in Shakespeare's relations with his wife, but they are entirely unsupported by known facts.

It is not known when Shakespeare left Stratford or came to London. The popular tradition that he was driven from home because of a poaching episode on the estate of Sir Thomas Lucy is no longer given much credence. Nor is the theory generally accepted that he joined Lord Leicester's company in a humble capacity when it played in Stratford in 1587 and accompanied it to London. Informed opinion now leans toward the belief that Shakespeare, in his early years, was, as one of the best traditions asserts, a schoolmaster in the country. It is generally assumed that Shakespeare came to London about 1586 or 1587 and soon attached himself to the theatre, perhaps as assistant to the book-keeper or prompter. His first plays may have been written even before he left the country.

Our first apparent glimpse of him as a well known figure in dramatic circles occurs in a scurrilous pamphlet written by Robert Greene, a young satirist and dramatist, which was published after Greene's death in the autumn of 1592. It contained a warning to three of his fellow dramatists, all, like himself, University men, to give up the trade of play-making, because, he said, certain actors, "puppets that speak from our mouths," have themselves become dramatists. He warns his friends in particular against "an upstart crow beautified with our feathers" who "supposes he is as well able to bumbast out a blank verse as the best of you and being an absolute Johannes Factotum (*i.e.*, Jack of all trades, — actor, dramatist and reviser of old plays) is in his own conceit the only Shake-scene in a country." This is commonly believed to refer to Shakespeare and to indicate that in 1592 he was chosen as the most successful of the new actor-playwrights to point Greene's moral.

Shortly afterward the publisher apologized for the unfriendly pamphlet, so far as it had offended " one or two " of the persons referred to. " With neither of them that take offence was I acquainted, and with one of them I care not if I never be. The other, whom at that time I did not so much spare as since I wish I had; . . . that I did not, I am as sorry as if the original fault had been my fault, because myself have seen his demeanour no less civil than he excellent in the quality [*i.e.,* profession] he professes. Besides, divers of worship [*i.e.,* persons of honour] have reported his uprightness of dealing, which argues his honesty, and his facetious grace in writing, that approves his art." Again, though without certain evidence, it is generally thought that this acquaintance to whom the publisher Chettle made such handsome amends can be none other than Shakespeare.

From June 1592 for almost two years, with only a brief interval during January 1592–1593, the theatres were closed because of a serious epidemic of the plague in London. The companies of actors were compelled to travel in the provinces with a reduced personnel. Shakespeare apparently resigned from his company for this interval and became an unattached playwright. This freedom from acting gave him a chance to develop his ambitions in more reputable forms of literature than the drama. At any rate, he issued, in 1593, *Venus and Adonis,* an amorous narrative poem in the rich decorated style then popular. Shakespeare called it " the first heir of my invention," meaning by the phrase that he regarded it as the first work of his that was intended for publication. It seems to have met instant success and enjoyed wide popularity. In the university play, *The Return from Parnassus,* one of the students of Cambridge University exclaims, "Let this duncified world esteem of Spenser and Chaucer, I'll worship sweet Master Shakespeare, and to honor him will lay his *Venus and Adonis* under my pillow." This poem was followed, in 1594, by *The Rape of Lucrece,* a poem in honor of chastity. The success of this more sober and moral work was equally great. Gabriel Harvey, the Cambridge scholar, wrote, "The younger sort take much delight in Shakespeare's *Venus and Adonis,* but his *Lucrece*" has qualities "to please the wiser sort." Each of these poems was dedicated to Henry Wriothesley, the Earl of Southampton. For such dedications a patron was supposed to pay handsomely. There is a tradition that Shakespeare received "many great and uncommon marks of favor from Southampton"; and Davenant, the playwright, asserted that the Earl "at one time gave him a thousand pounds to enable him to go through with a purchase he had a mind to." The dedication to *Lucrece* bears evidence that an intimate relationship had been established between the two by 1594. How long this patronage and friendship lasted we do not know. Many critics believe that Sonnet 107 was written to celebrate Southampton's release from prison in 1603, when James I came to the throne.

During these plague years, 1592–1594, Shakespeare also began to write his sonnet sequence. He did not have his sonnets printed; such poems were regarded as too intimate for indiscriminate publicity. Instead, he followed the custom of circulating them in manuscript among his friends. They were not published until 1609 and then probably without his knowledge and consent. Their originality is to be found in the drama which Shakespeare makes them reveal. The first 125 sonnets are addressed to his friend, a man; the 126th is not a sonnet, but an envoy or formal conclusion to this first group. Sonnets 127 to 152 are addressed to a dark lady, the poet's mistress, who has tempted his friend and, by inducing him to yield to her, made him false to friendship. Who the friend was, or the mistress, we can only conjecture. Some critics are of the opinion that the characters are all imaginary and that many of the sonnets have no place in the sequence which tells this story.

Some scholars have conjectured that, during these years of comparative leisure, Shakespeare spent some time in Northern Italy. This sojourn would explain the fact that when he began to write after the plague had subsided, he set the scene of most of his plays in Italy. Moreover, he seems able to give the proper atmosphere and local color to the Italian scene. However, this Italian journey must remain mere conjecture. His imagination working upon reports from travelers and from books was able to catch as effectively the spirit of Henri IV's court at Nerac in *Love's Labour's Lost* and of Danish Elsinore in *Hamlet*.

The companies with which Shakespeare was connected before 1592 cannot be determined. His early work shows that he must have had some close professional association with Marlowe. Until recently he has been supposed to be a disciple of Marlowe; now some of the critics believe that much of the influence passed in the other direction.

When normal theatrical activity began again in London after the Plague, Shakespeare became a member and a sharer in the company known as the Chamberlain's Men. From that year, 1594, to the end of his career he is never associated with any other company, either as actor or dramatist. The most famous members of this group were Will Kempe, the great buffoon and comedian, and Richard Burbage, the leading tragic actor of the age. On December 26 and 28 of that year, Shakespeare's name appears as one of those actors who performed two "comedies or interludes" before the Queen at Greenwich Palace; and on the 28th we have also a record of the performance of his own *Comedy of Errors* at Gray's Inn. By this time, then, we may think of him as established in reputation as actor, poet, and dramatist.

Shakespeare's first residence in London seems to have been in the parish of St. Helen's, Bishopgate, near the theatre where his company was then acting, and not far from the dwelling of Richard Burbage, the great tragic actor. By the autumn of 1596, he had moved across the Thames into Southwark. Professor Leslie Hotson has recently discovered that there he and Francis Langly, the owner of the Swan playhouse, had a serious altercation with a notoriously unjust local Justice of the Peace, named William Gardiner. In Justice Shallow of *The Merry Wives of Windsor,* Shakespeare caricatures this man and reveals himself as a master of personal satire.

About this time, tokens of his prosperity and social importance begin to appear. In 1596 he probably coöperated with his father in applying to the College of Heralds for a grant of arms, a request that was promptly granted. In 1597 he bought for £60, New Place, one of the largest houses in his native town. In 1598 his name appears on the title-page of published copies of his plays, the publishers of earlier issues not having troubled themselves to give the author's name. In 1599 a splendid new theatre, the Globe was built on the

Bankside, and a stock company was formed for the purpose of administering it, whereof Shakespeare was one of the chief partners. It was for the Globe stage that the great plays from *Julius Caesar* to *Coriolanus* were probably written, as well as a number of Ben Jonson's in which Shakespeare appeared. We have considerable evidence of the prosperity of this enterprise; Shakespeare's own income from his shares has been variously estimated at from seventy-five pounds a year to twice that amount. Besides this, there were profits which he received as actor-sharer in the company, fees from the Revels office for performances at court, and fees as author. This last item would not include any profit from the publication of his plays. Like other playwrights of the time, he sold all rights in his dramas to the company which bought them. Henslowe, the manager, paid from £5 to £20 for a new play. Shakespeare probably received more, because the company for which he wrote was the most prosperous of all those of the age. From all his sources of income he may have had, during his later years, a total annual income of perhaps one hundred and fifty pounds; and it should be remembered that the purchasing power of English money in his age was anywhere from four to seven times what it was at the beginning of the twentieth century. In 1602 Shakespeare bought a considerable addition to the Stratford property, 107 acres adjoining the town; and various local lawsuits, in which he sought to recover on loans, indicate his continued connection with his native community, though he probably remained primarily a resident of London. The accident of a lawsuit there in which he was called as a witness, shows that in 1604 he was living at the house of one Christopher Mountjoy, a Huguenot merchant, in the district called Cripplegate, and that he had helped in arranging a match between Mountjoy's daughter Mary and her father's apprentice.

In 1598 a writer named Francis Meres in his *Palladis Tamia,* composed an elaborate comparison of leading English authors with those of antiquity, in which he wrote: " As the soul of Euphorbus was thought to live in Pythagoras, so the sweet witty soul of Ovid lives in mellifluous and honey-tongued Shakespeare; " and again: " As Plautus and Seneca are accounted the best for comedy and tragedy among the Latins, so Shakespeare among the English is the most excellent in both kinds for the stage," for comedy, witness his *Gentlemen of Verona,* his *Errors,* his *Love's Labour's Lost,* his *Love's Labour's Wonne,* his *Midsummer Night's Dreame,* and his *Merchant of Venice;* for tragedy, his *Richard the Second, Richard the Third, Henry the Fourth, King John, Titus Andronicus,* and his *Romeo and Juliet.* In the same year a contemporary poet referred to the " honey-flowing vein " of his *Venus and Adonis* and *Lucrece* as poems which had placed his name " in fame's immortal book."

It has been supposed that Shakespeare was a friend and adherent of the Earl of Essex, whom he complimented in one of the Prologues in *Henry the Fifth,* and with whom Shakespeare's early patron, Lord Southampton, was concerned in the conspiracy of 1601 against the Queen. Some find in Shakespeare's Sonnet 107 a note of rejoicing over the accession of King James, at which time Southampton was released from prison. All this is quite uncertain; but it is true that Shakespeare's professional fortunes, with those of his company, were favored by the new reign. The king was a devotee of the theatre, and had been in London but a few weeks when he elevated the Lord Chamberlain's men to be " His Majesty's

Players." In March 1604, when the royal procession through the City was about to take place, Shakespeare's name headed a list of nine actors who, as Grooms of the Chamber, received grants of scarlet cloth to make them festal suits for the event. It may have been about this time that he retired from his active career on the stage; at any rate, the latest extant mention of his name in a list of performers comes from 1603, whereas in similar lists of 1605 and later it does not occur with those of his colleagues.

About 1600 the tone of Shakespeare's plays becomes more serious and sombre. For six or seven years he wrote only tragedies and satirical comedies like *All's Well that Ends Well* and *Measure for Measure*. The tone of these plays has often been thought to reflect grievous and bitter personal experiences in the life of the author. One is on safer ground in detecting signs of severe mental strain and exhaustion in plays like *Lear* and something bordering collapse in *Timon of Athens*. Some critics have thought it not unlikely that Shakespeare suffered some sort of nervous break-down or illness after the completion of *Timon of Athens* in 1607 or 1608. At any rate, in *Pericles* and the dramatic romances which followed, there is evidence that the author has attained a new serenity of spirit. The change in tone is so profound that it cannot be satisfactorily explained by a dramatist's effort to meet new theatrical conditions or to write in a fashionable manner recently established by Beaumont and Fletcher.

In 1608 Shakespeare was back at Stratford, after the death of his mother, serving as godfather to the infant son of a neighbor; and it seems probable that, from this time, his periods of residence in Stratford grew longer and those in London diminished correspondingly. We may set the year

1610 or 1611 as the date of his retirement from London. He still wrote plays for The King's Men, but probably not more than one a year. His last dramatic work was done in collaboration with John Fletcher, with whom he wrote *The Two Noble Kinsmen* and *Henry the Eighth*. It was during a performance of the latter play that the Globe theatre was burned. Shakespeare joined with his associates in plans for a new Globe, which was opened in the following year; but there is nothing to indicate that he wrote a line of new drama for its stage.

We know practically nothing of the last three years of his life. His name frequently appears in connection with municipal affairs in Stratford and he is referred to as "William Shakespeare, gentleman of Stratford-on-Avon." He disposed of his shares in the theatres before his death. His daughters may have caused him some worry during these last years. The elder, Susanna, had married John Hall, a Stratford physician, in 1607, and was forced in 1613 to bring action in an ecclesiastical court to protect her character against slander. His younger daughter, Judith, married Thomas Quiney on February 10, 1616, at a time prohibited by Canon law, so that the two were later excommunicated. In March 1616, he executed his will, leaving the bulk of his property to Susanna Hall. He died in April of the same year. John Ward, later vicar of Stratford, says that "Shakespear, Drayton, and Ben Jhonson had a merry meeting, and itt seems drank too hard, for Shakespear died of a feavour there contracted." There seems no reason to reject this tradition. He was buried in the chancel of the Church of the Holy Trinity, where he had been baptized, and his grave is still guarded by the old doggerel inscription:

Good friend, for Jesus' sake forbear
To dig the dust enclosed here;
Blest be the man that spares these stones,
And curst be he that moves my bones.

His fame continued after his death. Some years later, a poet named Digges recalled the days when Jonson and Shakespeare were rivals for first place on the London stage, and the greater popularity of the less learned dramatist. Sometimes, he said, even the comedies of Jonson would not pay the cost of heating the theatre and feeing the ushers; " when let but Falstaff come," with Prince Hal and the rest, or Benedick and Beatrice, or Malvolio, and

The cock-pit, galleries, boxes, are all full.

In 1623, seven years after his death, thirty-six of his plays were collected by two of his former colleagues, John Heminge and Henry Condell, who had long been actors in his company and stockholders in the Globe theatre, and published in an edition now called the First Folio. Perhaps the greatest tribute given to Shakespeare in his own time was that contributed by his friend and rival dramatist, Ben Jonson, to this collection. In this poem he dared compare his plays with

all that insolent Greece or haughty Rome
Sent forth, or since did from their ashes come.
Triumph, my Britain! thou hast one to show,
To whom all scenes of Europe homage owe.
He was not of an age, but for all time!

SHAKESPEARE'S DRAMATIC CAREER

DURING the first years of his career, Shakespeare wrote in almost all the dramatic forms then in vogue. The first period of his artistic activity, extending to the year 1593–1594, was thus one of experimentation. By 1589–1590, the approximate time at which he began to write, three types of drama were universally recognized — comedy, tragedy, and chronicle history plays. Moreover, each type had developed clearly defined forms.

In comic dramaturgy three traditions were in vogue: that of the Roman author Plautus (255 B.C.–184 B.C.), that of court comedy, and that of Italian romance and comedy. These three traditions were at first quite distinct. Shakespeare often combines elements from all of them in a single play, particularly during the later periods of his work. Of these conventions, those derived from Plautus were in 1590 the most authoritative, particularly in the comedies written for presentation in the public schools and universities. The Roman dramatist's plots, though largely farcical, gave opportunity for ready merry satire. The action, most of it composed of a series of tricks devised by a clever servant, depended for its effects upon disguises, mistakes in identity, and impossible coincidences. Shakespeare's first comedy, *The Comedy of Errors,* and perhaps the first play that he wrote, was derived from two of the comedies of Plautus, — the *Menæchmi* and the *Amphitruo.* He retained and even intensified the farcical spirit of his sources. In the *Menæchmi*, most of the confusions were due to the presence of one set of identical twins. Shakespeare introduced a second set and revelled in the increased speed and merriment which they gave to the action. But he introduced with the situation of good Ægeon condemned to death a serious and romantic note into the farce, thus showing, at the beginning of his career, not only an exuberant invention natural to youthful genius, but also one of the most strongly marked characteristics of his mature power, — his ability to cause the mingling of the grave and the gay in the same play, merely to heighten its predominant emotional tone.

The same fulness and diversity of invention is found in a second one of Shakespeare's early comedies, *Love's Labour's Lost*. This play, however, belongs to a very different dramatic tradition. It was devised for a courtly audience and was like court exhibitions in depending for its effects upon allegory, spectacle, music, and the witty repartee of cultivated ladies and gentlemen. John Lyly (1554?–1606), in plays written for the choir boys, had developed this type of entertainment into a definite dramatic form, but Shakespeare shows himself largely independent of Lyly's methods. He not only gives *Love's Labour's Lost* a new sparkle and brilliancy, but by importing a number of the stock figures of Italian comedy into his play and domesticating them, he also gives his work more comic substance and keener satiric edge. *A Midsummer Night's Dream,* written probably for a wedding, presents in perfected form the kind of comedy on which he tried his "prentice hand" in *Love's Labour's Lost*.

The third of his early comedies, *The Two Gentlemen of Verona,* represents a still third tradition. It is a typical

Italian comedy. The theme, the struggle of love versus friendship; the girl with three suitors; the heroine disguised as a page in the service of her lover; and the two serving men, one a wit and a roguish jester, the other a stupid lout; — these are all stock-devices of Italian comedy. The thought and generous sentiment expressed are also commonplaces of Renaissance idealism. Shakespeare's originality lay in the skill with which he developed authentic human feeling in these conventional figures, especially the women. Julia and Sylvia anticipate faintly some of his most radiant heroines.

In tragedy, at the beginning of Shakespeare's career, the formative influences were those of Seneca, a Roman tragic writer who lived from 3 B.C. to 65 A.D. Revenge was the theme of most of his plays, and the stories told were replete with violence, murder, and horror. Supernatural figures like ghosts and furies appeared in order to motivate and drive forward the action. These dramatic tales were told in a highly colored style, in which aphorism and other rhetorical devices played an important part in producing the melodramatic effects. The first imitation of Seneca in English plays was formal and scholastic and best represented by *Gorboduc* (1562) written by Norton and Sackville. Just before Shakespeare began to write, two dramatists, Marlowe and Kyd, gave some tragic dignity to the popular, loosely constructed medleys of adventure, romance and farce by submitting them to the discipline of Senecan dramatic principles. Marlowe in *Tamburlaine* (1587) retained the free structure of the popular plays, but he set at the center of his crowded action and startling scenes a figure of heroic proportions. To the ranging, unmoral ambitions of this protagonist come disappointment and defeat. In this misfortune of a boundlessly aspiring personality of the

Renaissance lay tragedy as Marlowe conceived it. His great contribution to Elizabethan drama was the depiction of character of depth and seriousness, in conflict with itself. He was the first Elizabethan writer to dramatize the tragic struggles of a human soul. He also filled his plays with a sense of Nemesis or of Fate working out its ends, indifferent to the ambitions of presumptuous men. His tragedies were written in blank verse. This was an eloquent medium for the lyrical utterances and the long, impassioned soliloquies into which his imagination transformed Seneca's carefully constructed rhetorical speeches.

At about the same time that *Tamburlaine* appeared, Thomas Kyd produced his *Spanish Tragedy*. The plot of this play is a more typical Senecan tale of crime and punishment than is Marlowe's masterpiece. It is the story of the revenge which Hieronomo takes for the murder of his son Horatio; of vengeance directed and stimulated by a ghost. The father feigns insanity, and while waiting for an opportunity to kill the murderer, indulges in numerous soliloquies in which he analyzes his feelings and gives them passionate expression. At length, under cover of acting in a masque which has been written for an entertainment at court, he kills his enemies and produces the final slaughter expected at the end of a "tragedy of blood."

The Senecan tradition as modified by these two dramatists was expressed in Shakespeare's first tragedies and indeed lay at the base of practically all of the plays of this genre that he ever wrote. *Titus Andronicus* contains all of the most repulsive elements of blood and horror of which the type was capable. If this is the first of Shakespeare's tragedies, it shows the uncritical exuberance of a young genius who delights in giving his invention free rein within the traditions of a popular type of melodrama. *Richard III* (1593) although in form a chronicle history, presents a Marlovian figure, a villain hero, striding toward the realization of his insatiable ambition through a sea of deceit, hypocrisy, and murder. Senecan Nemesis in the form of moral retribution stalks majestically through the play and gives it its ethical unity. Besides other prominent devices, such as the ghosts and Queen Margaret in the rôle of avenging Fury, the aphoristic dialogues and other rhetorical devices are Senecan in origin. Shakespeare's contribution to the type is here the creation of a character whose motives can be understood in human terms, — motives which bear a causal relation to the action.

The third type of play which Shakespeare wrote early in his career was chronicle history. This was, in origin, a naïve and popular form of art. Its primary purpose was at first not even to tell a story to be found in the English annals, but to present upon the stage those deeds for which historical characters were famous. The writer of the type did not set out to tell a well-composed and exciting story about one of the English sovereigns, but to dramatize as many of the events in his reign as he conveniently could. There were no traditions in this genre, as there were in tragedy and comedy, to suggest guiding principles to the dramatists. Consequently these history plays at first possessed almost no organic unity. They were a series of episodes bearing only a chronological relationship to each other. Authors of the type obtained their facts largely from the prose English chronicles, such as Holinshed. But the plays, being devised wholly for the people, derived some of their recurrent features from such popular forms of entertainment as the English ballad; the miracle and morality plays, which were, in their way, mere illustrations of the events in the life of some Biblical hero; and the pageants, in which historical characters were impersonated. Sure entertainment for the populace was provided by the scenes of low comedy introduced as interludes between the dramatized historical events.

The first part of *Henry VI,* probably a work by George Peele which Shakespeare revised slightly in 1599, is an excellent example of this sort of episodic play. It tells the story of England's war with France, making Talbot the central figure in the English army and Joan of Arc in the French. It also narrates briefly the struggles of different factions at the English court. Many scenes depend for their interest on spectacle and pageantry. Troops march across the stage with banners flying. Joan conjures up devils and offers to sell her soul to them. Talbot, apparently trapped by the Countess of Auvergne in her castle, blows his horn in Robin Hood's manner; and his merry men, concealed in the building, rush to his rescue. Calls to arms, scenes of defiance, bombastic boasts, and personal combats abound. All this is evidence that the play was written for unsophisticated minds and chauvinistic hearts.

Shakespeare began his work in the chronicle history with the second and third parts of *Henry VI*. The events treated in these plays were quite as complicated as those of the first part of *Henry VI,* and the dramatic method was as frankly episodic. But Shakespeare's originality at once asserts itself. The whole action is given a kind of epic unity by the character of Queen Margaret. The second part begins with her arrival at the English court; the third part ends with her defeat and capture on the battlefield at Tewksbury. Within the limits of this action, a number of strong, vital characters emerge. The greatest of these is the sinister Gloucester, who is to become King Richard III. The action thus becomes the expression of the personalities, — of these figures who seem to dominate and direct it. This establishment of an intrinsic relationship between the action and the dramatis personæ immediately revealed to Shakespeare dramatic possibilities in the history play which had not been before apparent. These he immediately realized in *Richard III,* in which the action, having become the characteristic deeds of a strong, wicked man, fully displays this villain's character and gives his tragedy ethical meaning.

Thus far Shakespeare had developed when the plague years of 1592 to 1594 closed the theatres and sent the companies travelling in the provinces. He used this interval, as has been indicated, for the trial of his literary powers in sonnets and ornate narrative poems. When he rejoined the Chamberlain's Company in 1594, he began what is frequently called the second period of his dramatic activity. This was the time in which he brought his chronicle history plays to a triumphant culmination. In *Richard II* he turned from the creation of strong, wicked kings to the depiction of one whose complicated, subjective nature made him weak in the management of practical affairs. This Richard is both an instinctive lyric poet and an actor playing with zest at any given moment the rôle which Fate has chosen for him. The emergence of such a subtly conceived character from the events of his reign as narrated in Holinshed's *Chronicles,* lifts the history play into a new sort of tragi-comedy of character. In the two parts of *Henry IV,* Shakespeare reverts to the episodic type of play in which the comic relief given through the buffoonery of low-comedy characters occupied an important place. He may have been attracted to this type because it offered him a chance to satisfy a new interest which his audiences had found in comedies of London life, such as Dekker's *The Shoemaker's Holiday.* At any rate, in his depiction of Falstaff and his familiars, particularly in their London haunts, Shakespeare made of a current theatrical interest immortal comedy. In the second part of *Henry IV,* written clearly to give his audiences further glimpses of their new stage hero, he first repeated situations in which Falstaff's humor had best revealed itself and then he provided him with a new set of foils in the ridiculous group of countrymen attached to the petty court of Justice Shallow. In *Henry V,* Shakespeare raised the chauvinism of the early chronicles into an eloquent imperialism. Yet the heroics of this play were interrupted at regular intervals by scenes of low comedy, in which representatives of different parts of the Empire appear and finally the King himself in disguise, to provoke farcical revelations of character.

This was Shakespeare's last chronicle history play, except for *Henry VIII,* written at the end of his career in collaboration with Fletcher. By the year 1600, the reigns of all the great monarchs from King John down to Tudor times had been ably dramatized. Moreover, at this time, Shakespeare's interest had become largely diverted from the deeds and problems of Kings, which had always been the subjects of these plays, to the realistic comedy which was strictly subordinate and incidental to historical events. This fact may explain why, when Shakespeare had completed his saga of the kings of England, he wrote with zest the jolly farce, *The Merry Wives of Windsor.* Though the play continually betrays the truth of the tradition that it was written hurriedly in a fortnight, to comply with a command of Queen Elizabeth, its action stirs into comical activity a vividly portrayed group of the sturdy citizens of an English village and also of the fools and eccentrics living there.

Strangely enough, the years in which Shakespeare was developing his powers as a writer of realistic comedy were precisely those in which he composed his greatest romantic comedies: *The Merchant of Venice, Much Ado About Nothing, As You Like It,* and *Twelfth Night.* Each one of them is a special and original development of one of the romantic formulas derived from Italian literature. The main plot of *The Taming of the Shrew* is also conventionally Italianate, but Shakespeare treats it, in the main, realistically and perfunctorily, while he makes little effort to lift the story of the shrew herself above brisk farce. The later comedies are the expression of a completely different literary temper. Each one has for its central plot an Italianate love story, but it is laid in a remote world which has been given a charmed atmosphere through the magic of Shakespeare's poetic imagination. In *The Merchant of Venice,* however, a vigorous form of dramatic life appears which is alien to this spirit. Shylock, introduced into the play in order to muddy the current of true love flowing from Belmont, becomes at once so sympathetic and sinister a picture of a Jewish usurer that his catastrophe seems to modern readers half tragic. Yet the moonlight world of the fifth act carries us back into the romance which is the proper element of the tale. The plot of *Much Ado About Nothing* also skirts tragedy, but is kept safely in a youthful world of high spirits and sanity by the spirited and mocking verbal exchange of the true lovers Benedick and

Beatrice. In *As You Like It* the artificial country of sensuous and decadent pastoral tradition has become a tract of English woodland on which the real sun shines and soft winds blow This is the proper setting for the romance incarnate which the play presents. In *Twelfth Night* the Italianate tale of the lovers is accompanied by a subplot, the comedy of which owes much to the recent innovations made by Ben Jonson in *Every Man in His Humour* (1597–1598) and *Every Man Out of His Humour* (1599). His " humour " figures were creatures dominated and rendered utterly ridiculous by a persistent bias or eccentricity. Malvolio, the victim of self-love, is Shakespeare's equivalent of those figures of Jonson whose ridiculous defect is psychological. The way in which the rogues lure him into an exaggerated exhibition of his folly and expose him, is also an adaptation of Jonson's comic method. Sir Andrew Aguecheek, for his part, is a representative of another Jonsonian type, the ridiculous would-be gentleman who is also gulled. *Twelfth Night* was probably the last of his joyous comedies and their culmination. But Shakespeare, in devoting much of his attention in this play to satire, good-natured though it be, prefigured the course that his comedy was to take in his third or so-called tragic period extending from 1600 to 1608–1609.

The three comedies written in this period, *Troilus and Cressida, All's Well That Ends Well,* and *Measure for Measure,* are so permeated with the satiric spirit and so grave, even cynical, in tone, that some recent critics call them " problem comedies." During the later fifteen nineties, many violent formal satires were written by Englishmen in the savage manner of the Roman satirist Juvenal. The authors, in particular Joseph Hall and Marston, treated sexual immorality, in the opinion of the licensing authorities, so scandalously that in 1599 they ordered all the satires suppressed and burned by the common hangman. However, this satiric spirit could not be thus easily destroyed. Forbidden to express itself in formal verse, it found drama to be an equally effective medium. Marston in his *Malcontent* (1600) showed that his power and his interests were easily accommodated to dramatic form. The three sombre comedies of Shakespeare are a part of this movement in satiric comedy. Each is a story involving sexual relationships which, in two of them, are frankly licentious and sordid. These plots are set in a society in which corruption and immorality are rampant. The temper of the plays, though clearly satiric, does not express itself in direct and savage personal attack. Shakespeare presents even the most dissolute of the denizens of unsavory London brothels with so much penetration and realistic fulness that they seem amusing even in the midst of their vice. His gentle spirit also appears in the creation of one of the most sympathetic of his heroines, Isabella who passes unsmirched through all the moral rottenness of *Measure for Measure*.

Shakespeare's great achievement during the first years of the 17th century was, of course, his supreme tragedies. In *Romeo and Juliet*, written in 1596, he had already signalized his emancipation from the more obvious and crude of the Senecan tragic devices, largely through his skill in relating the bloody action to human character and motive, and through his power of giving the ardor of the lovers transcendent lyric beauty. *Julius Caesar* approached nearer to the method of his subsequent tragedies. Caesar's death is treated in the Senecan manner, but the catastrophe of Brutus is of a different sort. He is at war with himself and ends his life tragically, because he cannot fit his nobility to the practical demands of a world in uproar. Yet his difficulties are intellectual rather than emotional. With *Hamlet* begins the miraculous series of tragedies in each of which a man is destroyed by one of his unruly passions. The plot of this tragedy is, in part at least, the story of the corroding power of melancholy induced by grief, upon a naturally affable and noble nature. *Othello* reveals the destructive power of jealousy; *King Lear,* of self-will and of wrath; *Macbeth,* of ambition and guilty fear; and *Coriolanus,* of pride. In *Anthony and Cleopatra,* his last tragic treatment of love, Shakespeare gives an unsurpassed picture of mature human passion devouring its victims, in an appropriate atmosphere of oriental opulence.

But these tragedies are more than terrifying dramas of the passions. They involve the deepest currents of individual life and reveal many of the profound secrets of human destiny. These mysteries they express in the most splendid rhetoric that has ever fallen upon human ears, filled with a meditative wisdom more satisfying than that of most philosophers.

Toward the end of this unparalleled series of masterpieces, Shakespeare betrays evidence of the great strain which their composition must have imposed upon him. His power to master the inevitable cruelties of human life seems to be nearly submerged in *Lear,* and completely so in *Timon of Athens. Coriolanus,* too, in its steady gloom and unbroken level of emotion and expression, suggests a mind and spirit wearied by the superhuman demands that they had met.

An unusually severe outbreak of the plague closed the London theatres from July 1608 to the end of November,

1609. During this interval, which he spent in Stratford, Shakespeare apparently ceased dramatic composition. When he began to write again, he produced work of an entirely new sort. It showed no trace of his former weariness and agitation of spirit. This recovery of mental poise may have been due merely to rest. But many critics believe that during these two years Shakespeare successfully passed through a major crisis of his life. Sir Edmund Chambers suggests that this experience was akin to religious conversion.

The dramas which Shakespeare wrote after this period of rest, *Cymbeline, The Winter's Tale,* and *The Tempest,* are called tragi-comedies or dramatic romances. To this group *Pericles* should perhaps be added. This type of play was probably invented by Francis Beaumont and John Fletcher, who, in *Philaster* (1608 or 1609), produced what is usually regarded as the first representative of the new genre. Their dramatic romances were at first written for the audiences who attended Blackfriar's theatre, but even this cultivated group of persons had apparently become tired of the intense emotional and intellectual concentration which Shakespeare's later tragedies had demanded. They preferred an easier sort of theatrical excitement. This the romances of Beaumont and Fletcher offered in abundance. They depended for their effects upon complicated and exciting situations, upon violent contrasts of character, upon masques and other stage spectacles and upon sheer surprise. Above all, these romances contained effective dénouements. The ending is usually happy, although the passions displayed in the first part of these works are such as would normally lead to tragedy.

It is possible that Shakespeare turned to the writing of dramatic romances merely because Beaumont and Fletcher's *Phi-*

laster was so popular that the audiences clearly wanted more dramas of a similar sort. The demand would have been the more explicit because, after the plague had subsided, Shakespeare's company leased Blackfriar's theatre, where the first Beaumont and Fletcher plays had been presented. The new lessees also retained at least one of the actors who had played acceptably there the young hero's part in these dramas. Therefore, Shakespeare's apparent change in dramatic interests may have been largely dictated by conditions in the theatre.

However, Shakespeare was clearly not satisfied merely to imitate these clever innovators. In *Cymbeline* he presents the melodramatic story, the hurry of events, the vivid contrasts, the surprises, and the carefully wrought and complicated dénouement of the type. He also invokes the atmosphere of a corrupt and decadent court. But even here in this play he contrives to present in Imogen his most complete picture of an ardent and devoted woman. In the two later romances he shifts the point of his dramatic emphasis. Surprising and exciting scenes still appear, but they are of less importance than the regions of remote beauty which serve as their setting, and the marvels are of less effect than the spirit which presides over them. All the action is patently in the control of a serene mind, confident of the triumph of good over evil, of faith over doubt and suspicion, of reason over passion. It is the prominence of this spirit that leads critics to affirm that these plays have come from a mind that has learned that even the turmoil and irrationality of existence can be made to contribute to the formation of a calm and happy human life.

Shakespeare, it appears from this survey, was in origin preëminently a man of the theatre. He wrote always the kind of play that the public demanded at the moment. He seems never to have devised a new sort of drama, seldom even to have invented a plot. He was willing to leave innovation to lesser men. In this way he conserved his energy for the most important aspects of literary creation. His power was bestowed upon his characters and their speech. By substituting them for the puppets that he found in his borrowed plots, he created a world of imaginative creatures more vital than those which direct experience provides. By realizing with poetic completeness the situations in which the tales presented these characters, he gave them a vivid and beautiful world to inhabit. Finally, by reflecting these men and women in his own intelligence, he has enabled us to share his deep understanding of the sources of human conduct, his delight in its infinite variety, and his profound explanation of the deepest problems that perplex and elevate the mysterious life of man.

ELIZABETHAN THEATRES

THROUGHOUT the sixteenth century interludes and other dramatic entertainments were presented occasionally both in public halls and in the private halls of noblemen's houses. Before actual theatres were built for London audiences, plays were given habitually in the courtyards of some of the great inns of the city. The owners of such places, seeing clearly the advantage of attracting the public to their hostelries by plays, evidently entered into regular contract with some one company of actors and even made alterations in their buildings, so that they became, in effect, permanent theatres. These courtyards were surrounded by galleries, the pillars of which formed a natural stage for the actors. Audiences could be assembled easily and quickly by the stairs leading from the galleries into the street and, when the play was finished, could be counted upon to remain for drinking and other deeds of darkness.

The actual theatres, when they came to be built were of two sorts, — public and private. The former were constructed on the model of the courtyards of the inns and of the covered rings which had been provided for the sport of bear-baiting. They were circular structures consisting of a central court or pit open to the sky and a stage and galleries, both of which were covered. The private theatres were halls in which the seats were set along three sides of the room. These buildings were entirely roofed and artificially lighted, so that performances could be given in the evening. The term "private" is a misnomer. The audiences which gathered in these theatres were, on the whole, more select and cultivated than the rabble who often were admitted to the pit of the public theatres; but the performances in these private theatres were open to all who paid their admission.

The Corporation, or governing body of the City, being Puritanical in sentiment and sympathy, as has been said, was hostile to the establishment of theatres within the limits of its jurisdiction. It considered them to be monuments of prodigal expenditure and nurseries of vice and civil disturbance. Therefore, the first builders of theatres erected them on land outside the city limits. In 1576 the Theatre and the Curtain were built "in the fields" to the north of the City proper, just outside the Bishopgate entrance, within the precincts of a dissolved priory. The first, built by James Burbage, the father of Richard, the tragic actor of Shakespeare's Company, was in use as early as August, 1577. The building was torn down in December, 1598, by the Burbages and some of the timbers carried across the river to build the Globe, the new habitation of Shakespeare's company. This was probably the "wooden O" referred to in the prologue to *Henry the Fifth.* The history of the Curtain is more obscure. It was for a time an "easer," or subsidiary of the Theatre, and the profits from the two houses were pooled. The Chamberlain's Company played in this playhouse for about a year between its occupancy of the Theatre and the Globe. It remained in use until 1624.

In this same year, 1576, some of the rooms of an old monastic building which had belonged to the Dominicans or Blackfriars were leased by Richard Farrant, Master of the Children of the Chapel Royal at Windsor. One of these chambers, probably not more than twenty feet wide, was made into a theatre in which to house the performances of the choir boys who appeared in theatrical history as the Children of the Chapel, and other companies of children. During part of the years 1583–1584 this first Blackfriar's theatre was under the control of the dramatist John Lyly. About 1596 James Burbage, fearing that he might lose his lease on the Theatre, purchased some buildings in Blackfriars and constructed a theatre out of the old refectory, a room 107 by 52 feet. The district, although within the city walls, formed a liberty, that is, it retained most of the extensive legal privileges originally held by the friars. Consequently Burbage knew that a theatre safely within the precints of the old monastery was exempt from the drastic regulations of the authorities of the City. No plays were presented here until 1600, when the Children began in it the period of their greatest significance for theatrical history. From 1608, when it became the winter house of the King's Men, until the closing in 1642 of all of the London playhouses by the edict of the Puritans, the second Blackfriar's theatre remained the most fashionable of all the London playhouses.

Either in the latter part of 1576 or early in 1577, a third public theatre was opened in the butts, that is, the place in which archery was practiced, at Newington, a village on the south side of the river, about one mile from London Bridge. This building was too far away from the City to prove a serious rival to the other two theatres. The fields to the north of London in which they were situated remained the acknowledged theatrical center until the Rose was built in 1587 in the liberty of the Clink on the south bank of the river in the borough of Southwark. From this time on this so-called Bankside became a serious rival to the older district and eventually superseded it as a popular centre. Philip Henslowe was one of the builders of this playhouse. In 1592 he begins his famous diary, which was an account of his financial dealings with the companies occupying the Rose up to 1603 and with playwrights composing for him and his tenants. Henslowe's lease on the Rose expired in 1605 and the subsequent history of the theatre is obscure, except that after 1620 it was used for prize-fights.

In 1595, the Swan was built in Paris Garden, a name given to various rings used for bear-baiting. It was situated on the Surrey side of the Thames, also within the liberty of the Clink. From a contemporary drawing of the theatre, it appears that its stage was moveable, a fact which shows that the building was designed for entertainments other than dramatic.

All four of these public theatres, the Theatre, the Curtain, the Rose and the Swan remained in use until July 28, 1597, when the *Isle of Dogs* was presented at the Swan by Pembroke's Company. Seditious political satire was sensed in the play; it was suppressed, and Thomas Nashe, the author, disciplined. Subsequently, even more drastic measures of reform were taken by the Privy Council, which issued a decree limiting the number of London Companies to two, — the Admiral's and the Chamberlain's. The former then was housed at the Rose until 1600 when it moved to the new Fortune. The Chamberlain's Men occupied the Curtain until 1599, when they moved to the Globe.

The Globe theatre was built in the newly fashionable theatre district on the Bankside. It was held by a syndicate, half the shares of which were owned by Richard Burbage and his brother and the other half by other members of the Chamberlain's Company, of whom Shakespeare was one. In 1613, during a performance of Shakespeare's *Henry the Eighth,* the thatched straw roof of the theatre caught fire when certain cannon were shot off at the entry of King Henry to Cardinal Wolsey's masque. The whole house burned to the ground in less than two hours. By good luck the actors and audience all escaped without injury by two very narrow exits. A serious accident was averted when the breeches of one unfortunate man which had caught fire were put out by a " provident wit " with a " bottle ale." The theatre was at once rebuilt in a more substantial fashion and re-opened in June, 1614. Here the King's Men continued to act during the summers, as a secondary place to their winter house of Blackfriars, until the Civil War. The building was pulled down in 1644.

At least four other famous theatres were built in London between 1600 and 1642. They were the Fortune and the Hope, both erected by the famous Henslowe, and the Cockpit and the Red Bull, both originally housing the Queen's Men. These last two buildings remained standing until the Restoration, and by serving as models for the theatres built after 1660, formed a link between the Elizabethan theatre and the modern theatre, which is a direct development from that of the Restoration.

All of the public theatres were approximately alike. Except for the square Fortune theatre, they were large, round, wooden buildings. In the center was the pit open to the air, in which standing room was provided for a penny. This pit was surrounded on three sides by three galleries one above another. On the fourth side was the stage, a large, almost square platform, which projected some distance into the pit. The stage, like the galleries, was covered by a roof, usually supported by pillars. Seats were furnished for the audience in the galleries and on the stage, and cost as much as half a crown. Above the stage was a hut, which contained apparatus for lowering heavy properties to the stage or raising them from it. On this machine the throne on which the King was to sit came creaking down " the boys to please," and by means of the same pulley, celestial beings descended or ascended as the action directed. For example, in Greene's *Alphonsus, King of Arragon,* Venus is let down from the top of the stage, and at one of her exits the stage direction reads: " If you conveniently can, let a chaire come downe from the top of the stage and draw her up."

The platform or outer stage, unprovided with a curtain, was open on three sides to the audience. This was usually conceived as representing unlocalized, or only vaguely localized, territory. It represented, for example, open country or a setting for scenes of battle or siege, a garden or an orchard, a street at the threshold of a house, the confluence of two or more streets, or the hall of a house. The properties used for such scenes were few. When it represented an interior, usually a hall of state, convention apparently allowed the servitors of the " tireman " to carry on some properties before the eyes of the audience. The chair of state, we have seen, came down from above, and smaller articles of furniture might be carried on in the procession with which such scenes were often opened. In a similar way a sick man could be carried or even a banquet spread as for example, in *Macbeth.* When the outer stage served as an interior, the back of the stage was probably hung with arras or painted cloths.

The few properties needed to represent an out-of-door scene were more difficult to manage. Some large objects were evidently drawn forwards and backwards with the aid of some machine provided with wheels. Trees were probably made to ascend or descend by means of trapdoors, as were also ghosts. At the rear of the stage was a wall pierced on each side by a door each leading to a tiring room. Part of the rear wall was formed by a curtain, which on being drawn would reveal the comparatively small inner stage. In the Fortune Theatre this was seven feet deep, seventeen feet wide and twelve feet high. Above the rear stage was a balcony, sometimes partly occupied by spectators. It served for such places as the battlements of a town in the war plays or for the balcony used with so much effect in *Romeo and Juliet*.

Definitely localized scenes were set in the inner stage. Behind the protecting curtains the tireman could work to set chamber scenes with enough properties to give verisimilitude. It could represent such interiors as the chamber in which Desdemona was strangled or the still more confined space of the tomb of Juliet. The inner stage was also used for all the scenes which required what the Elizabethan called discovery. Prospero, by drawing the curtain in the last act of *The Tempest*, " discovers " to Alonso " Ferdinand and Miranda playing at chess." Characters discovered in this inner stage might later in the scene move out and occupy the outer stage. This is probably the way that the scenes of the dance in *Romeo and Juliet* was managed.

Sometimes the outer stage represented a street through which the actor had to pass in order to knock at the door of a house. To show the character gaining admittance, the curtains were drawn and the interior of the house revealed on the inner stage. At other times the inner stage served as the propertied background for the outer stage. In *As You Like It,* for example, the trees and rocks of the forest probably occupied the inner stage, while the characters did most of their acting on the outer stage.

It has sometimes been supposed that in Elizabethan plays there was a regular alternation of scenes between the inner and outer stage. This is not so; but, for obvious reasons, no two successive scenes representing different places could be set upon the inner stage. These arrangements of Shakespeare's stage allowed for easy change of locality and so for diversity and speed of action. The position of the outer stage in relation to the audience was suitable for the delivery of the soliloquies and other forms of dramatic lyricism which glorify Shakespeare's plays.

Performances in the out-of-door theatres were given in the afternoon of every day except Sundays and Saints' Days, if the weather permitted. For certain seasons plays were not given on the Thursdays on which a bear-baiting was scheduled at one of the neighboring rings. A flag flying from the top of the hut of a theatre announced to the public that a performance was to be given on that day.

ELIZABETHAN DRAMATIC COMPANIES

THE history of Elizabethan and Jacobean drama, from one point of view, is a history of the professional companies of actors for whom the plays of this great age were written. These organizations were the direct descendants of the wandering bands of acrobats and jugglers which toured the countries of western Europe during the Middle Ages. Early in the fifteenth century these itinerants seem to have become definitely devoted to the drama and became skillful enough actors to present interludes in the great halls of English gentlemen. Indeed, at this time some of the richest noblemen began to organize companies and to attach them to their own households. As servants of their patron, such actors enjoyed his protection. They wore his livery, and when they moved about the country, they traveled under his license. Without this protection they would have been liable to arrest as vagabonds. This is the reason that Elizabethan companies of actors were always, at least in theory, under the protection of some great lord and were known by such names as the Lord Chamberlain's Servants, or the King's Men. The patron did assume some responsibility for the conduct of his actors and often interceded with the authorities on their behalf. When he desired to have a play presented as part of the festivities of a wedding or other elaborate entertainment, he naturally ordered his own men to provide the desired drama.

THE CHILDREN'S COMPANIES

The first companies to establish themselves in favor during Queen Elizabeth's reign were organizations of children formed from the choir boys of the Chapel Royal and St. Paul's Cathedral. During most of the 16th century schoolboys used regularly to present at their school plays in Latin or in English, as part of their instruction in literature and ethics. This custom was naturally adopted in the schools founded for the instruction of choir boys, where permanent organizations of these talented youth were established. They played habitually in their own quarters, probably in the auditorium commonly used as a singing school. From 1559 to 1576, when the adult companies, as yet owning no theatres, were probably considered not refined enough for courtly taste, the children frequently presented their plays at court. The Children of St. Paul's were particular favorites of Queen Elizabeth, and from her accession until 1581 and they continued to appear before her intermittently until 1590. When the first indoor theatre was constructed in the old Blackfriar's monastery in 1576, the two principal choirs combined to form a quasi-professional organization to occupy the place. For this group John Lyly wrote some of his plays, which were presented both to the general public and at the Court.

From 1590 to 1600 the dramatic activity of the children, at least in the theatres, ceased almost entirely. In the later year, however, the children of the Chapel reëstablished themselves at Blackfriar's and for a time became serious rivals of the adult companies. To this competition Shakespeare refers in *Hamlet,* when he has Rosencrantz explain that the actors have been compelled to travel in the provinces because of the

" late innovation," " the aery of children," the " little eyases " (fledglings) who have superseded them in popular favor. At first this reconstituted company presented plays like Ben Jonson's *Cynthia's Revels,* in which opportunity was given for the dancing, singing, and pageantry in which the boys traditionally excelled. But they soon produced dramas of the same sort as those of the adult companies, except that they came to specialize in satire and realistic comedies which were filled with personal attacks and bitter social criticism. Many of the plays of Chapman, Marston, and Middleton formed a part of their repertory. At the accession of James I, this company became known as " The Children of the Queen's Revels." The actors among the boys were then separated from the actual choir boys and formed a company exploited for the profit of their managers. These men were frequently in legal difficulties for kidnapping boys to serve in their organizations and for presenting offensive satiric comedies. After many vicissitudes, the boy actors ceased to be of any importance in the history of the stage by the year 1612–1613.

THE QUEEN'S MEN

The history of the adult companies becomes important to a student of Shakespeare's stage in the year 1583. Then the Master of Revels, the official Director of Court Entertainments of all sorts, was ordered to recruit a company to act under the direct patronage of Her Majesty, Queen Elizabeth. This royal project was the Queen's countermove to a recent order of the City which forbade all dramatic performances in the Inn Yards. During the entire career of Elizabethan drama, the authorities of the City proper showed persistent hostility to the drama. Their regulations were a constant threat to the existence of the theatre. If the Court had not been consistently on the side of the actors in this long duel, some of the greatest work in English literature might never have been written.

The Queen's Men, as this new organization was called, were recruited from the best actors of the four or five important companies of the time. Therefore it became at once the leading theatrical organization. Its most famous members were Robert Wilson and Richard Tarlton, both of whom, as actors, were renowned for their "extemporal wit." Tarlton was the most famous clown and buffoon of his age. Both of these actors composed for the Queen's Company plays that were designed to appeal to a distinctly popular taste. Among them were pieces which served as partial sources for some of Shakespeare's own plays, notably the two early episodic Chronicle Histories, *The Famous Victories of Henry V*, and *The True Tragedy of Richard III*. After Tarlton's death in 1588, the Queen's Company gradually lost its popularity, and by 1592 it had ceased to be the favorite at Court. This loss of prestige accelerated the rise of two important new organizations; the Lord Admiral's Men and Lord Strange's Men.

THE LORD ADMIRAL'S MEN

As early as 1576 Lord Howard appears as a patron of a company of actors which appeared at Court. In 1585 he became Admiral and his players adopted the name which they have made famous, — the Lord Admiral's Men. The career of this company becomes of first importance shortly before 1590, when Edward Alleyn, the most famous actor of his day, assumed control of the group. Almost at once he established between his men and Lord Strange's Servants an association so close that it amounted to a kind of amalgamation. This proved a fortunate arrangement for both companies during the years 1592–1594, when the severity of the plague in London forced the closing of all the theatres there. Then, with Alleyn as manager, the actors successfully toured the provinces.

In May 1594, Alleyn married the stepdaughter of Henslowe, the owner of more than one London theatre. This connection and the subsidence of the plague led to a separation of the two companies and the reëstablishment of the Admiral's Men as a distinct organization. It began at once to play at Henslowe's new theatre on the Bankside, — the Rose. Thanks to Henslowe's famous *Diary* or *Account Book*, in which he entered systematically all of his financial dealings with his actors and playwrights, we possess a more accurate record of the career of this company than of any other of Shakespeare's time.

By presenting all of Marlowe's plays with Alleyn in the principal rôles, this troupe quickly gained a position of great popularity, and for years formed the only serious rival to Shakespeare's company. They continued to act at the Rose until 1600 when they moved to Henslowe's new theatre, the Fortune. Shortly after the accession of James I in 1603, they became Prince Henry's Servants and remained under his patronage until his death in 1612, when they became the servants of the Elector Palatine, who had come to England to marry the Princess Elizabeth. After the birth of Prince Charles (Charles II) in 1630, they became the Prince's Men and so pass beyond the range of our immediate interest.

EARL OF PEMBROKE'S COMPANY

Pembroke's Company, in service of which some critics believe Shakespeare to have begun his career, was, according to Sir Edmund K. Chambers, a name given to a group of actors of the amalgamated Admiral's-Lord Strange's Company who were separated from the main group during the plague years 1592–1594, in order to travel more widely in the provinces. To such an organization both of the parent companies naturally handed over some of their plays. These facts explain how Shakespeare could have been a member of Lord Strange's Company, at least from the year 1592, and yet have had a share in composing plays, like *Henry the Sixth, Part I,* which we know were the property of Pembroke's Company. By the summer of 1593, this organization was bankrupt. In 1597 a new company, under the same patron, recruited from the actors of the Admiral's and Strange's Men was acting at the Swan Theatre. It promptly involved itself in difficulties with the Court by playing a political satiric comedy of Thomas Nashe's called *The Isle of Dogs*. In October 1600, the checkered and obscure career of this company apparently came to an end.

LORD STRANGE'S — THE CHAMBERLAIN'S COMPANY

The company to which Shakespeare was attached during almost his entire career bore successively the names of Lord Strange, the Earl of Derby, the Chamberlain, and the King. Although a group of actors and acrobats had appeared in the provinces as early as 1576, under the patronage of Ferdinando Stanley, Lord Strange, the company with which Shakespeare's name is associated, was not formed until 1588.

In this year the Earl of Leicester died and some of his actors joined a group from the company of Lord Hunsdon to form a new organization of which Lord Strange became the patron. At first, and probably up to the time of its reorganization in 1594, this company consisted of five men and six apprentices or boys, some young enough to play the women's parts and some old enough to take minor male rôles. This was apparently the size of the company when Shakespeare began to write for it. Some of the actors of this troupe played very definite " lines." This was true of Will Kempe, the most famous actor in the group. He invariably took the part of a slow-witted lout or clown, a part to which he could bring many " lazzi," or tricks of physical farce, and much improvisation. Launce in *The Two Gentlemen of Verona* was one of the most typical of his rôles. The " line " of Thomas Pope was almost as definite as this. He was habitually the quick-witted servant, the master of clever verbal exchange, the opponent and foil for Kempe. For example, he played Speed to the latter's Launce.

The other men in this early company were John Heminge, Augustine Phillips, and George Bryane. Their rôles were not so clearly fixed and stereotyped as those of the two clowns. They divided between them the usual comic parts of the two young men or lovers, like those of Proteus and Valentine in *The Two Gentlemen of Verona,* and the rôle of the old man, often an opinionated and downright father, like that of the Duke of Milan in the same comedy. When Shakespeare began to write for Lord Strange's Company, he had to provide in each play parts suitable for these five principal actors composing the troupe. Practically all of them were men of greater reputation and authority than the young poet and, for that reason, able to exercise a formative control over the parts written for them.

In 1594 important changes took place in the organization of this company. In April of that year Lord Strange, who for a few months had been the Earl of Derby, died suddenly and his actors obtained the patronage of Henry, Lord Hunsdon, Lord Chamberlain. At approximately the same time they severed their connection with Alleyn and the Admiral's Men. They became again an entirely independent company and increased their numbers, for whom parts had to be provided from six to eight men. Moreover, about 1593–1594, Richard Burbage, then twenty-four years of age, began to reveal his great abilities as a tragic actor. These changes in the personnel of the company were reflected at once in the nature of the plays which Shakespeare now composed. He began to write dramas containing more parts, including always one extended rôle of somewhat heroic proportions for Burbage, such as Richard the Third, Richard the Second or the early Hamlet.

After the division of the Admiral's-Lord Strange's group into two distinct units, the two companies enjoyed for a number of years a practical monopoly of the London stage. Naturally they became vigorous rivals for the favor of the public. When one of them produced a hit, the other immediately sought a play that would appeal to the same taste. Thus, when Shakespeare's *Henry the Fourth, Part I,* first became a popular favorite, with Falstaff bearing the name of Oldcastle, The Admiral's Men promptly presented a play called *Sir John Oldcastle.* On the other hand, when the Admiral's Company opened a vein of new popular interest in dramas dealing with Robin Hood, the Chamberlain's Men countered with

Shakespeare's *As You Like It.* This monopoly of the two organizations was broken by the revival of the two companies of boy actors in 1599 and 1600, which has been described above.

When James I came to the throne, he took the Chamberlain's Men under his protection and they became known as the King's Men. This mark of royal favor was clearly a recognition of the commanding position which the company of Shakespeare and Burbage had attained by 1603. In 1608 it gave further evidence of its prosperity by assuming control of Blackfriar's Theatre, which, being enclosed and heated, it used during the winter months. The change in the nature of Shakespeare's plays written subsequent to this date can be partly explained by the fact that they were written for the more cultivated audiences of this private theatre. *Cymbeline, The Winter's Tale,* and *The Tempest* all possess elements designed to appeal to the greater refinement of the ladies and gentlemen accustomed to attend Blackfriar's Theatre.

Part of the growing success of this company and its stability was due to the character of its financial organization. The members of the company were sharers, that is owners, not only of the stock of the company of actors, but also of the leases of the theatres in which they acted. From 1599 on, for example, Shakespeare owned one-tenth interest in the playhouse of his company. The sharers, after meeting the various current expenses, divided the profits. Not all of the members of the organization were sharers. Some of them owned no stock at all in the theatrical enterprises, but were merely "hired servants" or men paid fixed salaries. This was the status of some of the minor actors, of the tiremen or property men, of the book-keepers or prompter, of the stage-keeper or stage-manager, and of the musicians. The costumes used in the Elizabethan period were never historically accurate, but they were uniformly gorgeous and costly, as much as nineteen pounds being given for a single coat. They supplied the color and splendor lacking in the scenery and stage properties. The individual actors may have possessed their own private wardrobes, although the companies did accumulate stock of their own. The owner of the theatre also possessed a wardrobe which was his personal property. In spite, then, of inevitable changes in the share-holders, the actors and the playwrights, this King's Company enjoyed a career of unbroken prestige and distinction from 1594 until the closing of the theatres in 1642.

CANON AND CHRONOLOGY OF THE PLAYS

IN Shakespeare's lifetime there were published eighteen of the plays attributed to him, in nearly forty cheap quarto editions. The nineteenth in order of printing was *Othello,* which did not appear until 1622. The First Folio (1623), described in the second chapter, was the first professedly complete collection of the plays "according to the true original copies." Of the thirty-six plays contained in the volume, eighteen had already appeared in separate quarto editions and eighteen, as far as we know, had not been printed before. One of those attributed to Shakespeare when issued as a quarto, *Pericles, Prince of Tyre,* was not included in the collection. It is now generally given a place in the Shakespeare canon, but is believed to have been written only in part by Shakespeare. The same thing is true of at least six of the plays which were admitted to the First Folio: namely the first part of *Henry VI, Titus Andronicus, The Taming of the Shrew, Troilus and Cressida, Timon of Athens* and *Henry the Eighth;* and to this list of composite authorship, some would add the second and third parts of *Henry VI* and also *Richard III.* The accepted Shakespeare canon, then, consists of thirty-seven plays, of which about thirty are now viewed as of substantially single authorship.

The attempt to arrange these plays in the order of their composition is by no means easy. The order of original publication gives us almost no help, except, of course, from the fact that it may indicate the latest limit of original production of certain of the plays. A few seeming allusions to contemporary events may furnish clues, but Shakespeare was very sparing in his use of such references. In certain cases we find contemporary mention of the plays, or allusions to characters or passages therein, again furnishing a late limit of date; of this sort of evidence the most important is that of Meres, who in the pamphlet of 1598, cited on page 23 above, enumerated eleven of the known plays of Shakespeare, together with one called *Love's Labour's Won,* which has never been clearly identified. There are also records of the performance of certain plays at court, in the books of the Master of the Revels. The following outline of the chief reasons which have led scholars to suggest the commonly accepted dating of some of the more familiar plays, will best illustrate the character of the evidence.

Antony and Cleopatra. On May 20, 1608, the publisher Blount entered in the *Stationers' Register* " A Book called Antony and Cleopatra "; and although there is no evidence that Shakespeare's play was actually published before the folio of 1623, this entry is commonly thought to refer to its proposed publication at about the time of its first appearance.

As You Like It. This play, too, was entered in the *Stationers' Register* for separate publication, but no copy of any such separate issue has survived; the date of the entry is August 4, 1600. In Act III, sc. v, there is a quotation (" Who ever loved that loved not at first sight? ") from Marlowe's poem, " Hero and Leander," which was published in 1598. A similar early limit for the play is suggested by the fact that its name was not included in Meres' list of 1598. Interesting but less reliable evidence has been drawn from the nature of the personnel of Shakespeare's Company. The part of Touchstone was almost surely devised not for Will Kempe, but for Robert Armin. In the *Second Part of Tarleton's Jests,* entered in the *Stationers' Register* on August 4, 1600, we learn that Armin was then acting in Shakespeare's Company. In Armin's *Quips,* written in February-March 1599/1600, he described himself as an actor in another company. Therefore, *As You Like It* must have been written between February and August, 1600.

The Comedy of Errors. A book, *Gesta Grayorum,* gives us the history of the revels carried on at Gray's Inn during the year 1594. From this account we learn that *The Comedy of Errors* (" like to Plautus in his *Menaechmus* ") was acted there by Shakespeare's Company on December 28, 1594. The tone of narrative shows that this comedy was put on as a makeshift and so not composed for the occasion. A reference in the play (III, ii, 126) to France " armed and reverted, making war against her heir " fixes the date of the play between August 12, 1589, when Henry IV became legally heir to the throne, and July 19, 1593, when he was acknowledged king.

Cymbeline. This play appeared for the first time in the folio of 1623, and there is no evidence of even an earlier effort at publication. Dr. Simon Forman, who recorded some of his visits to the theatre in a *Book of Plaies,* records a performance of *Cymbeline* which he saw, at least before his death, September 12, 1611, probably between the twentieth and thirtieth of April of this year. The authenticity of this document has been lately called into question and it may be a forgery. The plot of the play is much like that of Beaumont and Fletcher's *Philaster*, which was written at least as early as October 8, 1610, when it is mentioned in John Davies's *Scourge of Folly*, registered on that date. But it is not possible to determine which play was written or presented first.

Hamlet. A play of Hamlet, not marked as new, was given, probably by Shakespeares' Company on June 11, 1594. This drama evidently existed as early as 1589, for in that year Nashe makes a reference in his *Epistle to Greene's Menaphon*, which suggests that the work was written by Thomas Kyd. The popularity of this play is shown by frequent contemporary references, like the following in Lodge's *Wit's Miserie* (1596), "The Visard of ye ghost which cried so miserably at ye Theator, like an oister wife, 'Hamlet Revenge.'" This old play is not generally thought to be Shakespeare's work, although some critics have discerned traces of it in the First Quarto of *Hamlet*. An entry in *The Stationers' Register* for July 26, 1602, of "a booke called *The Revenge of Hamlet*" places us upon surer ground. In 1603 the First Quarto edition of the play, evidently the work of a bungling reporter, appeared, and in 1604 a second quarto, "enlarged to almost as much again as it was, according to the true and perfect copy." This is commonly thought to represent a rewriting of the earlier version which is imperfectly represented by the First Quarto.

Henry the Fourth. The First Part of this play was published in quarto in 1598; the Second Part in 1600. In Johnson's *Every Man out of his Humour*, which was acted in 1599, there is an allusion to Justice Silence, a character in the Second Part. Meres, in his list of 1598, includes *Henry the Fourth,* without indication of parts.

Henry the Fifth. This play was published in quarto in 1600. Lines 30–34 of the Chorus prefixed to Act V contain an allusion to the absence of the Earl of Essex on an expedition to Ireland, which left England in April, 1599 and returned September 28th of the same year.

Julius Caesar. This play was not published until 1623; it was not mentioned by Meres in 1598. In a poem published in 1601, Weever's " Mirror of Martyrs," is a stanza seemingly based on the most famous scene in the drama:

> The many-headed multitude were drawn
> By Brutus' speech that Cæsar was ambitious.
> When eloquent Mark Antony had shown
> His virtues, who but Brutus then was vicious?

It is also probable that, Clove, a character in *Every Man out of his Humour* (1599) alludes to a passage in Act III, sc. ii, when he says, " Reason long since is fled to animals."

King Lear. On November 26, 1607, this play was entered in the *Stationers' Register,* with the descriptive addition, " as it was played before the King's Majesty at Whitehall upon Saint Stephen's night at Christmas last "; the quarto appeared in 1608. An early limit of date for composition is suggested by the fact that Shakespeare probably borrowed the devil's names uttered by Edgar in one of his scenes of pretended madness (IV, i) from Harsnett's *Declaration of Popish Impostures,* published in 1603.

Macbeth. This play was not published till 1623. References to King James (as in the " twofold balls and treble sceptres" of Act IV, sc. i) indicates 1603, the date of his accession and the union of the English and Scottish crowns, as an early limit of composition. A late date limit is found in a contemporary record of a performance at the Globe in April 1610. Some words of the drunken porter in Act II, sc. iii. have been thought to allude to the Jesuit doctrine of "equivocation," as brought out in the trial of Henry Garnet for Complicity with the Gunpowder Plot on March 28, 1606.

Merchant of Venice. On July 22, 1598, this play was entered on the *Stationers' Register,* though it did not appear until 1600. It has been thought that its composition may have been stimulated by the trial and execution of Lopez, a Jewish physician of London, in 1594 for the attempted poisoning of Queen Elizabeth and Don Antonio of Portugal and the resulting anti-Jewish feeling. A reference in a letter of Francis Davidson written in October 1596, to an enemy of Essex's as Saint Gobbo, was clearly inspired by this play. Henslowe's mention of the first performance of "The Venesyon Comodey" in August 1594, is now regarded as too vague to be accepted as a reference to *The Merchant of Venice.*

Midsummer Night's Dream. This play was mentioned by Meres in 1598, and published in 1600. It has been thought plausible that it was composed for the festivities connected with the marriage of the Earl of Derby at Greenwich Palace in 1594, and that a passage in Act II, sc. i, alludes to the exceptional storms of that year.

Much Ado about Nothing. This play was published in 1600, the title-page stating that it had been "sundry times publicly acted." It was not mentioned by Meres in 1598 (unless possibly under the name *Love's Labour's Won*").

Othello. This play was not published till 1622. There is a record of a performance at Whitehall on November 1, 1604. A passage in Act III, sc. iii, is apparently based on Holland's translation of Pliny, published in 1601. There is an apparent echo of Othello's murder in *The Honest Whore* (I, i, 37) written by Dekker and Middleton in 1604.

Richard the Second. This play was published in quarto in 1597. Certain scenes appear to be based in part on Daniel's poem on the *Civil Wars between Lancaster and York,* published in 1595; but since Elizabethan books were often circulated in manuscript before being printed, this is not regarded as fixing certainly the early limit of date. In 1595 Sir Edward Hoby wrote a letter to Sir Robert Cecil in which he invited him to a performance of *King Richard* on December 9 of this year. This is usually assumed to be *Richard II*.

Richard III. The only external evidence for the date of this play is the publication of the first quarto in 1597. John Weever's reference to "Romea Richard" in his *Epigrammes* may be as early as 1594, but the numerous contemporary allusions to the play are all subsequent to 1597.

Romeo and Juliet. This play was published in 1597, and the title-page bore the statement that it had been often "played publicly by the right Honourable the L[ord] of Hunsdon his servants." It happens that we know that it was only between July 1596 and April 1597 that Shakespeare's company was so named. The Nurse's reference in Act I, sc. iii, to an earthquake of eleven years before has been thought to imply an original date of composition as early as 1591, because of the prominence of the earthquake of 1580.

The Tempest. This play was not published till 1623. There is a record of its performance at Whitehall Palace on November 1, 1611. Certain details in the account of the shipwreck and in the description of the island were drawn from narratives of the wreck on the Bermudas of one of the ships of an expedition to Virginia led by Sir George Somers on July 25, 1609. Accounts of this first appeared in England in 1610.

Twelfth Night. This play was not published till 1623. In the diary of John Manningham, a law student of London, is a record of a performance at the Middle Temple on February 2, 1602. It was not mentioned by Meres in 1598. The song " O mistress mine," introduced in Act II, sc. iii, was published in a musical collection in 1599; but we have no means of being sure whether this preceded or followed its use on the stage.

The Winter's Tale. This play was not published till 1623. Dr. Simon Forman, who kept a manuscript " book of plays " seen in London, recorded a performance at the Globe on May 15, 1611. A reference in Act IV, sc. iv., to a dance of satyrs " before the king " has been thought to be based on such a dance as that introduced in Johnson's *Masque of Oberon,* performed at court on January 1, 1611.

From such facts it appears that in the case of certain plays we may be reasonably sure, within a year or two, of the date of composition or first production; in other cases the evidence is ambiguous or largely wanting. For *Coriolanus,* for example, there is no definite evidence of date, and our estimate of its chronological position must be based only on general impressions of its style.

In the case of all the plays the evidence drawn from style is valued as corroborative of that of a more definite character; and there is now such general agreement respecting the main characteristic of Shakespeare's writing at different periods of his career, that, if a new play of his were suddenly discovered, with no external indication of the time of its production, there would be little difficulty in placing it within a few years of the date when it might be assumed to have been written. In general, Shakespeare's development as an artist seems to have been regular, normal and representative; he began by being primarily an imitator and assimilator of the methods of composition familiar in his youthful period, and developed his more individual traits experimentally and progressively. The traits of his early style are those naturally expected, then, of a young writer: an interest in *words,* and their possibilities for both beauty and wit, with some disposition to use them with a fluency and abundance out of proportion to the number and importance of the ideas concerned. In particular, a fondness for puns and other verbal quips, and for rime and other elements of chiming poetic sound, is characteristic of this period. In the middle period there is a balance between word and idea — an adaptation of each to the other — which represents the perfection of equilibrium in style. In the later period the interest in ideas tends to exceed that in phrasing and the richness and intricacy of the thought to increase, to an extent which sometimes impairs both beauty and clearness.

These more general qualities of style, in the various periods of Shakespeare's development, are specifically represented in his versification. That of the earliest period is relatively conventional, ornamental, and intrinsically pretty; it exists for its own sake, so to say, and is easier to read as verse than as dramatic speech. The technical signs of these qualities are an abundance of rime, and a disposition to make the sense follow closely the regular metrical divisions. In the final period the opposite extreme is noticed: rime is wholly abandoned, and the poet prefers to set the structure of his thought across that of the verse, running sentences over the ends of verses, sometimes even ending a verse on a syllable where one cannot make even the slightest phrase pause, and beginning and ending paragraphs and speeches in the middle of metrical lines. Verse of this character may be said to exist only as completely subordinated to dramatic expression, and it is hard to read rhythmically. In the middle period there is again an equilibrium between these extremes: the verse runs rhythmically, but with some freedom; and the greater part of the text can be read easily, at one and the same time, as verse and as dramatic speech.

One also notes a difference in the type of play chiefly represented in the various periods of Shakespeares' career. Three types were commonly recognized as the chief on the Elizabethan stage: comedy, tragedy, and history (or "chronicle-history"); later a somewhat distinctive type, called tragi-comedy, became familiar. Shakespeare's first editors classified all his plays under the three forms above indicated; modern critics find it convenient to distinguish some as "tragi-comedies," or (a term of more recent and doubtful use) as "dramatic romances." So soon as one notes these distinctions of type, it becomes obvious that in his earliest period Shakespeare experimented with history, comedy, and tragedy, doing rather more work in the first named form than in either of the others; that somewhat later he devoted himself increasingly to comedy; somewhat later, again, to tragedy; and that his final period was one of new experimentation in the tragi-comic form. These facts have led to a common practice of dividing the plays, and their writer's career, among four distinctive periods, roughly dated 1590–1594, 1594–1601, 1601–1608 and 1608–1612. While it proves convenient to employ such a division, one should do so cautiously, remembering, first, that the dates on which they are based are partly inaccurate and conjectural, second, that there is no definite boundary between any two of the assumed periods, and third, that we have no ground for assuming that they represent anything definite in the life or consciousness of Shakespeare. A neglect of these cautions has led to the familiar assumption that he passed through a "happy" period of composition of comedies, a sombre period when he preferred tragic themes and ideas, and a final period of reconciliation. The most we can say is that there was a time when he was relatively uninterested in tragic drama, and a later time when he became so deeply interested in it that he gave only his minor energies to other forms.

It is clear from all the foregoing considerations that we can form a fairly clear idea of the general chronological arrangement of Shakespeare's plays, and the types of dramatic art they represent in his career, but that we can rarely be certain, of any two plays of the same period, which was the earlier and which the later. The following list of plays, then, while exhibiting the consensus of critical opinion respecting their order of composition in a general way, must not be regarded as an attempt to date the individual plays with accuracy.

The type of play is indicated by the initial C for comedy, H for history, T for tragedy, and T-C for tragi-comedy. An asterisk indicates probable composite authorship.

CHRONOLOGY OF PLAYS

H	Henry the Sixth (Parts II, III)	1590–1591
C	Comedy of Errors	1589–1592
T	*Titus Andronicus	1589–1594
C	Love's Labour's Lost	1591
	(Revision)	1597–98
H	*Henry the Sixth (Part I)	1591–2
C	Two Gentlemen of Verona	1592
H	Richard the Third	1593
C	*Taming of the Shrew	1593–4
H	King John	1594
H	Richard the Second	1595
C	Midsummer Night's Dream	1595
T	Romeo and Juliet	1596
C	Merchant of Venice	1596
H	Henry the Fourth (Parts I, II)	1597–98
C	Merry Wives of Windsor	1598–99
H	Henry the Fifth	1599
C	Much Ado about Nothing	1599
C	As You Like It	1600
T	Julius Caesar	1599–1600
C	Twelfth Night	1601
C	*Troilus and Cressida	1601–02
C	All's Well that Ends Well	1602
T	Hamlet	1602–03
C	Measure for Measure	1603
T	Othello	1604
T	King Lear	1605–06
T	Macbeth	1606
T	Antony and Cleopatra	1607–08
T	*Timon of Athens	1607
T–C	*Pericles	1607–08
T	Coriolanus	1609

T–C	Cymbeline........................	1610
T–C	Winter's Tale......................	1611
T–C	The Tempest......................	1611
H	*Henry the Eighth..................	1612
C	*Two Noble Kinsmen..............	1612–13

NOTE. — Of the tragi-comedies, all but *Cymbeline* were classified as comedies in the First Folio; *Cymbeline* as a tragedy. *Troilus and Cressida* was classified as a tragedy, but by modern editors is commonly put among the comedies.

SHAKESPEARE'S TEXT

THE plays of the first professional companies were written mainly by actors themselves. In the fifteen-eighties a group of university men, of whom Christopher Marlowe, Robert Greene, and George Peele are the most famous, turned their hand to writing this form of popular literature. Their work was so superior to that of the actor-playwrights that these free-lance writers were soon the principal source of a new drama. The older practice did continue, to find its great exemplar in William Shakespeare of the Chamberlain's Company.

The plays which he wrote became the property of his company and existed in its possession in two manuscript forms. There was, first, the one called " the book " of the play. This was the authoritative stage-copy, the acting version which served as the prompt-copy for the book-holder, who was both librarian of the company and prompter. This " book " was probably not identical in all respects with the author's " original " or his " papers," to which the editors of the First Folio edition of Shakespeare refer when they write, " We have scarce received from him a blot in his papers." The " book " of the play, we know from contemporary testimony, often omitted from the original passages and even whole scenes which were thought to be ineffective as acting drama. In the case of Shakespeare's plays, this excision must have been made with his consent and possibly even at his suggestion. Neither the " book " nor the " original " of any one of Shakespeare's plays is extant. Other manuscripts existed in the form of the " parts " of the various actors. They were written out by the book-holder and contained the lines and cues which each actor had to memorize. The source of the only text of *The Two Gentlemen of Verona,* for example, was evidently established by fitting together or assembling the " parts " of the various actors in the comedy. One other interesting document of the play in possession of the company was a plot or skeleton of the action in outline. On it were indicated all of the entrances and exits, the properties, and the off-stage noises, and business required. Six manuscripts of these " plots " survive.

The players were reluctant to allow their dramas to be printed. They apparently thought that if a play could be read, few people would wish to see it acted. They may also have feared that their plays, if printed, would be appropriated for acting by rival companies. This reluctance explains the fact that only eighteen of Shakespeare's plays were printed during his lifetime. They were published in small pamphlets called quartos, which sold for only sixpence a piece. Eight of the first quartos and the second quartos of *Romeo and Juliet, Hamlet* and *Love's Labour's Lost* were clearly printed from copies owned by the play-house and published at the instance of the players. Such authorized publication was apt to occur, first, when theatrical activity had been interrupted by the plague. In the second place, the company might publish an authentic quarto of a play when a bad pirated edition of the same play had been put into circulation. In all, fourteen quartos are regarded as having been published under the auspices of the company and so " good."

The first quartos of at least six or seven of the plays were clearly unauthorized, " surreptitious and stolne," as the editors of the Folio call them. They were the *Second and Third Parts of Henry the Sixth,* (called the *First Part of the Contention of York and Lancaster* and *The True Tragedy of Richard Duke of York*), *Romeo and Juliet, Henry the Fifth, The Merry Wives of Windsor, Hamlet* and perhaps *Love's Labour's Lost.* They were based on no manuscript in the possession of the playhouse. The methods of obtaining them and preparing them for the printer probably varied, and different explanations of their origin have been suggested. Some of the texts were evidently stolen by a note-taker sent into the theatre to write down by ear the lines as they were spoken on the stage. Others were patched together from the parts of one or more dishonest actors and what they could remember of the parts of others on the stage at the same time. The most considerable mistakes in these texts would be due either to lapses in memory, to inability to write with sufficient speed to follow the speech of a fluent actor, or to mistakes of the ear. Besides being garbled for the reasons just described, the texts of these quartos were often greatly abbreviated and obviously incomplete. Naturally, texts put together in any such manner are thoroughly unreliable and are usually designated as " bad " quartos.

The authors of plays and the dramatic companies which owned them were insufficiently protected against such unauthorized editions. No copyright law existed. However, there was a number of laws regulating the printing of books. In the first place, no work could be published until licensed by the Archbishop of Canterbury and the Bishop of London, or their representatives. All London publication was controlled by the Company of Stationers, a closed corporation, made up of all the booksellers and most of the printers and publishers in London. A publisher, by entering a book which he had legally acquired in the official *Stationers' Register,* secured the sole right of selling it and was protected to this extent against piracy. A book never entered in this *Register,* as was the case of the first quarto of *Romeo and Juliet* and that of *Henry the Fifth,* was undoubtedly pirated. Those quartos that were entered to other firms than those publishing them, as was the case with the first quarto of *Hamlet,* were also clearly unauthorized.

In 1623, appeared the First Folio edition edited by John Heminge and Henry Condell, the only two survivors of the company of Shakespeare which had built and operated the Globe Theatre. They announced to the public that their volume included all of Shakespeare's comedies, histories, and tragedies. The book consisted of 908 pages, each of which measures in the largest copy extant 13⅜ inches in height by 8½ inches in breadth. The original edition has been estimated to consist of between 500 to 750 copies, of which between 150 and 200 are now extant. In 1623 the volume sold for twenty shillings; in 1922 a copy was sold in London for £8600 pounds. Of the 36 plays contained in the First Folio, eighteen had never appeared before in printed form. The editors evidently made every effort to base their texts on the best playhouse manuscripts available, or, as they phrased the matter, to have the texts "truly set forth according to their first original." They probably used prompt-books or transcripts made from the author's manuscripts, perhaps in his autograph. Manuscripts of both sorts would have been available to Heminge and Condell, both of whom were Shakespeare's friends and his colleague-actors. Because of this zeal to have their texts represent the author's originals, they based the texts of only six of the plays upon quartos already printed. These were *Love's Labour's Lost, Romeo and Juliet, The Merchant of Venice, Midsummer Night's Dream, Henry the Fourth, Part I,* and *Much Ado about Nothing.*

In spite of the apparent care of Heminge and Condell, numerous errors appeared in their text. Some of the causes of such misreadings were illegibility in the manuscripts used for the published edition, and, after the manuscripts came into the printer's hands, errors of the compositor. Other ambiguities and variations in the texts are due to cuts, and to additions and alterations made in the theatre when an acting version of the drama was prepared. These errors in the text subsequent editors have sought to detect and to eliminate. Consequently, hundreds of emendations have been suggested, many of which have been adopted by all modern editors. Perhaps the most brilliant of these is that suggested by the eighteenth century editor, Lewis Theobald. For the meaningless phrase " a table of greenfields " in Mistress Quickly's account of Falstaff's death in *King Henry V,* Act II, iii, 17, he suggested the sympathetic, revealing phrase, " a babbled of green fields." Recently a group of critics, of whom Mr. A. W. Pollard was the pioneer, has thrown much light upon the study of Shakespeare's text by seeking to determine the kind of copy that was used by the printer of a given play. For example, if these critics discover by bibliographical study that a copy was made for the printer by stringing together players' parts, they can make this fact explain certain of the peculiarities of the text. A text founded on such a document, for example, would be free from ambiguities, because an actor would have to set down clearly in his part the exact words he was to speak. But it might be corrupted by interpolations and " gags " introduced by the same man. Again, a copy representing a text which had been shortened or revised for a special performance might contain anomalies and ambiguities due to cuts or to carelessly or imperfectly excised passages. This kind of study, though built upon much conjecture, has put examination of Shakespeare's text upon a new basis, the results of which can best be seen in the textual essays contributed by J. Dover Wilson to the New Cambridge Edition. The earliest of the texts now in general use is that of the Cambridge Shakespeare originally issued in 1863 to 1866 and revised in 1891–1893 by Dr. W. A. Wright. It is reprinted in the Globe edition. Others equally popular and reliable are those of the Oxford Shakespeare edited by W. J. Craig in 1892, of Dr. W. A. Neilson, which was first published in 1906 and appears in the Students Cambridge edition (published by Houghton Mifflin Company), and finally of the New English Cambridge edition being issued by Sir Arthur Quiller-Couch and Professor J. Dover Wilson.

LANGUAGE AND VERSIFICATION

ALTHOUGH many words in Shakespeare's vocabulary are no longer in use and the meaning of many others has changed since his day, his language in most essentials was the same as ours. However, if we should hear it pronounced as it was on his stage, we should probably find it difficult to understand. Almost all of the consonants were pronounced as they are now, but most of the vowels and diphthongs were sounded more or less differently. Though something would doubtless be added to the melody of Shakespeare's verse and some of his doubtful rhymes made perfect to one who had learned to pronounce his language exactly as he did, still this knowledge is not essential, even to the thorough student. Certain peculiarities of his pronunciation such as variations in stress, or placing the accent on syllables different from those receiving it in modern speech, are, however, of fundamental importance. Indeed a mastery of these peculiarities is essential if one is to apprehend correctly the rhythm of Shakespeare's lines.

§ 1. The most important class of constant differences in Shakespeare's language is made up of the preterits and participles in " ed," where, in full or formal utterance, the termination was regularly pronounced as a separate syllable. Since the abbreviated form of utterance was also in common colloquial use, it was constantly availed of in dramatic poetry where metrical convenience indicated; in such cases the Elizabethan printers usually spelled the participle *liv'd, purchas'd* (or sometimes *purchast*), etc. The best modern printing of Shakespeare reverts to this practice, using the full spelling *lived*, etc., only where the *-ed* has its full syllabic value, though some printers follow the opposite course, and mark the full pronunciation thus: *livèd*. The better method is exemplified as follows:

And that the lean abhorred monster keeps; (*R. & J.*, V, iii, 104)
There to be crowned England's royal king; (*3 H. 6*, II, vi, 88)
O masters, if I were dispos'd to stir: (*J. C.*, III, ii, 126)
Led him, begg'd for him, sav'd him from despair.
(*Lear*, V, iii, 191)

§ 2. A second class of words now regularly shortened, but in Shakespeare's English often pronounced with fulness, is made up of those ending in *-ion, -ious, -ience,* and similar terminations. Such terminations, to preserve the metre, must often be pronounced as fully dissyllabic. Thus:

The most you sought was her promo*tion:* (*R. & J.*, IV, v, 71)
Hath told you Caesar was ambi*tious;* (*J. C.*, III, ii, 83)
And she in mild terms begg'd my pat*ience;* (*M. N. D.*, IV, i, 61)
Your mind is tossing on the oc*ean.* (*M. V.*, I, i, 8)

§ 3. Medial *r* and *l* were evidently pronounced more fully than with us, so as frequently to form an additional syllable (compare the *r* of modern Scots, as in Burns's line, " And man to man, the *world* o'er," where " world " is dissyllabic).

That croaks the fatal ent*r*ance of Duncan; (*Macb.*, I, v, 40)
Grace and rememb*r*ance be to you both; (*W. T.*, IV, iv, 76)
Than Bolingbroke's return to Eng*l*and. (*R. 2*, IV, i, 17)

§ 4. On the other hand, certain contractions, such as we still have in *e'er* for *ever*, etc., were used more freely than at present. Thus *whether* was apparently pronounced, at times, *whe'er,* and spelled *where; evil* pronounced *e'il,* and sometimes spelled *eale; having* pronounced (and spelled) *ha'ing,* etc.

And see whe'er Brutus be alive or dead; (*J. C.*, V, iv, 30)
[spelled *where* in the Folio]
From that particular fault, The dram of *eale* etc.
(*Haml.*, I, IV, 36)
[Here the meaning of *eale* is not certainly known, but it is generally thought to stand for *e'il* = evil.]

§ 5. The position of the accent has altered, in certain words, from that used by Shakespeare. Thus we find *aspect* accented on the second syllable, *character* on the second (though more commonly on the first, as now), *complete* on the first, *detestable* on the first, *contract* on the second, *exile* on the second, *record* (noun) on the second, *sepulchre* on the second, etc.

Than in a nuncio's of more grave aspect; (*T. N.*, I, iv, 28)
See thou character. Give thy thoughts no tongue;
(*Haml.*, I, iii, 59)
That thou dead corse, again in complete steel; (*Haml.*, I, iv, 52)
Thou detestable maw, thou womb of death. (*R. & J.*, V, iii, 45)

§ 6. The standard verse of Shakespeare's plays, as of the English poetic drama in general, is what is commonly called *iambic pentameter,* the type line being composed of ten syllables, of which the even-numbered syllables are accented (not always strongly, but more than those adjacent to them) and the odd-numbered syllables unaccented. Such a line is —

May all to Athens back again repair. (*M. N. D.*, IV, i, 70)

But such perfectly regular lines are in fact less common than those showing some variation from the type. Most of such variations are conveniently grouped according as they concern the number of *syllables* or the arrangement of the *accents*.

LINES CONTAINING MORE THAN TEN SYLLABLES

§ 7. An additional light syllable added to the tenth is common, giving the line what is usually called a *feminine ending;* as —

To be or not to be: that is the question. (*Hamlet,* III, i, 56)

Less commonly, two additional light syllables are found, forming a *triple ending;* as —

And so doth mine. I muse why she's at liberty. (*R. 3,* I, iii, 305)

§ 8. An extra light syllable may also be found preceding any of the regular unaccented syllables in the line, forming what is often called a *trisyllabic foot.* We may distinguish cases where the normal pronunciation of the two consecutive light syllables is so rapid that no marked change in the rhythm results from the presence of the extra syllable, and those where a perceptible change results from the rapid utterance designed to bring the two syllables into the time of one. Of the former sort, especially, are words of which the first ends with a vowel and the second begins with one, so that the two naturally coalesce; or, in like manner, single words in which there are adjacent vowels, or in which the letter *r* stands between two vowels. Thus —

It is too hard a knot for me to untie. (*T. N.*, II, ii, 42)
Hath shook and trembled at the ill neighbourhood.
(*H. 5*, I, ii, 154)
And move in that obedient orb again. (*1 H. 4*, V, i, 17)
Of what your reverence shall incite us to. (*H. 5*, I, ii, 20)

[In former periods, such lines were often printed "for me t' untie," "at th' ill neighbourhood," etc., to indicate the partial elision of sound.]

Of the second sort examples are the following:

But mine own safeties. You may be rightly just.
(*Macb.*, IV, iii, 29)
I beseech your Graces both to pardon me. (*R. 3*, I, i, 84)
Let me see, let me see, is not the leaf turn'd down.
(*J. C.*, IV, iii, 273)

§ 9. Rarely twelve full syllables are found, in such form as to suggest the six-foot line or alexandrine, though they are not numerous enough to make us certain that Shakespeare clearly recognized this as a normal variant in his verse. Examples are the following:

And these does she apply for warnings and portents.
(*J. C.*, II, ii, 80)
Besides, I like you not. If you will know my house.
(*A. Y. L.*, III, v, 74)
So to esteem of us, and on our knees we beg.
(*W. T.*, II, iii, 149)

Rather more common are instances where the verse is divided equally between two dramatic speeches:

Shall I attend your lordship?
At any time 'fore noon. (*M. for M.*, II, ii, 160)
To what I shall unfold.
Speak; I am bound to hear. (*Haml.*, I, v, 6)

LINES CONTAINING FEWER THAN TEN SYLLABLES

§ 10. The omission of one syllable, though exceedingly common in lyrical verse, is a rare occurrence in the iambic pentameter. A sufficient number of examples are found in the Shakespeare plays to require our attention, but it remains uncertain whether they may not be due to errors in the transmission of the text. Thus —

In drops of sorrow. Sons, kinsmen, thanes. (*Macb.*, I, iv, 35)
Stay! The king hath thrown his warder down. (*R. 2,* I, iii, 118)
Than the soft myrtle; but man, proud man.
(*M. for M.*, II, ii, 117)

We also find the omission of two syllables after a pause, and the omission of the last foot, or last two syllables, of the line; though here also it is often likely that the exceptions may be due to abbreviation or corruption of the text:

And leave eighteen. Alas, poor princess. (*Cymb.*, II, i, 61)
Than your good words. But who comes here? (*R. 2,* II, iii, 20)
A lad of life, an imp of fame. (*H. 5,* IV, i, 45)

§ 11. There also appear, especially at the end of speeches and scenes, lines of only six syllables or three feet:

You look but on a stool. (*Macb.*, III, iv, 68)
Applauding our approach. (*A. & C.*, IV, viii, 39)

There are also apparent lines of only four syllables or two feet:

Thou hast not lov'd. (*A. Y. L.*, II, iv, 36)
Could great men thunder. (*M. for M.*, II, ii, 110)

LINES WITH MORE OR FEWER THAN FIVE ACCENTS

§ 12. The increase in accent is simply the normal means of dramatic emphasis; as —

Together with *all forms, moods, shows* of grief. (*Haml.*, I, ii, 82)
After life's fitful fever *he sleeps well.* (*Macb.*, III, ii, 23)
So old and white as this. *Oh! oh!* 'tis foul! (*Lear,* III, iii, 24)
Ring the alarum-bell! *Blow, wind! come, wrack!*
(*Macb.*, V, v, 51)

§ 13. Much more common is the reduction of the number of accents to four or three, when the sense requires it:

Nor let no comforter delight mine ear. (*M. Ado,* V, i, 6)
You that look pale and tremble at this chance.
(*Haml.*, V, ii, 345)
And Brutus is an honourable man. (*J. C.*, III, ii, 92)
The lunatic, the lover, and the poet. (*M. N. D.*, V, i, 7)
To-morrow, and to-morrow, and to-morrow. (*Macb.*, V, v, 19)

LINES WITH ALTERED POSITION OF ACCENT

§ 14. The accented and unaccented syllables of a foot often exchange positions at the beginning of the line; less commonly, after the principal pause; rarely in other positions. Thus:

Gorged with the dearest morsel of the earth.
(*R. & J.*, V, iii, 46)
Woe to the hand that shed this costly blood! (*J. C.*, III, i, 258)
Finds tongues in trees, *books in* the running brooks.
(*A. Y. L.*, II, i, 16)

And yet dark night *strangles* the travelling lamp. (*Macb.*, II, iv, 7)

Pale as his shirt, his knees *knocking* each other. (*Haml.*, II, i, 81)

PHRASING

§ 15. Besides the number and position of accents and syllables, the structure of Shakespeare's verse is dependent on *phrasing,* — that is, the grouping of syllables and words, according to their grammatical significance, by means of lesser and greater pauses such as are normal in our speech. In the line

Is crimson in thy lips and in thy cheeks (*R. & J.*, V, iii, 95)

there is no pause of sufficient importance to be indicated by a mark of punctuation, yet there are three distinct phrases separated by very slight pauses after "crimson" and "lips." The structure of the verse is therefore perceptibly different from that of the line

Domestic fury and fierce civil strife, (*J. C.*, III, i, 263)

where there is a single point of phrasing after "fury," or the line

Is sicklied o'er with the pale cast of thought, (*Haml.*, III, i, 85)

where the phrasing is divided after the fourth syllable instead of after the fifth. Phrasing divided after an accented syllable is called *masculine,* after an unaccented syllable *feminine*. If a verse is divided into two phrases by a single pause, sufficiently marked to be indicated by a comma or other stop (or regarded as equivalent in rhythmic time to a punctuation pause), the pause is called a *cesura* (literally, a cutting). The cesura, as already implied, may be either masculine, as in the line

Though justice be thy plea, consider this, (*M. V.*, IV, i, 198)

or feminine, as in the line

Assume a virtue, if you have it not. (*Haml.*, III, iv, 160)

§ 16. Besides these internal phrase-pauses, there is the metrical pause at the end of the line, which commonly coincides with a pause due to grammatical phrasing. If the pause in the sense at this point is strong enough to be indicated by a comma or other mark of punctuation, the line is said to be *end-stopped*. If the sense is such as to demand no pause at the end of the line, it is said to be *run-on;* thus

He brings great news. The raven himself is hoarse
That croaks the fatal entrance of Duncan
Under my battlements. Come, you spirits
That tend on mortal thoughts, unsex me here.
(*Macb.*, I, v, 39–42)

§ 17. If the line ends on a word which permits no phrase-pause whatever, so that the voice (unless arrested artificially for purely metrical purposes) must proceed instantly to the following line, the run-on effect is greatly increased. Such a line is said to have a *light* or a *weak ending;* [1] as —

[1] J. K. Ingram, who first systematized this subject, distinguished the two terms by using " light " of words on which " the voice can to a small extent dwell," as, *am, are, be, can, does, has, I, they,* etc., and " weak " of words which force the reader " to run them, in pronunciation no less than in sense, into the closest connection with the opening words of the succeeding line," as, *and, for, from, if, in, or.*

To feeling as to sight? or art thou but
A dagger of the mind, a false creation; (*Macb.*, II, i, 37)
Who needs must know of her departure and
Dost seem so ignorant, we'll enforce it from thee;
(*Cymb.*, IV, iii, 10)

Whose ignorant credulity will not
Come up to the truth. So have we thought it good;
(*W. T.*, II, i, 192)

And that most deeply to consider is
The beauty of his daughter. He himself [etc.].
(*Temp.*, III, ii, 106)

RHYME, ALLITERATION, ETC.

§ 18. In Shakespeare's earlier dramas, in accordance with the dramatic custom of the period, he frequently used the iambic pentameter in the rhymed couplet form. In the later plays the couplet appears only occasionally, as a kind of tag marking the close of a scene, or to point a saying of a proverbial or epigrammatic character. Thus:

This fellow pecks up wit as pigeons pease,
And utters it again when God doth please.
He is wit's pedlar, and retails his wares
At wakes and wassails, meetings, markets, fairs:
And we that sell by gross, the Lord doth know,
Have not the grace to grace it with such show.
(*L. L. L.*, V, ii, 315–320)

Things base and vile, holding no quantity,
Love can transpose to form and dignity.
Love looks not with the eyes but with the mind,
And therefore is wing'd Cupid painted blind.
Nor hath Love's mind of any judgment taste;
Wings and no eyes figure unheedy haste;

And therefore is Love said to be a child,
Because in choice he is so oft beguil'd.
(*M. N. D.*, I, i, 232–239)

Then shall I swear to Kate, and you to me;
And may our oaths well kept and prosperous be!
(*H. 5,* V, ii, 401–402; end of play.)

Till then sit still, my soul. Foul deeds will rise
Though all the earth o'erwhelm them, to men's eyes.
(*Haml.*, I, ii, 257–258; end of scene.)

I gin to be aweary of the sun,
And wish the estate o' the world were now undone.
Ring the alarum-bell! Blow, wind! come, wrack!
At least we'll die with harness on our back.
(*Macb.*, V, v, 49–52; end of scene.)

§ 19. Besides the couplet, Shakespeare sometimes introduced into his plays rhymed verse in forms drawn from lyrical poetry. Thus in the dialogue of *Romeo and Juliet,* in *R. & J.*, I, v, 95–108, we find fourteen lines arranged in the form of the Shakespearean sonnet, with the rhyme-scheme *ababcdcdefefgg;* and in some other early plays the verse falls occasionally into quatrain and other rhymed stanza forms. There are also, of course, various rhymed forms introduced as lyrics in other metres than the iambic pentameter; for examples, see the fairy lyrics in the *Midsummer Night's Dream,* and the songs introduced into a great number of the plays.

§ 20. Alliteration (that is, the use of neighboring words beginning with the same initial consonant) does not appear in Shakespeare's verse according to any plan or with any frequently conspicuous effect. It often, however, adds to the beauty or expressiveness of the lines; thus —

The country cocks do crow, the clocks do toll;
(*H. 5,* IV, 15, Prologue)
The honey-bags steal from the humble-bees;
(*M. N. D.*, III, i, 171)
And churlish chiding of the winter's wind; (*A. Y. L.*, II, i, 7)
My bounty is as boundless as the sea; (*R. & J.*, II, ii, 133)
To-morrow, and to-morrow, and to-morrow
Creeps in this petty pace from day to day; (*Macb.*, V, v, 19–20)
Will plead like angels, trumpet-tongu'd, against
The deep damnation of his taking-off. (*Macb.*, I, vii, 19–20)

In some of these examples, notably the first and fourth, it will be observed that there is repetition of vowel sounds as well as consonants; and in general, for the finest effects of Shakespeare's blank verse, "vowel colour," and "consonant colour," as they are sometimes called, are blended in ways which are obviously effective but often difficult to analyze.

The development in Shakespeare's versification corresponded to the growth in his control of his poetic medium. In the first experimental period of his writing, he clearly regarded the single line as the unit of his poetical composition. It was usually end-stopped and coincided exactly with a grammatical or rhetorical phrase. Verse so composed tended toward monotony and toward forcing the speech of the characters to assume the artificial formality of a series of almost self-sufficient lines. Rhyme was a natural embellishment of this sort of poetic structure.

As Shakespeare grew in mastery of his medium, he freed his verse more and more from the shackles of the individual line. Run-on lines and feminine endings began to appear more frequently. The verse thus more easily accommodated itself to the rhythms of the thought and emotion which informed it. In this way, the balance between form and content became more perfect. The poetry ceased to be obviously rhetorical and yet was not too heavily freighted with thought to be easily grasped as it came from the lips of the actors. During Shakespeare's later period of writing, this balance was again broken. The lines became surcharged with meaning. Indeed they became so close-packed with thought that they are difficult to understand except after close study. By this time the line had completely ceased to be the unit of his poetic form. Instead, Shakespeare composed in units consisting of a series of lines or groups which are sometimes called poetic paragraphs. This sort of writing gave his verse much more variety and complexity of metrical movement. It also created a form of dramatic utterance that possessed the structure and rhythms of natural speech and yet gave it all the imaginative reach of sublime poetry. The two following passages, representing the characteristic verse of Shakespeare's early and late dramatic period respectively, exemplify his simple, and his complex type of poetic structure.

> Welcome, good Robin. See'st thou this sweet sight?
> Her dotage now I do begin to pity;
> For, meeting her of late behind the wood,
> Seeking sweet favours for this hateful fool,
> I did upbraid her and fall out with her.
> For she his hairy temples then had rounded
> With coronet of fresh and fragrant flowers;
> And that same dew, which sometimes on the buds
> Was wont to swell like round and orient pearls,
> Stood now within the pretty flowerets' eyes
> Like tears that did their own disgrace bewail,
> When I had at my pleasure taunted her,
> And she in mild terms begg'd my patience,
> I then did ask of her her changeling child;

Which straight she gave me, and her fairy sent
To bear him to my bower in fairy land.
(*M. N. D.*, IV, i, 49–64)

I pray thee, mark me.
I, thus neglecting worldly ends, all dedicated
To closeness and the bettering of my mind
With that which, but by being so retir'd
O'er-prized all popular rate, in my false brother
Awak'd an evil nature; and my trust,
Like a good parent, did beget of him
A falsehood, in its contrary as great
As my trust was; which had indeed no limit,
A confidence sans bound. He being thus lorded,
Not only with what my revenue yielded,
But what my power might else exact, like one
Who having into truth, by telling of it,
Made such a sinner of his memory
To credit his own lie, he did believe
He was indeed the Duke. (*Temp.*, I, ii, 88–103)

TABLE OF VERSE ELEMENTS OF CHRONOLOGICAL SIGNIFICANCE

It has appeared from the foregoing outline of Shakespeare's versification that certain definite elements in the verse of his dramas are found to vary with a high degree of progressiveness, from the beginning to the end of his dramatic career, so that they become of chronological significance. They are sometimes, indeed, spoken of as "tests" for the dating of plays, though no one would wish to use them for this purpose with a sense of entire certainty, or unaided by evidence of other kinds. In particular, groups of statistics must be considered with reference to the special circumstances of any play concerned: thus the amount of rhyme in the *Midsummer*

Night's Dream is excessive for its period, for the obvious reason that the style of the play, particularly in the fairy scenes, is peculiarly appropriate to rhyme and other lyrical elements. There is no such ground of explanation for the also excessive appearance of rhyme in *Richard the Second;* we can only say, in that instance, that the verse style differs from that which would be expected in the period when the play is believed, for reasons of a different character, to have been written. The same thing applies, in lesser degree, to the rhymes in *Macbeth.* But in general, we note a remarkably sustained tendency, on Shakespeare's part, to develop his dramatic verse in the following directions: a diminishing use of rhyme, an increasing use of feminine endings and run-on lines, and an increasing complexity of structure resulting from the conflict of the verse pattern with that of grammatical and rhetorical phrasing. These tendencies are exhibited statistically in the following table, in which the plays are arranged in the same conjecturally chronological order as that given on page 71.

	Total Number Lines	Blank Verse	Ten-syllable Rhymes	Per Cent Feminine Endings (in B. V.)	Per Cent Run-on Lines	Per Cent Light and Weak Endings	Per Cent Speeches Ending within Lines
Henry VI (I).........	2693	2379	314	8.2	10.4	0.2	0.5
Henry VI (II)........	3032	2562	122	13.7	11.4	0.1	1.1
Henry VI (III).......	2904	2749	155	13.7	9.5	0.1	0.9
Comedy of Errors.....	1770	1150	380	16.6	12.9	0.0	0.6
Love's Labour's Lost..	2789	579	1028	7.7	18.4	0.5	10.0
Two Gent. Verona....	2060	1510	116	18.4	12.4	0.0	5.8
Richard III..........	3599	3374	170	19.5	13.1	0.1	2.9
King John...........	2553	2403	150	6.3	17.7	0.3	12.7
Titus Andronicus.....	2525	2338	144	8.6	12.0	0.2	2.5
Mids. Night's Dr......	2251	878	731	7.3	13.2	0.0	17.3
Romeo and Juliet.....	3002	2111	486	8.2	14.2	0.3	14.9
Richard II...........	2644	2107	537	11.0	19.9	0.2	7.3
Merchant of Venice...	2705	1896	93	17.6	21.5	0.4	22.2
Taming of Shrew.....	2671	1971	169	17.7	8.1	0.7	3.6
Henry IV (I).........	3170	1622	84	5.1	22.8	0.4	14.2
Henry IV (II)........	3437	1417	74	16.3	21.4	0.0	16.8
Merry Wives of W....	3018	227	69	27.2	20.1	0.0	20.5

Henry V	3320	1678	101	20.5	21.8	0.1	18.3
Much Ado	2823	643	40	22.9	19.3	0.3	20.7
As You Like It	2904	925	71	25.5	17.1	0.2	21.6
Julius Caesar	2440	2241	34	19.7	19.3	0.5	20.3
Twelfth Night	2684	763	120	25.6	14.7	0.5	36.3
Troilus and Cressida	3423	2025	196	23.8	27.4	0.3	31.3
Hamlet	3924	2490	81	22.6	23.1	0.3	51.6
Measure for Measure	2809	1574	73	26.1	23.0	0.4	51.4
All's Well	2981	1234	280	29.4	28.4	1.0	74.0
Othello	3324	2672	86	28.1	19.5	0.1	41.4
King Lear	3298	2238	74	28.5	29.3	0.3	60.9
Macbeth	1993	1588	118	26.3	36.6	1.4	77.2
Antony and Cleopatra	3064	2761	42	26.5	43.3	3.6	77.5
Timon of Athens	2358	1560	184	24.7	32.5	1.9	62.8
Pericles	2386	1436	225	20.2	18.2	4.1	71.0
Coriolanus	3392	2521	42	28.4	45.9	4.1	79.0
Cymbeline	3448	2505	107	30.7	46.0	5.1	85.0
Winter's Tale	2750	1825	0	32.9	37.5	5.5	87.6
Tempest	2068	1458	2	35.4	41.5	4.6	84.5
Henry VIII	2754	2613	16	47.3	46.3	3.5	72.4

(This table is based upon the percentages given by Neilson and Thorndike in *The Facts about Shakespeare* — which percentages are themselves derived from previous countings; the low percentage of light and weak endings for Henry the Eighth is due to the fact that these rarely occur in the Fletcher scenes.)

GRAMMAR

IN GENERAL, the literary English of Shakespeare's time was in a more flexible state, closer to the looseness or freedom of colloquial speech, than in ours; and in the dialogue of drama this characteristic is particularly evident.

The following notes indicate only the more common or more important differences of usage which are likely to demand attention from the student.

§ 1. One part of speech is frequently used for another; in particular, a noun or a verb is made up, for the nonce, from some other word-form.

In the dark *backward* and abysm of time. (*Temp.*, I, ii, 50)
The fair, the chaste, and unexpressive *she*. (*A. Y. L.*, III, ii, 10)
He *childed* as I *fathered*. (*Lear*, III, vi, 117)
That may repeat and *history* his loss. (*2 H. 4*, IV, i, 203)
This day shall *gentle* his condition. (*H. 5*, IV, iii, 63)
Grace me no grace, nor *uncle* me no uncle. (*R. 2*, II, iii, 87)
My death's sad tale may yet *undeaf* his ear. (*R. 2*, II, i, 16)

§ 2. There is much irregularity in the inflection of pronouns; especially, the nominative is found where strict or modern usage would require the objective case.

And *he* (= him) my husband best of all affects.
(*M. W. W.*, IV, iv, 87)
Yes, you have seen Cassio and *she* together. (*Oth.*, IV, ii, 3)
Making night hideous, and *we* fools of nature
So horridly to shake our disposition. *Haml.*, I, iv, 54)
Pray you, *who* does the wolf love? (*Cor.*, II, i, 8)

§ 3. There is similar irregularity in the agreement of subject and verb; in particular, the third person singular of the verb frequently appears with a plural subject.[1]

These high wild hills and rough uneven ways
Draws out our miles, and makes them wearisome.
(*R. 2,* II, iii, 4–5)

Their encounters, though not personal, *hath* been royally attorneyed. (*W. T.*, I, i, 28)

Three parts of him
Is ours already. (*J. C.*, I, iii, 154–55)

§ 4. The practice of omitting the relative pronoun, familiar in modern English in the objective case (as in "The man I love"), is widespread, and includes the nominative.

I have a *brother is* condemn'd to die (*M. for M.*, II, ii, 34)

Besides, our nearness to the King in love
Is near the hate of *those love* not the King. (*R. 2,* II, ii, 129)

§ 5. The subjunctive mood is used more widely than in modern English, not only in conditional and other subordinate clauses, but in independent clauses expressive of possibility (modern "would" with infinitive), desire, or command.

And lead these testy rivals so astray
As one *come* not within another's way. (*M. N. D.*, III, ii, 359)

She *were* an excellent wife for Benedick. (*Much Ado,* II, i, 366)

Sleep *dwell* upon thine eyes, peace in thy breast!
(*R. & J.*, II, ii, 187)

Run one before, and let the Queen know of our gests.
(*A. & C.*, IV, viii, 1)

[1] This is often spoken of as an example of the influence of the northern dialect, in which the plural form of the verb commonly ended in *s*. But it is found in verbs to which this does not apply.

§ 6. A possible condition may be expressed by the subjunctive with *so* instead of *if*, or by the inverted order (subjunctive preceding its subject) without any introductory conjunction.

Whate'er Lord Harry Percy then had said . . .
May reasonably die and never rise
To do him wrong or any way impeach
What then he said, *so he unsay* it now. (*1 H. 4*, I, iii, 76)
Hold out my horse, and I will first be there. (*R. 2*, II, i, 300)

§ 7. In a condition contrary to fact the simple pluperfect form may be used in the principal clause (the conclusion) as well as in the introductory subordinate clause.

§ 8. The infinitive (with *to*) is used as a noun more freely than in modern English; also, in an "indefinite" or "absolute" construction, following adjectives and verbs, where we should require a preposition with the gerund.

Could you on this fair mountain leave *to feed* [*i.e.*, leave off feeding]. (*Haml.*, III, iv, 66)
Ah, who shall hinder me *to wail* and weep? (*R. 3*, II, ii, 34)
Too proud *to be* so valiant (= of being so valiant). (*Cor.*, I, i, 262)

You know me well, and herein spend but time
To wind about my love with circumstance [*i.e.*, in winding about, etc.]. (*M. V.*, I, i, 154)

§ 9. Two negative words are often used, not as the equivalent of an affirmative, but as maintaining or intensifying the negation.

Nor never could the noble Mortimer
Receive so many, and all willingly. (*1 H. 4*, I, iii, 110)

You may *deny* that you were *not* the mean
Of my Lord Hastings' late imprisonment [*i.e.*, deny that you were the mean]. (*R. 3,* I, iii, 90)

§ 10. The comparative and superlative endings are often used in addition to the adverbs *more* and *most.*

And his *more braver* daughter could control thee. (*Temp.*, I, ii, 439)

With the *most boldest* and best hearts of Rome. (*J. C.*, III, i, 121)

§ 11. Both the adverbial termination *-ly* and the superlative *-est* are sometimes used only once though logically required for two or more words.

Good gentlemen, look *fresh* and *merrily.* (*J. C.*, II, i, 224)
And she will speak most *bitterly* and *strange.* (*M. for M.*, V, i, 36)

The *generous* and *gravest* citizens. (*M. for M.*, IV, vi, 13)

§ 12. The dative of a personal pronoun, and the possessive *your,* are frequently used (like the "ethical dative" in Latin) in a vague colloquial implication of advantage or interest.

He pluck'd *me* ope his doublet. (*J. C.*, I, ii, 267)
There was a little quiver fellow, and 'a would manage *you* his piece thus; and 'a would about and about, and come *you* in and come *you* in. (*2 H. 4,* III, ii, 300)
Your serpent of Egypt is bred now of *your* mud by the operation of *your* sun. So is *your* crocodile. (*A. & C.*, II, vii, 29)
As I was smoking a musty room, comes *me* the Prince and Claudio, hand in hand. (*Much Ado.*, I, iii, 61)
[Note that all these passages are from colloquial prose.]

§ 13. The dative of the personal pronoun is also used at times (as in Latin) to express advantage and disadvantage, or other relationships for which modern English would require a preposition such as *to* or *for*. [This survives, of course, in some uses, such as "Do me a favour."]

But here *me* this. (*T. N.*, V, i, 123)
Who calls me villain, . . .
Tweaks me by the nose, gives *me* the lie i' the throat,
As deep as to the lungs, who does *me* this? (*Haml.*, II, ii, 601)
Let me remember thee what thou hast promis'd,
Which is not yet perform'd *me*. (*Temp.*, I, ii, 244)

§ 14. The possessive of the neuter pronoun *it* is regularly *his*, sometimes *it* (an early provincial genitive).

How far that little candle throws *his* beams! (*M. V.*, V., i, 90)
Since nature cannot choose *his* origin. (*Haml.*, I, iv, 26)
The innocent milk in *it* most innocent mouth.
(*W. T.*, III, ii, 101)
It hath *it* original from much grief. (*2 H. 4*, I, ii, 131)

§ 15. A clause of result may be introduced by *that*, where modern English requires "so that."

The hum of either army stilly sounds,
That the fix'd sentinels almost receive
The secret whispers of each other's watch. (*H. 5*, IV, Chorus, 6)
Have you not made an universal shout,
That, Tiber trembled underneath her banks. (*J C.*, I, i, 50)

§ 16. The word *that* is also used with the meanings "in that," "why," and "when," because it represents various adverbial uses of cases of the old relative pronoun (compare *quod* in Latin).

O spirit of love, how quick and fresh art thou,
That, notwithstanding thy capacity
Receiveth as the sea, nought enters there . . .
But falls into abatement. (*T. N.*, I, i, 10)

Albeit I will confess thy father's wealth
Was the first motive *that* I woo'd thee, Anne.
(*M. W. W.*, III, iv, 14)

Is not this the day
That Hermia should give answer of her choice?
(*M. N. D.*, IV, i, 140)

§ 17. *Other* is used as a pronoun of plural as well as singular meaning.

For the *other,* Sir John, let me see. (*2 H. 4,* III, ii, 131)

And therefore is the glorious planet Sol
In noble eminence enthron'd and spher'd
Amidst the *other.* (*T. & C.*, I, iii, 91)

§ 18. *Near* sometimes appears in a contracted form of the comparative, unchanged from the positive; and in like manner some nouns ending in the sound *s* take no change of form for the plural.

Nor *near* (= nearer) no farther off, my gracious lord.
(*R. 2*, III, ii, 64)

My lord your son had only but the *corpse* (= corpses),
The shadows and the shows of men to fight.
(*2 H. 4,* I, i, 192)

§ 19. Adjectives whose form indicates an active meaning are sometimes used with passive sense, and those of passive form with active meaning; also, those properly signifying effect sometimes signify cause.

Wherever in your *sightless* (= invisible) substances.
(*Macb.*, I, v, 50)

There's something in 't
That is *deceivable* (= deceptive). (*T. N.*, IV, iii, 21)

Oppressed with two *weak* (= weakening) evils, age and hunger.
(*A. Y. L.*, II, vii, 132)

SOURCE MATERIAL

IN THE following pages the effort has been made to indicate, for the plays represented, the general character of their principal sources, and to present the source material in some detail in those cases where it is significant for the method of Shakespeare's art. Since to give the sources in full is usually impracticable, the method is sometimes that of summary, sometimes that of selective extracts. It must not be considered as complete; therefore the student should not infer that a Shakespearean scene or passage which does not closely parallel material given in this section can be assumed to be essentially Shakespeare's. But enough is reproduced to make it possible to trace the main outlines of the dramatist's method in adapting his material; and frequently the workmanship even of verbal details of an important scene may be interpreted in the light of the details of the source.[1]

[1] No source material is given for *A Midsummer Night's Dream* or *The Tempest,* since for neither of these plays has any principal literary source been established; so far as we know, the main plot in each case was of Shakespeare's invention. For the Dream he may have drawn, for the story of Theseus, upon North's Plutarch and Chaucer's " Knight's Tale," and upon various sources for hints concerning the fairies. The account of the storm in *The Tempest* was probably based on narratives of the great storm of July 1609, in which a British fleet en route to Virginia was wrecked in the Bermudas; in one of these narratives the Bermudas are called " the Devil's Island," " it being counted of most that they can be no habitation for men but rather given over to devils and wicked

ROMEO AND JULIET

THE story of this tragedy is found in more than one Italian tale of the Renaissance, for example, in the novelle of Bandello (1544), which were translated into French by Boiseau and Belleforest in 1559, and thence into English by Painter in *The Palace of Pleasure,* 1567. There is also some evidence of a lost English play on the theme, the method of which may be represented by a Dutch play of about 1630. But Shakespeare's principal source seems to have been Arthur Brooke's poem, *Romeus and Juliet,* published 1562, from which extracts are here given. The entire poem contained about 3000 lines.

ROMEUS AND JULIET

This barefoot friar girt with cord his grayish weed,
For he of Francis' order was, a friar, as I rede.
Not as the most was he, a gross unlearned fool,
But doctor of divinity proceeded he in school.
The secrets eke he knew in Nature's works that lurk;
By magic's art most men supposed that he could wonders work. . . .
The bounty of the friar and wisdom had so won
The townsfolks' hearts, that well nigh all to Friar Laurence run,

---

spirits." There are also indications that a number of the plot elements of *The Tempest* may have been suggested by certain Italian plays whose scenarios were outlined in a recently published manuscript (see Neri: *Scenari delle Maschere in Arcadia*).

To shrive themself; the old, the young, the great and small;
Of all he is beloved well, and honoured much of all.
And, for he did the rest in wisdom far exceed,
The prince by him, his counsel craved, was holp at time of need.
Betwixt the Capulets and him great friendship grew,
A secret and assurèd friend unto the Montague.
Loved of this young man more than any other guest,
The friar eke of Verone youth aye liked Romeus best;
For whom he ever hath in time of his distress,
As erst you heard, by skilful lore found out his harm's redress. . . .

Young Romeus poureth forth his hap and his mishap
Into the friar's breast; but where shall Juliet unwrap
The secrets of her heart? To whom shall she unfold
Her hidden burning love, and eke her thought and cares so cold?
The nurse of whom I spake, within her chamber lay,
Upon the maid she waiteth still; to her she doth bewray
Her new receivèd wound, and then her aid doth crave,
In her, she saith, it lies to spill, in her, her life to save.
Not easily she made the froward nurse to bow,
But won at length with promised hire, she made a solemn vow
To do what she commands, as handmaid of her hest;
Her mistress' secrets hide she will within her covert breast.

To Romeus she goes; of him she doth desire
To know the mean of marriage, by counsel of the friar.

"On Saturday," quod he, "if Juliet come to shrift,
She shall be shrived and married; how like you, nurse, this drift?"
"Now by my truth," quod she, "God's blessing have your heart,
For yet in all my life I have not heard of such a part.
Lord, how you young men can such crafty wiles devise,
If that you love the daughter well, to blear the mother's eyes.
An easy thing it is with cloak of holiness
To mock the seely mother, that suspecteth nothing less.
But that it pleasèd you to tell me of the case,
For all my many years, perhaps, I should have found it scarce." . . .
And then she swears to him, the mother loves her well;
And how she gave her suck in youth, she leaveth not to tell.
"A pretty babe," quoth she, "it was when it was young;
Lord, how it could full prettily have prated with its tongue" . . .
And thus of Juliet's youth began this prating nurse,
And of her present state to make tedious, long discourse.

. . . .

A servant Romeus had, of word and deed so just,
That with his life, if need required, his master would him trust.
His faithfulness had oft our Romeus proved of old;
And therefore all that yet was done unto his man he told,
Who straight, as he was charged, a corden ladder looks,
To which he had made fast two strong and crooked iron hooks.

The bride to send the nurse at twilight faileth not,
To whom the bridegroome given hath the ladder that he got.
And then to watch for him appointeth her an hour;
For whether Fortune smile on him, or if she list to lower,
He will not miss to come to his appointed place,
Where wont he was to take by stealth the view of Juliet's face.
How long these lovers thought the lasting of the day,
Let other judge that wonted are like passions to assay:
For my part, I do guess each hour seems twenty year:
So that I deem, if they might have, as of Alcume we hear,
The sun bound to their will, if they the heavens might guide,
Black shade of night and doubled dark should straight all over hide.

Th' appointed hour is come; he, clad in rich array,
Walks toward his desirèd home: good fortune guide his way.
Approaching near the place from whence his heart had life,
So light he wox, he leapt the wall, and there he spied his wife,
Who in the window watchèd the coming of her lord;
Where she so surely had made fast the ladder made of cord,
That dangerless her spouse the chamber window climbs,
Where he ere then had wished himself above ten thousand times.
The windows close are shut; else lóok they for no guest;
To light the waxen quariers, the ancient nurse is pressed,

Which Juliet had before preparèd to be light,
That she at pleasure might behold her husband's beauty bright.
A kerchief white as snow ware Juliet on her head,
Such as she wonted was to wear, attire meet for the bed.
As soon as she him spied, about his neck she clung,
And by her long and slender arms a great while there she hung.
A thousand times she kissed, and him unkissed again,
Ne could she speak a word to him, though would she ne'er so fain.
And like betwixt his arms to faint his lady is;
She fets a sigh and clappeth close her closèd mouth to his;
And ready then to sownd she lookèd ruthfully,
That lo, it made him both at once to live and eke to die. . . .
"O Romeus," quoth she, "in whom all virtues shine,
Welcome thou art into this place where from these eyes of mine
Such teary streams did flow, that I suppose well-nigh
The source of all my bitter tears is altogether dry.
Absence so pined my heart, which on thy presence fed,
And of thy safety and thy health so much I stood in dread.
But now what is decreed by fatal destiny,
I force it not; let Fortune do, and death, their worst to me.
Full recompensed am I for all my passèd harms,
In that the gods have granted me to clasp thee in mine arms."

. . . .

[*The Friar to Juliet:*]

Cast off from thee at once the weed of womanish dread,
With manly courage arm thyself from heel unto the head;
For only on the fear or boldness of thy breast
The happy hap or ill mishap of thy affair doth rest.
Receive this vial small and keep it as thine eye;
And on thy marriage day, before the sun do clear the sky,
Fill it with water full up to the very brim,
Then drink it off, and thou shalt feel throughout each vein and limb
A pleasant slumber slide, and quite dispread at length
On all thy parts, from every part reave all thy kindly strength;
Withouten moving thus thy idle parts shall rest,
No pulse shall go, ne heart once beat within thy hollow breast,
But thou shalt lie as she that dieth in a trance:
Thy kinsmen and thy trusty friends shall wail the sudden chance;
Thy corpse then will they bring to grave in this churchyard,
Where thy forefathers long ago a costly tomb prepared,
Both for themself and eke for those that should come after,
Both deep it is, and long and large, where thou shalt rest, my daughter,
Till I to Mantua send for Romeus, thy knight;
Out of the tomb both he and I will take thee forth that night. . . .

"What do I know," quoth she, "if that this powder shall
Sooner or later than it should, or else, not work at all?

And then my craft descried as open as the day
The people's tale and laughing-stock shall I remain for aye.
And what know I," quoth she, "if serpents odious,
And other beasts and worms that are of nature venomous,
That wonted are to lurk in dark caves underground
And commonly, as I have heard, in dead man's tombs are found,
Shall harm me, yea or nay, where I shall lie as dead?
Or how shall I that alway have in so fresh air been bred,
Endure the lothsome stink of such an heapèd store
Of carcases not yet consumed, and bones that long before
Intombèd were, where I my sleeping-place shall have,
Where all my ancestors do rest, my kindred's common grave?
Shall not the friar and my Romeus, when they come,
Find me, if I awake before, y-stifled in the tomb?"
And whilst she in these thoughts doth dwell somewhat too long,
The force of her imagining anon did wax so strong,
That she surmised she saw, out of the hollow vault,
A grisly thing to look upon, the carcase of Tybalt;
Right in the selfsame sort that she few days before
Had seen him in his blood embrued, to death eke wounded sore.
And then when she again within herself had weighed
That quick [2] she should be buried there, and by his side be laid,
All comfortless, for she shall living fere [3] have none,
But many a rotten carcase, and full many a naked bone;

[2] Alive. [3] Companion.

Her dainty tender parts 'gan shiver all for dread,
Her golden hairs did stand upright upon her childish head. . . .
But when she felt her strength began to wear away,
By little and little, and in her heart her fear increasèd aye,
Dreading that weakness might, or foolish cowardice,
Hinder the execution of the purposed enterprise,
As she had frantic been, in haste the glass she caught,
And up she drank the mixture quite, withouten farther thought.
Then on her breast she crossed her arms long and small,
And so, her senses failing her, into a trance did fall.

. . . .

An apothecary sat unbusied at his door,
Whom by his heavy countenance he guessèd to be poor.
And in his shop he saw his boxes were but few,
And in his window, of his wares, there was so small a shew;
Wherefore our Romeus assuredly hath thought,
What by no friendship could be got, with money should be bought;
For needy lack is like the poor man to compel
To sell that which the city's law forbiddeth him to sell.
Then by the hand he drew the needy man apart,
And with the sight of glitt'ring gold inflamèd hath his heart:
"Take fifty crowns of gold," quoth he, "I give them thee,
So that, before I part from hence, thou straight deliver me
Some poison strong, that may in less than half an hour
Kill him whose wretched hap shall be the potion to devour."

The wretch by covetise is won, and doth assent
To sell the thing, whose sale ere long, too late, he doth repent.
In haste he poison sought, and closely he it bound,
And then began with whispering voice thus in his ear to round:
"Fair sir," quoth he, "be sure this is the speeding gear,
And more there is than you shall need; for half of that is there
Well serve, I undertake in less than half an hour
To kill the strongest man alive; such is the poison's power."
Then Romeus, somewhat eased of one part of his care,
Within his bosom putteth up his dear unthrifty ware. . . .

And then our Romeus (the vault-stone set upright),
Descended down, and in his hand he bare the candle light
And then with piteous voice the body of his wife
He 'gan behold, who surely was the organ of his life;
For whom unhappy now he is, but erst was blissed,
He watered her with tears, and then a hundred times her kissed;
And in his folded arms full straitly he her plight,
But no way could his greedy eyes be fillèd with her sight:
His fearful hands he laid upon her stomach cold,
And them on divers parts beside the woeful wight did hold.
But when he could not find the signs of life he sought,
Out of his cursed box he drew the poison that he bought;
Whereof he greedily devoured the greater part,
And then he cried, with deadly sigh fetched from his mourning heart:

"O Juliet, of whom the world unworthy was,
From which, for world's unworthiness thy worthy ghost did pass,
What death more pleasant could my heart wish to abide
Than that which here it suff'reth now, so near thy friendly side?
Or else so glorious tomb how could my youth have craved,
As in one self-same vault with thee haply to be ingraved?
What epitaph more worth, or half so excellent,
To consecrate my memory, could any man invent,
As this our mutual and our piteous sacrifice
Of life, set light for love?" But while he talketh in this wise,
And thought as yet awhile his dolours to enforce,
His tender heart began to faint, pressed with the venom's force;
Which little and little 'gan to overcome his heart,
And whilst his busy eyne he threw about to every part,
He saw, hard by the corse of sleeping Juliet,
Bold Tybalt's carcase dead, which was not all consumèd yet;
To whom, as having life, in this sort speaketh he:
"Ah, cousin dear, Tybalt, whereso thy restless sprite now be,
With stretchèd heands to thee for mercy now I cry,
For that before thy kindly hour I forcèd thee to die.
But if with quenchèd life not quenchèd be thine ire,
But with revenging lust as yet thy heart be set on fire,
What more amends, or cruel wreak desirest thou
To see on me, than this which here is showed forth to thee now?

Who reft by force of arms from thee thy living breath,
The same with his own hand, thou seest doth poison himself to death.
And for he causèd thee in tomb too soon to lie,
Too soon also, younger than thou, himself he layeth by."
These said, when he 'gan feel the poison's force prevail,
And little and little mastered life for aye began to fail,
Kneeling upon his knees, he said with voice full low, —
" Lord Christ, that so to ransom me descendedst long ago
Out of thy Father's bosom, and in the Virgin's womb
Didst put on flesh, oh, let my plaint out of this hollow tomb,
Pierce through the air, and grant my suit may mercy find;
Take pity on my sinful and my poor afflicted mind!
For well enough I know, this body is but clay,
Nought but a mass of sin, too frail, and subject to decay."
Then pressed with extreme grief he threw with so great force
His overpressèd parts upon his lady's wailed corse,
That now his weakened heart, weakened with torments past,
Unable to abide this pang, the sharpest and the last,
Remainèd quite deprived of sense and kindly strength,
And so the long imprisoned soul hath freedom won at length.

THE MERCHANT OF VENICE

THE principal elements of the plot of this play (excluding the story of the three caskets) are found in an Italian novella by Giovanni Fiorentino, one of a collection called *Il Pecorone,* made in the fourteenth century, and published in 1565. Of this there is not known to have been an English translation in Shakespeare's time, and one cannot say whether he went directly to the Italian source for his material. It has been conjectured that he followed an early lost drama on the same theme, such as one referred to as a play "of the Jew" in a pamphlet of 1579. The following is a condensed outline of Fiorentino's story.

THE FIRST NOVEL OF THE FOURTH DAY IN "IL PECORONE"

A young gentleman of Florence, named Giannetto, was adopted by a wealthy merchant of Venice named Ansaldo, who bestowed on him everything that the youth could desire. At length Giannetto desired to accompany certain friends on a merchandizing expedition to Alexandria, and Ansaldo fitted him out with a splendid ship and goods to that end. But passing near the port of Belmonte, he was persuaded to leave his companions and try his fortune in winning the hand of the beautiful lady who reigned over that place. This lady, when any suitor failed to meet the conditions she imposed, had the invariable custom of dismissing him and seizing all his possessions; and so it fared with Giannetto. For by a device of drugged wine he was made helpless, and meantime his ship and all it contained was taken possession of by the people of Belmonte. So he returned penniless to Venice; but Ansaldo forgave him everything, and not only so, but when next the young men were setting out again for Alexandria he bought Giannetto another ship to try his fortune a second time. Then everything happened as before; and a second time Giannetto returned to Venice in disgrace.[4] Such, however, was Ansaldo's love for the youth that even a third time he bade him go on the voyage. But on this occasion, having exhausted all his resources, Ansaldo was forced to sell all he had and in addition to borrow ten thousand ducats of gold of a Jew at Mestri. And the condition of the loan was that, if it were not paid on the feast of St. John in the following June, the Jew might take a pound of flesh from any part of Ansaldo's body. So the bond was signed, a ship finer and better freighted than either of the others was made ready, and Giannetto set out with Ansaldo's blessing. On this occasion he was so fortunate as to win what he sought; for, being warned by an attendant of the lady of Belmonte respecting the drugged wine, he drank it only in pretense, and so saved his senses and his possessions. For the lady, accepting his success, wedded him with great pomp, and he was proclaimed sovereign of the country.

All then went most happily with Giannetto and his bride until there came a day when it was mentioned in his presence that the people were celebrating the festival of St. John. Instantly Giannetto recalled Ansaldo's bond, and was stricken with fear lest the ten thousand ducats had not been paid. Whereupon his lady bade him ride all speed to Venice, taking attendants and an hundred thousand ducats to cancel the debt. Meantime, the time having expired, the Jew had seized Ansaldo and made demand

4 Fiorentino gives in detail the story of Giannetto's adventures at Belmonte, and his ultimate success in winning the lady; but of all this Shakespeare made no use, introducing as substitute the story of the three caskets, a well known medieval tale, — found, for example, in the famous collection called *Gesta Romanorum*.

for the pound of flesh. There were merchants of Venice, greatly concerned for their friend, who offered to pay the money, but the Jew would not listen to them, wishing only for the satisfaction of saying that he had put to death the greatest of the Christian merchants. And when Giannetto arrived, bearing ten times the amount required under the bond, the Jew was equally obdurate, saying that if he would give him as much gold as the city of Venice was worth, he would not receive it.

Now when Giannetto had left his lady she followed him to Venice, dressed in the garb of a lawyer, and with two attendants. Putting up at an inn, she bade her servant relate that his master was a young man who had just completed his law studies at Bologna, and was returning homeward; thereupon the stranger was received with great civility. And when she inquired of the landlord respecting the administration of justice in that city, he answered that it was too severe, and proceeded to tell her the circumstances of Ansaldo's bond and its forfeiture. Thereupon the lawyer caused a proclamation to be made that whoever had any questions of law to determine should have recourse to him; and Giannetto won the consent of the Jew that the famous lawyer should be called in consultation.

"Giannetto and the Jew each told the merits of the cause to the judge; who, when he had taken the bond and read it, said to the Jew, 'I must have you take the hundred thousand ducats, and release this honest man, who will always have a grateful sense of the favor done to him.' The Jew replied, 'I will do no such thing.' The judge answered, 'It will be better for you.' The Jew was positive he would yield nothing. Upon this they went to the appointed tribunal, and the judge spoke in favor of Ansaldo. Desiring the Jew to stand forth, 'Now,' says he to the Jew, 'do you cut off a pound of this man's flesh where you choose.' The Jew ordered him to be stripped naked, and took in his hand a razor which had been made on purpose. Giannetto, when he saw this, turning to the judge, said, 'This is not the favor I asked of you.' 'Be quiet,' says he; 'the pound of flesh is not yet cut off.' As soon as the Jew was going to begin 'Take care what you do,' says the judge; 'if you take more or less than a pound, I will order your head to be struck off; and I tell you beside, that if you shed one drop of blood you shall be put to death. Your paper makes no mention of the shedding of blood, but says expressly that you may take a pound of flesh, neither more nor less; and if you are wise, you will take great care what you do.' And he immediately sent for the executioner to bring the block and axe, saying, 'If I see one drop of blood, off goes your head.' The Jew then began to be in great fear, and Giannetto in as great joy. At length the Jew, after much wrangling, told him, 'You are more cunning than I can pretend to be; however, give me the hundred thousand ducats, and I am content.' 'No,' said the judge, 'cut off your pound of flesh according to your bond; I will not give you a farthing; why did you not take the money when it was offered?' The Jew came down to ninety thousand and then to eighty, but the judge was still resolute. . . . 'Give me at least,' said the Jew,' 'my own ten thousand ducats, and a curse confound you all!' The judge replied, 'I will give you nothing; if you will have the pound of flesh, take it; if not, I will order your bond to be protested and annulled.' Every one present was greatly pleased, and, deriding the Jew, said 'He who laid traps for others is caught himself.' The Jew, seeing he could do nothing, tore in pieces the bond in a great rage. So Ansaldo was released, and conducted home in great joy by Giannetto."

But first Giannetto took the hundred thousand ducats to the lawyer, urging him to accept them in reward for his service. The lawyer refused all money, but sent his respects to Giannetto's lady, bade him give the money to her, and said his only reward should be the ring he saw on Giannetto's finger. This ring was one which had been given Giannetto by his lady, and, though he yielded to the lawyer's request, he said he feared she would think he had given it to some other woman. Then he took leave of his friends at Venice, and returned to Belmonte, bringing Ansaldo with him. Now his wife had arrived some days ahead of him, pretending to have spent her absence at the baths. Then Giannetto and his friends were received with great pomp of welcome, and the lady ran to embrace her lord; but presently, seeing that she did not receive him with her accustomed warmth, he inquired the reason. Then she accused him of having lavished his caresses on former mistresses at Venice, and asked him where the ring was which she had given him. "I swear by all that is sacred," said he, "that I gave it to the lawyer who gained our cause." "And I can swear," said she, "that you gave it to a woman." So after much talk in this manner she began to laugh, showing him the ring, and revealing that she herself was the lawyer of Bologna. All this heightened greatly the love between Giannetto and his lady; and to add to their content he gave the attendant who had helped him to win her, to Ansaldo for a wife.

RICHARD THE SECOND, HENRY THE FOURTH, AND HENRY THE FIFTH

FOR these historical plays Shakespeare chiefly used Raphael Holinshed's *Chronicles of England* (1578; but there is evidence that it was the second edition, 1587, which Shakespeare followed); from this the principal following selections are taken. Further, for the story of Prince Henry, afterward Henry the Fifth, Shakespeare followed an old popular chronicle drama, of unknown authorship, *The Famous Victories of Henry the Fifth,* which was on the stage as early as 1588.

[From Holinshed's *Chronicles of England*]

RICHARD THE SECOND

[Richard] was of good disposition and towardness, but his age being ready to incline which way soever a man should bend it, those that were appointed to have the government of his person, did what lay in them now at the first, to keep him from all manner of light demeanor. But afterwards, when everyone began to study more for his own private commodity, than for the advancement of the common-wealth, they set open the gates to other, which being ready to corrupt his good nature, by little and little grew familiar with him, and dimming the brightness of true honor, with the counterfeit shine of the contrary, so maskered his understanding, that in the end they brought him to tract the steps of lewd demeanor, and so were causers both of his and their own destruction. . . .

It fell out that in this Parliament holden at Shrewsbury, Henry Duke of Hereford accused Thomas Mowbray, Duke of Norfolk, of certain words which he should utter in talk had betwixt them, as they rode together lately before betwixt London and Brainford sounding highly to the king's dishonor. And for further proof thereof, he presented a supplication to the king, wherein he appealed the Duke of Norfolk in field of battle, for a traitor, false and disloyal to the king, and enemy unto the realm. This supplication was read before both the dukes, in presence of the king: which done, the Duke of Norfolk took upon him to answer it, declaring that whatsoever the Duke of Hereford had said against him other than well, he lied falsely like an untrue knight as he was. . . .

[On the day appointed for the combat at Coventry] the Duke of Norfolk hovered on horseback at the entry of the lists, his horse being barded with crimson velvet, embroidered richly with lions of silver and mulberry trees; and when he had made his oath before the constable and marshall that his quarrel was just and true, he entered the field manfully, saying aloud: "God aid him that hath the right;" and then he departed from his horse, and sat him down in his chair, which was of crimson velvet, curtained about with white and red damask. The lord marshall viewed their spears, to see that they were of equal length, and delivered the one spear himself to the Duke of Hereford, and sent the other unto the Duke of Norfolk by a knight. Then the herald proclaimed that the traverses and chairs of the champions should be removed, commanding them on the king's behalf to mount on horseback, and address themselves to the battle and combat.

The Duke of Hereford was quickly horsed, and closed his bavier, and cast his spear into the rest, and when the trumpet sounded set forward courageously towards his enemy six or seven paces. The Duke of Norfolk was not fully set forward, when the king cast down his warder, and the heralds cried, "Ho, ho!" Then the king caused their spears to be taken from them, and commanded them to repair again to their chairs, where they remained two long hours, while the king and his council deliberately consulted what order was best to be had in so weighty a cause. Finally, after they had devised and fully determined what should be done therein, the heralds cried silence; and Sir John Bushy, the king's secretary, read the sentence and determination of the king and his council in a long roll, the effect whereof was, that Henry Duke of Hereford should within fifteen days depart out of the realm, and not to return before the term of ten years were expired, except by the king he should be repealed again, and this upon pain of death; and that Thomas Mowbray Duke of Norfolk, because he had sown sedition in the realm by his words, should likewise avoid the realm, and never to return again into England, nor approach the borders or confines thereof, upon pain of death. . . .

The Duke of Norfolk departed sorrowfully out of the realm into Almanie, and at the last came to Venice, where he for thought and melancholy deceased. . . . The Duke of Hereford took his leave of the king at Eltham, who there released four years of his banishment: so he took his journey over into Calais, and from thence went into France, where he remained. A wonder it was to see what number of people ran after him in every town and street where he came, before he took the sea, lamenting and bewailing his departure, as who would say that when he departed, the only shield, defence and comfort of the commonwealth was faded and gone. . . .

In the meantime the Duke of Lancester departed out of this life at the Bishop of Ely's place in Holborn, and lieth buried in the cathedral church of St. Paul in London. . . . The death of this duke gave occasion of increasing more hatred in the people of this realm toward the king, for he seized into his hands all the goods that belonged to him, and also received all the rents and revenues of his lands which ought to have descended unto the Duke of Hereford by lawful inheritance, in revoking his letters patents which he had granted to him before, by virtue whereof he might make his attorneys general to sue livery for him, of any manner of inheritances or possessions that might from thenceforth fall unto him, and that his homage might be respited with making reasonable fine; whereby it was evident that the king meant his utter undoing. This hard dealing was much misliked of all the nobility, and cried out against of the meaner sort: but namely the Duke of York was therewith sore moved, who before this time had borne things with so patient a mind as he could, though the same touched him very near, as the death of his brother the Duke of Gloucester, the banishment of his nephew the said Duke of Hereford, and other mo injuries in great number, which for the slippery youth of the king he passed over for the time, and did forget as well as he might. But now perceiving that neither law, justice nor equity could take place, where the king's wilful will was bent upon any wrongful purpose, he considered that the glory of the public wealth of his country must needs decay, by reason of the king his lack of wit, and want of such as would (without flattery) admonish him of his duty: and therefore he thought it the part of a wise man to get him in time to a resting place, and to leave the following of such an unadvised captain, as with a leaden sword would cut his own throat. Hereupon he, with the Duke of Aumarle his son, went to his house at Langley, rejoicing that nothing had mishappened in the common-wealth through his device or consent. The common bruit ran, that the king had set to farm the realm of England unto Sir William Scroop, Earl of Wiltshire, and then treasurer of England, to Sir John Bushy, Sir John Bagot, and Sir Henry Green, knights. . . . Moreover, this year he caused seventeen shires of the realm, by way of putting them to their fines, to pay no small sums of money for redeeming their offenses, that they had aided the Duke of Gloucester, the earls of Arundel and Warwick, when they rose in armor against him. . . . Moreover, the king's letters patents were sent into every shire within this land, by virtue whereof an oath was demanded of all the king's liege people for a further assurance of their due obedience, and they were constrained to ratify the same in writing under their hands and seals. Moreover they were compelled to put their hands and seals to certain blanks, whereof ye have heard before, in the which, when it pleased him, he might write what he thought good. . . .

[While the king was absent on an expedition to Ireland] divers of the nobility as well prelates as other, and likewise many of the magistrates and rulers of the cities, towns, and commonalty, here in England, perceiving daily how the realm drew to utter ruin, not like to be recovered to the former state of wealth, whilst King Richard lived and reigned (as they took it), devised with great deliberation and considerate advice, to send and signify by letters unto Duke Henry, whom they now called (as he was indeed) Duke of Lancaster and Hereford, requiring him with all convenient speed to convey himself into England, promising him all their aid, power, and assistance, if he, expelling King Richard, as a man not meet for the office he bare, would take upon him the sceptre, rule, and diadem of his native land and region. . . .

[Richard, returned from Ireland after much delay,] taking with him such Cheshire men as he had with him at that present (in whom all his trust was reposed), he doubted not to revenge himself of his adversaries, and so at the first he passed with a good courage: but when he understood as he went thus forward, that all the castles, even from the borders of Scotland unto Bristow, were delivered unto the Duke of Lancaster, and that likewise the nobles and commons, as well of the south parts as the north, were fully bent to take part with the same duke against him; and further, hearing how his trusty counselors had lost their heads at Bristow, he became so greatly discomforted that, sorrowfully lamenting his miserable state, he utterly despaired of his own safety, and, calling his army together, which was not small, licensed every man to depart to his home. The soldiers, being well bent to fight in his defense, besought him to be of good cheer, promising with an oath to stand with him against the Duke and all his partakers unto death: but this could not encourage him at all; so that in the night next ensuing he stole from his army, and with the Dukes of Exeter and Surrey, the Bishop of Carlisle, and Sir Stephen Scroop, and about half a score others, he got him to the castle of Conway, where he found the Earl of Salisbury, determining there to hold himself, till he might see the world at some better stay; for what counsel to take to remedy the mischief thus pressing upon him he wist not. On the one part he knew his title just, true, and infallible; and his conscience clean, pure, and without spot of envy or malice: he had also no small affiance in the Welshmen and Cheshire men. On the other side he saw the puissance of his adversaries, the sudden departure of them whom he most trusted, and all things turned upside down: he evidently saw, and manifestly perceived, that he was forsaken of them by whom in time he might have been aided and relieved, where now it was too late, and too far overpassed.

This surely is a notable example, and not unworthy of all princes to be well weighed and diligently marked, that this Henry Duke of Lancaster should be thus called to the kingdom, and have the help and assistance (almost) of all the whole realm, which perchance never thereof thought or yet dreamed; and that King Richard should thus be left desolate, void, and in despair of all hope and comfort, in whom if there were any offense, it ought rather to be imputed to the frailty of wanton youth than to the malice of his heart. But such is the deceivable judgment of man, which, not regarding things present with due consideration, thinketh ever that things to come shall have good success, with a pleasant and delightful end. . . .

[When the king had come to Flint Castle, the Archbishop of Canterbury] willed him to be of good comfort, for he should be assured not to have any hurt as touching his person; but he prophesied not as a prelate, but as a Pilate. For was it no hurt (think you) to his person to be spoiled of his royalty, to be deposed from his crown, to be translated from principality to prison, and to fall from honor into horror? All which befell him to his extreme heart grief (no doubt); which to increase, means alas! there were many, but to diminish, helps (Got wot) but a few. So that he might have said with the forlorn man in the merciless seas of his miseries:

Ut fera nimboso tumuerunt aequora vento,
In mediis lacera nave relinquor aquis.

Some write . . . that the Archbishop of Canterbury went with the Earl of Northumberland unto Conway, and there talked with him; and further, that even then the king offered, in consideration of his insufficiency to govern, freely to resign the crown, and his kingly title to the same, unto the Duke of Hereford. . . . But wheresoever this offer was made, after that the Archbishop had now here at Flint communed with the king, he departed, and taking his horse again rode back to meet the Duke, who began at that present to approach the castle, and compassed it round about, even down to the sea, with his people ranged in good and seemly order at the foot of the mountains. . . .

Forthwith as the Duke got sight of the king, he shewed a reverend duty as became him, in bowing his knee, and coming forward did so likewise the second and third time, till the king took him by the hand and lift him up, saying, " Dear cousin, ye are welcome." The Duke, humbly thanking him, said, " My sovereign lord and king, the cause of my coming at this present is (your honor saved) to have again restitution of my person, my lands and heritage, through your favorable license." The king hereunto answered, " Dear cousin, I am ready to accomplish your will, so that ye may enjoy all that is yours, without exception." . . .

As for the Duke, he was received with all the joy and pomp that might be of the Londoners, and was lodged in the Bishop's palace, by Paul's Church. . . . In every town and village where he passed, children rejoiced, women clapped their hands, and men cried out for joy. But to speak of the great numbers of people that flocked together in the fields and streets of London at his coming, I here omit. . . . The next day after his coming to London the king from Westminster was had to the Tower, and there committed to safe custody. . . .

[A session of Parliament] began the thirteenth day of September, in the which many heinous points of misgovernance and injurious dealings in the administration of his kingly office were laid to the charge of this noble prince King Richard, the which (to the end the commons might be persuaded that he was an unprofitable prince to the commonwealth, and worthy to be deposed) were engrossed up in thirty-three solemn articles, heinous to the ears of all men, and to some almost incredible. . . .

Then for so much as these articles, and other heinous and detestable accusations, were laid against him in open parliament, it was thought by the most part that he was worthy to be deposed from all kingly honor and princely government; and to bring the matter without slander the better to pass, divers of the king's servants, which by license had access to his person, comforted him (being with sorrow almost consumed, and in manner half dead) in the best wise they could, exhorting him to regard his health and save his life. . . . The king, being now in the hands of his enemies, and utterly despairing of all comfort, was easily persuaded to renounce his crown and princely pre-eminence, so that, in hope of life only, he agreed to all things that were of him demanded. . . .

THE TENOR OF THE INSTRUMENT WHEREBY KING RICHARD RESIGNETH THE CROWN TO THE DUKE OF LANCASTER

In the name of God Amen: I Richard, by the grace of God king of England and of France, &c., lord of Ireland, acquit and assoil all archbishops, bishops, and other prelates, secular or religious, of what dignity, degree, state, or condition so ever they be, and also all dukes, marquesses, earls, barons, lords, and all my liege men, both spiritual and secular, of what manner or degree they be, from their oath of fealty and homage, and all other deeds and privileges made unto me, and from all manner bonds of allegiance, regality and lordship, in which they were or be bounden to me, or any otherwise constrained; and them, their heirs and successors for evermore, from the same bonds and oaths I release, deliver, and acquit, and set them for free, dissolved, and acquit, and to be harmless, for as much as longeth to my person by any manner, way or title of right, that to me might follow of the foresaid things, or any of them. And also I resign all my kingly dignity, majesty, and crown, with all the lordships, power, and privileges to the foresaid kingly dignity and crown belonging, and all other lordships and possessions to me in any manner of wise pertaining, of what name, title, quality, or condition soever they be, except the lands and possessions for me and mine obits purchased and bought. . . .

And also I renounce the name, worship, and regality and kingly highness, clearly, freely, singularly and wholly, in the most best manner and form that I may, and with deed and word I leave off and resign them, and go from them for evermore; saving always to my successors, kings of England, all the rights, privileges, and appurtenances to the said kingdom and lordships above said belonging and appertaining. For well I wot and knowledge, and deem myself to be and have been insufficient and unable, and also unprofitable, and for my open deserts not unworthy to be put down. And I swear upon the holy Evangelists, here presently with my hands touched, that I shall never repugn to this resignation, demission or yielding up, nor never impugn them in any manner by word or deed, by my self nor none other: nor I shall not suffer it to be impugned, in as much as in me is, privily or apertly. But I shall have, hold, and keep this denouncing, demission, and giving up for firm and stable for evermore in all and every part thereof, so God me help and all saints, and by this holy evangelist by me bodily touched and kissed. And for more record of the same, here openly I subscribe and sign this present resignation with mine own hand.

. . . Thus was king Richard deprived of all kingly honor and princely dignity, by reason he was so given to follow evil council, and used such inconvenient ways and means, through insolent misgovernance and youthful outrage, though otherwise a right noble and worthy prince. . . . Shortly after his resignation, he was conveyed to the castle of Leeds in Kent, and from thence to Pomfret, where he departed out of this miserable life, as after you shall hear. He was seemly of shape and favor, and of nature good enough, if the wickedness and naughty demeanor of such as were about him had not altered it. His chance verily was greatly infortunate, which fell into such calamity that he took it for the best way he could devise to renounce his kingdom, for the which mortal men are accustomed to hazard all they have to attain thereunto. But such misfortune, or the like, oftentimes falleth unto those princes which, when they are aloft, cast no doubt for perils that may follow. He was prodigal, ambitious, and much given to the pleasure of the body. He kept the greatest port, and maintained the most plentiful house, that ever any king in England did either before his time or since. . . . Furthermore, there reigned abundantly the filthy sin of lechery and fornication, with abominable adultery, specially in the king, but most chiefly in the prelacy, whereby the whole realm, by such their evil example, was so infected that the wrath of God was daily provoked to vengeance for the sins of the prince and his people. . . .

Thus have ye heard what writers do report touching the state of the time and doings of this king. But if I may boldly say what I think; he was a prince the most unthankfully used of his subjects, of any one of whom ye shall lightly read. For although, through the frailty of youth, he demeaned himself more dissolutely than seemed convenient for his royal estate, and made choice of such counsellors as were not favored of the people, whereby he was the less favored himself; yet in no king's days were the commons in greater wealth, if they could have perceived their happy state: neither in any other time were the nobles and gentlemen more cherished, nor churchmen less wronged. But such was their ingratitude towards their bountiful and loving sovereign, that those whom he had chiefly advanced were readiest to control him. . . . [The Duke of Hereford, seeking to avenge the death of his uncle Duke of Gloucester,] wanted moderation and loyalty in his doings, for the which both he himself and his lineal race were scourged afterwards, as a due punishment unto rebellious subjects; so as deserved vengeance seemed not to stay long for his ambitious cruelty, that thought it not enough to drive King Richard to resign his crown and regal dignity over unto him, except he also should take from him his guiltless life.

HENRY THE FOURTH

One writer . . . saith that King Henry, sitting on a day at his table, sore sighing, said: "Have I no faithful friend which will deliver me of him whose life will be my death, and whose death will be the preservation of my life?" This saying was much noted of them which were present, and especially of one called Sir Piers of Exton. This knight incontinently departed from the court, with eight strong persons in his company, and came to Pomfret, commanding the esquire that was accustomed to sew and take the assay before King Richard, to do so no more, saying: "Let him eat now, for he shall not long eat." King

Richard sat down to dinner, and was served without courtesy or assay, whereupon, much marveling at the sudden change, he demanded of the esquire why he did not his duty. "Sir," said he, "I am otherwise commanded by Sir Piers of Exton, which is newly come from King Henry." When King Richard heard that word, he took the carving knife in his hand, and strake the esquire on the head, saying, "The devil take Henry of Lancaster and thee together!" And with that word Sir Piers entered the chamber, well armed, with eight tall men likewise armed, every of them having a bill in his hand. King Richard perceiving this put the table from him, and stepping to the foremost man, wrung the bill out of his hands, and so valiantly defended himself that he slew four of those that thus came to assail him. Sir Piers, being half dismayed therewith, leaped into the chair where King Richard was wont to sit, while the other four persons fought with him, and chased him about the chamber. And in conclusion, as King Richard traversed his ground from one side of the chamber to another, and coming by the chair where Sir Piers stood, he was felled with the stroke of a poleax which Sir Piers gave him upon the head, and therewith rid him out of life, without giving him respite once to call upon God for mercy of his past offenses. It is said that Sir Piers of Exton, after he had thus slain him, wept bitterly, as one stricken with the prick of a guilty conscience, for murdering him whom he had so long time obeyed as king. . . .

Henry Earl of Northumberland, with his brother Thomas Earl of Worcester, and his son the Lord Henry Percy, surnamed Hotspur, which were to King Henry in the beginning of his reign both faithful friends and earnest aiders, began now to envy his wealth and felicity; and especially they were grieved because the king demanded of the earl and his son such Scottish prisoners as were taken at Homeldon and Nesbit. . . . Insomuch that Henry Hotspur said openly, "Behold, the heir of the realm is robbed of his right, and yet the robber with his own will not redeem him." So in this fury the Percies departed, minding nothing more than to depose King Henry from the high type of his royalty, and to place in his seat their cousin Edmund Earl of March, whom they did not only deliver out of captivity, but also (to the high displeasure of King Henry) entered in league with the foresaid Owen Glendower. Herewith they by their deputies, in the house of the Archdeacon of Bangor, divided the realm amongst them, causing a tripartite indenture to be made and sealed with their seals, by the covenants whereof all England from Severn and Trent, south and eastward, was assigned to the Earl of March; all Wales, and the lands beyond Severn westward, were appointed to Owen Glendower; and all the remnant from Trent northward, to the Lord Percy. . . .

Resolved to go forwards with their enterprise, they marched towards Shrewsbury, upon hope to be aided (as men thought) by Owen Glendower and his Welshmen, publishing abroad throughout the countries on each side that King Richard was alive. . . . And to speak a truth, no marvel it was if many envied the prosperous state of King Henry, sith it was evident enough to the world that he had with wrong usurped the crown, and not only violently deposed King Richard, but also cruelly procured his death, for the which undoubtedly both he and his posterity tasted such troubles as put them still in danger of their states, till their direct succeeding line was quite rooted out by the contrary faction, and in Henry the Sixth and Edward the Fourth it may appear. . . . King Henry, advertised of the proceedings of the Percies, forthwith gathered about him such power as he might make, and . . . passed forward with such speed that he was in sight of his enemies, lying in camp near to Shrewsbury, before they were in doubt of any such thing. . . . By reason of the king's sudden coming in this sort, they stayed from assaulting the town of Shrewsbury, which enterprise they were ready at that instant to have taken in hand; and forthwith the Lord Percy, as a captain of high courage, began to exhort the captains and soldiers to prepare themselves to battle, sith the matter was grown to that point that by no means it could be avoided, so that (said he) this day shall either bring us all to advancement and honor, or else, if it shall chance us to be overcome, shall deliver us from the king's spiteful malice and cruel disdain; for playing the men, as we ought to do, better it is to die in battle for the common-wealth's cause, than through coward-like fear to prolong life which after shall be taken from us by sentence of the enemy. Hereupon the whole army, being in number about 14,000 chosen men, promised to stand with him so long as life lasted. . . .

Then suddenly blew the trumpets, the king's part crying, "Saint George! Upon them!", the adversaries cried "Esperance Percy!"; and so the two armies furiously joined. The archers on both sides shot for the best game, laying on such load with arrows that many died, and were driven down that never rose again. . . . The Lord Henry

Percy and the Earl Douglas, a right stout and hardy captain, not regarding the shot of the king's battle, nor the close order of the ranks, pressing forward together bent their whole forces towards the king's person, coming upon him with spears and swords so fiercely that the Earl of March, the Scot, perceiving their purpose, withdrew the king from that side of the field (as some write) for his great benefit and safeguard, as it appeared; for they gave such a violent onset upon them that stood about the king's standard that, slaying his standard-bearer Sir Walter Blount, and overthrowing the standard, they made slaughter of all those that stood about it. . . . The prince that day holp his father like a lusty young gentleman; for although he was hurt in the face with an arrow, so that divers noblemen that were about him would have conveyed him forth of the field, yet he would not suffer them so to do, lest his departure from amongst his men might happily have stricken some fear into their hearts; and so, without regard of his hurt, he continued with his men, and never ceased either to fight where the battle was most hot or to encourage his men where it seemed most need. This battle lasted three long hours, with indifferent fortune on both parts, till at length the king, crying, "St. George! Victory!" brake the array of his enemies, and adventured so far that (as some write) the Earl Douglas strake him down, and at that instant slew Sir Walter Blount and three other apparelled in the king's suit and clothing, saying, "I marvel to see so many kings thus suddenly arise, one in the neck of another." The king indeed was raised, and did that day many a noble feat of arms; for, as it is written, he slew that day with his own hands six and thirty persons of his enemies. The other on his part, encouraged by his doings, fought valiantly, and slew the Lord Percy, called Sir Henry Hotspur. To conclude, the king's enemies were vanquished and put to flight. . . .

The Lord Henry, Prince of Wales, eldest son of King Henry, got knowledge that certain of his father's servants were busy to give informations against him, whereby discord might arise betwixt him and his father. . . . [After a meeting with the king, requested by the prince, father and son were] reconciled, betwixt whom the said pickthanks had sown disunion, insomuch that the son, upon a vehement conceit of unkindness sprung in the father, was in the way to be worn out of favor. Which was the more likely to come to pass, by their informations that privily charged him with riot and other uncivil demeanor unseemly for a prince. Indeed he was youthfully given, grown to audacity, and had chosen him companions agreeable to his age; with whom he spent the time in such recreations, exercises, and delights as he fancied. But yet (it should seem by the report of some writers) that his behavior was not offensive, or at least tending to the damage of any body; sith he had a care to avoid doing of wrong, and to tedder his affections within the tract of virtue, whereby he opened unto himself a ready passage of good liking among the prudent sort, and was beloved of such as could discern his disposition, which was in no degree so excessive as that he deserved in such vehement manner to be suspected. In whose dispraise I find little, but to his praise very much. . . .

[King Henry now being stricken with an apoplexy,] during this his last sickness he caused his crown (as some write) to be set on a pillow at his bed's head; and suddenly his pangs so sore troubled him, that he lay as though all his vital spirits had been from him departed. Such as were about him, thinking verily that he had been departed, covered his face with a linen cloth. The prince his son, being hereof advertised, entered into the chamber, took away the crown, and departed. The father, being suddenly revived out of that trance, quickly perceived the lack of his crown; and having knowledge that the prince his son had taken it way, caused him to come before his presence, requiring of him what he meant so to misuse himself. The prince with a good audacity answered: "Sir, to mine and all men's judgments you seemed dead in this world; whereof I as your next heir apparent took that as mine own, and not as yours." "Well, fair son," said the king with a great sigh, "what right I had to it, God knoweth." "Well," said the prince, "if you die king, I will have the garland, and trust to keep it with the sword against all mine enemies, as you have done." Then said the king, "I commit all to God, and remember you to do well." With that he turned himself in his bed, and shortly after departed to God, in a chamber of the Abbot's of Westminster called Jerusalem, the twentieth day of March, in the year 1413, and in the year of his age forty-six, when he had reigned thirteen years, five months and odd days, in great perplexity and little pleasure. . . . This king was of a mean stature, well proportioned, and formally compact, quick and lively, and of a stout courage. In his latter days he showed himself so gentle that he gat more love amongst the nobles and people of this realm than he had purchased malice and evil will in the beginning. But yet to speak a truth, by his proceedings, after he had attained to the crown, what with such taxes, tallages, subsidies, and exactions as he was constrained to charge the people with; and what by punishing such as, moved with disdain to see him usurp the crown (contrary to the oath taken at his entering into this land, upon his return from exile), did at sundry times rebel against him, he won himself more hatred than in all his lifetime, if it had been longer by many years than it was, had been possible for him to have weeded out and removed.

HENRY THE FIFTH

THIS king even at first appointing with himself to show that in his person princely honors should change public manners, he determined to put on him the shape of a new man. For whereas aforetime he had made himself a companion unto misruly mates of dissolute order and life, he now banished them all from his presence (but not unrewarded, or else unpreferred), inhibiting them upon a great pain not once to approach, lodge, or sojourn within ten miles of his court or presence; and in their places he chose men of gravity, wit, and high policy, by whose wise counsel he might at all times rule to his honor and dignity; calling to mind how once, to high offense of the king his father, he had with his fist stricken the Chief Justice for sending one of his minions, upon desert, to prison, when the Justice commanded himself also strait to ward, and he (then prince) obeyed. The king after expelled him out of his Privy Counsel, banished him the court, and made the Duke of Clarence, his younger brother,

President of Council in his stead. This reformation in the new king Christ[opher] Okl[and] hath reported, fully consenting with this. For saith he,

> Ille inter iuvenes paulo lascivior ante,
> Defuncto genitore gravis constans que repente,
> Moribus ablegat corruptis regis ab aula
> Assuetos socios, et nugatoribus acrem
> Poenam (si quisquam sua tecta reviserit) addit,
> Atque ita mutatus facit omnia principe digna,
> Ingenio magno post consultoribus usus, &c.

[When a bill providing for the forfeiture to the king of certain lands held by the church was under consideration in Parliament, the clergy] thought best to try if they might move the king's mood with some sharp invention, that he should not regard the importunate petitions of the commons. Whereupon, on a day in the Parliament, Henry Chichely, Archbishop of Canterbury, made a pithy oration wherein he declared how not only the duchies of Normandy and Aquitaine, with the counties of Anjou and Maine, and the country of Gascoigne, were by undoubted title appertaining to the king, as to the lawful and only heir to the same, but also the whole realm of France, as heir to his great-grandfather King Edward the third. Herein did he much inveigh against the surmised and false-feigned law Salic, which the Frenchmen allege ever against the kings of England in bar of their just title to the crown of France. . . .

The king sent over into France his uncle the Duke of Exeter, the Lord Gray, Admiral of England, the Archbishop of Dublin, and the Bishop of Norwich, ambassadors unto the French king, with five hundred horse. . . .

The French king received them very honorably and banqueted them right sumptuously, showing to them jousts and martial pastimes. . . . When the triumph was ended, the English ambassadors, having a time appointed to declare their message, admitted to the French king's presence, required of him to deliver unto the king of England the realm and crown of France, with the entire duchies of Aquitaine, Normandy, and Anjou, with the countries of Poitou and Maine. Many other requests they made; and this offered withal, that if the French king would without war, and effusion of Christian blood, render to the king their master his very right and lawful inheritance, that he would be content to take in marriage the Lady Katharine, daughter to the French king, and to endow her with all the duchies and countries before rehearsed. And if he would not do so, then the king of England did express and signify to him that, with the aid of God and help of his people, he would recover his right and inheritance wrongfully witholden from him, with mortal war and dint of sword. . . .

[When the Archbishop of Bruges came to England as ambassador from the king of France, King Henry said to him:] "I little esteem your French brags, and less set by your power and strength. I know perfectly my right to my region, which you usurp; and except you deny the apparent truth, so do yourselves also; if you neither do nor will know it, yet God and the world knoweth it. The power of your master you see, but my puissance ye have not yet tasted. If he have loving subjects, I am (I thank God) not unstored of the same: and I say this unto you, that before one year pass, I trust to make the highest crown of your country to stoop, and the proudest mitre to learn his humiliatedo. In the mean time tell this to the usurper your master, that within three months I will enter into France, as into mine own true and lawful patrimony, appointing to acquire the same not with brag of words but with deeds of men and dint of sword, by the aid of God, in whom is my whole trust and confidence." . . .

After this, when the wind came about prosperous to his purpose, he caused the mariners to weigh up anchors and hoist up sails, and to set forward with a thousand ships, on the vigil of our Lady day the Assumption, and took land at Caux, commonly called Kidcaux, where the river of Seine runneth into the sea, without resistance. At his first coming on land he caused proclamation to be made that no person should be so hardy, on pain of death, either to take anything out of any church that belonged to the same, or to hurt or do any violence either to priests, women, or any such as should be found without weapon or armor and not ready to make resistance; also that no man should renew any quarrel or strife, whereby any fray might arise to the disquieting of the army. [The siege of Harfleur followed. After its capitulation,] the king ordered captain to the town his uncle the Duke of Exeter, who established his lieutenant there, one Sir John Fastolfe, with fifteen hundred men. . . .

The Englishmen were brought into some distress in this journey [from the river Somme to Calais], by reason of their victuals in manner spent, and no hope to get more; for the enemies had destroyed all the corn before they came. Rest could they none take, for their enemies with alarms did ever so infest them. Daily it rained, and nightly it freezed; of fuel there was great scarcity, of fluxes plenty; money enough, but wares for their relief to bestow it on had they none. Yet in this great necessity the poor people of the country were not spoiled, nor anything taken of them without payment, nor any outrage or offense done by the Englishmen, except one, which was, that a soldier took a pyx out of a church, for which he was apprehended, and the king not once removed till the box was restored and the offender strangled. The people of the countries thereabout, hearing of such zeal in him to the maintenance of justice, ministered to his army victuals and other necessaries, although by open proclamation so to do they were prohibited. . . .

[The king] rode forth to view his adversaries, and that done, returned to his people, and with cheerful countenance caused them to be put in order of battle, assigning to every captain such room and place as he thought convenient, and so kept them still in that order till night was come, and then determined to seek a place to encamp and lodge his army in for that night. . . . Order was taken by commandment from the king, after the army was first set in battle array, that no noise or clamor should be made in the host; so that in marching forth to this village every man kept himself quiet, but at their coming into the village, fires were made to give light on every side, as there likewise were in the French host, which was encamped not past two hundred and fifty paces distant from the English. . . .

[The French] were lodged even in the way by which the Englishmen must needs pass towards Calais, and all that night, after their coming thither, made great cheer, and were very merry, pleasant, and full of game. The

Englishmen also for their parts were of good comfort, and nothing abashed of the matter, and yet they were both hungry, weary, sore traveled, and vexed with many cold diseases. Howbeit, reconciling themselves with God by housel and shrift, requiring assistance at his hands who is the only giver of victory, they determined rather to die than to yield or flee. The day following was the five and twentieth of October in the year 1415, being then Friday, and the feast of Crispin and Crispinian, a day fair and fortunate to the English, but most sorrowful and unlucky to the French. . . .

[When the king] had thus ordered his battles, he left a small company to keep his camp and carriage, which remained still in the village, and then, calling his captains and soldiers about him, he made to them a right grave oration, moving them to play the men, whereby to obtain a glorious victory, as there was hope certain they should, the rather if they would but remember the just cause for which they fought, and whom they should encounter, such faint-hearted people as their ancestors had so often overcome. To conclude, many words of courage he uttered, assuring them that England should never be charged with his ransom, nor any Frenchman triumph over him as a captive; for either by famous death or glorious victory would he, by God's grace, win honor and fame.

It is said that as he heard one of the host utter his wish to another thus, "I would to God there were with us now so many good soldiers as are at this hour within England!" the king answered: "I would not wish a man more here than I have. We are indeed in comparison to the enemies but a few, but if God of his clemency do favor us, and our just cause (as I trust he will), we shall speed well enough. But let no man ascribe victory to our own strength and might, but only to God's assistance, to whom I have no doubt we shall worthily have cause to give thanks therefore. And if so be that, for our offenses' sakes, we shall be delivered into the hands of our enemies, the less number we be, the less damage shall the realm of England sustain. But if we should fight in trust of multitude of men, and so get the victory, our minds being prone to pride, we should thereupon, peradventure, ascribe the victory not so much to the gift of God as to our own puissance, and thereby provoke his high indignation and displeasure against us; and if the enemy get the upper hand, then should our realm and country suffer more damage and stand in further danger. But be you of good comfort, and show yourselves valiant: God and our just quarrel shall defend us, and deliver these our proud adversaries, with all the multitude of them which you see (or at least the most of them) into our hands." . . .

About four of the clock in the afternoon, the king, when he saw no appearance of enemies, caused the retreat to be blown, and, gathering his army together, gave thanks to almighty God for so happy a victory, causing his prelates and chaplains to sing this psalm, *In exitu Israel de Aegypto;* and commanded every man to kneel down on the ground at this verse, *Non nobis Domine, non nobis, sed nomini tuo da gloriam.* Which done, he caused the Te Deum, with certain anthems, to be sung, giving laud and praise to God, without boasting of his own force or any human power. . . .

[Arrived at London,] the king, like a grave and sober

personage, and as one remembering from whom all victories are sent, seemed little to regard such vain pomps and shows as were in triumphant sort devised for his welcoming home from so prosperous a journey; in so much that he would not suffer his helmet to he carried with him, whereby might have appeared to the people the blows and dints that were to be seen in the same; neither would he suffer any ditties to be made and sung by minstrels of his glorious victory, for that he would wholly have the praise and thanks altogether given to God.

. . . This Henry was a king of life without spot, a prince whom all men loved and of none disdained, a captain against whom Fortune never frowned, nor mischance once spurned; whose people him, so severe a justicer, both loved and obeyed, and so humane withal, that he left no offense unpunished nor friendship unrewarded; a terror to rebels and suppresser of sedition, his virtues notable, his qualities most praiseworthy. In strength and nimbleness of body from his youth few to him comparable, for in wrestling, leaping, and running no man well able to compare. In casting of great iron bars and heavy stones he excelled commonly all men; never shirnking at cold nor slothful for heat; and when he most labored, his head commonly uncovered; no more weary of harness than a light cloak; very valiantly abiding at needs both hunger and thirst; so manful of mind as never seen to quinch at a wound, or to smart at the pain; not to turn his nose from evil favor, nor close his eyes from smoke or dust; no man more moderate in eating and drinking, with diet not delicate, but rather more meet for men of war than for princes or tender stomachs. Every honest person was permitted to come to him, sitting at meal, where either secretly or openly to declare his mind. High and weighty causes, as well between men of war and other, he would gladly hear, and either determined them himself or else for end committed them to others. He slept very little, but that very soundly, in so much that when his soldiers sung at nights, or minstrels played, he then slept fastest. Of courage invincible, of purpose unmutable, so wisehardy always, as fear was banished from him; at every alarm he first in armour, and foremost in ordering. In time of war such was his providence, bounty and hap, as he had true intelligence not only what his enemies did, but what they said and intended; of his devices and purposes few, before the thing was at the point to be done, should be made privy. He had such knowledge in ordering and guiding an army, with such a gift to encourage his people, that the Frenchmen had constant opinion he could never be vanquished in battle. Such wit, such prudence, and such policy withal, that he never enterprised anything before he had fully debated and forecast all the main chances that might happen, which done, with all diligence and courage he set his purpose forward. What policy he had in finding present remedies for sudden mischiefs, and what engines in saving himself and his people in sharp distresses, were it not that by his acts they did plainly appear, hard were it by words to make them credible. Wantonness of life and thirst in avarice had he quite quenched in him; virtues indeed, in such an estate of sovereignty, youth, and power, as very rare, so right commendable in the highest degree. So staid of mind and countenance beside, that never jolly or triumphant for victory, nor sad or damped for loss or misfortune. For bountifulness and liberality, no man more free, gentle, and frank in bestowing rewards to all persons, according to their deserts; for his saying was that he never desired money to keep, but to give and spend. . . . Of person and form was this prince rightly representing his heroical affects; of stature and proportion tall and manly, rather lean than gross, somewhat long-necked and black-haired, of countenance amiable; eloquent and grave was his speech, and of great grace and power to persuade. For conclusion, a majesty was he that both lived and died a pattern in princehood, a lodestar in honor and mirror of magnificence; the more highly exalted in his life, the more deeply lamented at his death, and famous to the world alway.

THE FAMOUS VICTORIES OF HENRY THE FIFTH

[*After the Prince has been sent to prison by order of the Chief Justice, enter Derrick* (*the clown*) *and John Cobbler.*]

Derrick. Zounds, masters! here's ado, when princes must go to prison. Why, John, didst ever see the like?

John. O Derrick, trust me, I never saw the like.

Derrick. Why, John, they mayest see what princes be in choler: a judge a box on the ear! I'll tell thee, John, O John, I would not have done it for twenty shillings.

John. No, nor I; there had been no way but one with us: we should have been hanged.

Derrick. Faith, John, I'll tell thee what: thou shalt be my Lord Chief Justice, and thou shalt sit in the chair, and I'll be the young prince, and hit thee a box in the ear;

and then thou shalt say, "To teach you what prerogatives mean, I commit you to the Fleet."

John. Come on, I'll be your judge; but thou shalt not hit me hard.

Derrick. No, no.

John. What hath he done?

Derrick. Marry, he hath robbed Derrick.

John. Why, then, I cannot let him go.

Derrick. I must needs have my man.

John. You shall not have him.

Derrick. Shall I not have my man? say no and you dare! How say you, shall I not have my man?

John. No, marry, shall you not.

Derrick. Shall I not, John?

John. No, Derrick.

Derrick. Why, then, take you that, till more come! Zounds! shall I not have him?

John. Well, I am content to take this at your hand; but I pray you, who am I?

Derrick. Who art thou? Zounds, dost not know thy self?

John. No.

Derrick. Now away, simple fellow. Why man, thou art John the cobbler.

John. No, I am my Lord Chief Justice of England.

Derrick. Oh, John! Mass, thou sayest true, thou art indeed.

John. Why, then, to teach you what prerogatives mean, I commit you to the Fleet.

Derrick. Well, I will go; but, i'faith, you graybeard knave, I'll course you.

Exit, and straight enters again.

Oh John, come, come out of thy chair! why, what a clown wert thou, to let me hit thee a box on the ear, and now thou seest they will not take me to the Fleet!

. . . .

Enter the young Prince with Ned and Tom.

Henry. Come away, sirs. Gogs wounds, Ned! didst thou not see what a box on the ear I took my Lord Chief Justice?

Tom. By gogs blood, it did me good to see it; it made his teeth jar in his head.

Enter Sir John Oldcastle.

Henry. How now, Sir John Oldcastle? What news with you?

Sir John. I am glad to see your grace at liberty. I was come to visit you in prison.

Henry. To visit me! Didst thou not know that I am a Prince's son? Why, 'tis enough for me look into a prison, though I come not in my self. But here's such ado nowadays, — here's prisoning, here's hanging, whipping, and the devil and all; but I tell you, sirs, when I am king, we will have no such things; but, my lads, if the old king my father were dead, we would all be kings.

Sir John. He is a good old man; God take him to His mercy the sooner!

Henry. But Ned, so soon as I am king, the first thing I will do shall be to put my Lord Chief Justice out of office, and thou shalt be my Lord Chief Justice of England.

Ned. Shall I be Lord Chief Justice? By gogs wounds, I'll

be the bravest Lord Chief Justice that ever was in England.

Henry. Then, Ned, I'll turn all these prisons into fence schools, and I will endue thee with them, with lands to maintain them withal. Then I will have a bout with my Lord Chief Justice. Thou shalt hang none but pickpurses and horse-stealers, and such base-minded villains; but that fellow that will stand by the highway side, courageously with his sword and buckler, and take a purse, that fellow give him commendations; beside that, send him to me and I will give him an annual pension out of my exchequer, to maintain him all the days of his life.

Sir John. Nobly spoken, Harry! We shall never have a merry world till the old king be dead.

Ned. But whither are ye going now?

Henry. To the court, for I hear say my father lies very sick.

Tom. But I doubt he will not die.

Henry. Yet will I go thither, for the breath shall be no sooner out of his mouth, but I will clap the crown on my head.

. . . .

Enter knights.

Tom. Gogs wounds, the king is dead!

Sir John. Dead? Then, gogs blood, we shall be all kings.

Ned. Gogs wounds, I shall be Lord Chief Justice of England! . . .

Sir John. Oh, how it did me good to see the king when he was crowned! Methought his seat was like the figure of heaven, and his person like unto a god.

Ned. But who would have thought that the king would have changed his countenance so?

Sir John. Did you not see with what grace he sent his embassage into France? to tell the French king that Harry of England hath sent for the crown, and Harry of England will have it.

Tom. But 'twas but a little to make the people believe that he was sorry for his father's death.

The trumpet sounds.

Ned. Gogs wounds! the king comes! Let's all stand aside.

Enter the king, with the Archbishop and the Lord of Oxford.

Sir John. How do you, my lord?

Ned. How now, Harry? Tut, my lord! put away these dumps; you are a king, and all the realm is yours. What, man, do you not remember the old sayings? You know I must be Lord Chief Justice of England. Trust me, my lord, methinks you are very much changed; and 'tis but with a little sorrowing, to make folks believe the death of your father grieves you; and 'tis nothing so.

Henry. I prethee, Ned, mend thy manners, and be more modester in thy terms; for my unfeigned grief is not to be ruled by thy flattering and dissembling talk. Thou sayest I am changed: so I am indeed, and so must thou be, and that quickly, or else I must cause thee to be changed.

Sir John. Gogs wounds! how like you this? Zounds! 'tis not so sweet as music.

Tom. I trust we have not offended your Grace no way.

Henry. Ah, Tom, your former life grieves me, and makes me to abandon and abolish your company for ever; and therefore not upon pain of death to approach my presence by ten miles space. Then, if I hear well of you, it may I will do somewhat for you; otherwise look for no more favor at my hands than at any other man's. And therefore be gone; we have other matters to talk on.

Exeunt knights.

Now, my good Lord Archbishop of Canterbury, what say you to our embassage into France?

. . . .

Henry (speaks to himself). Ah Harry, thrice unhappy Harry, hast thou now conquered the French king, and begins a fresh supply with his daughter? But with what face canst thou seek to gain her love, which hath sought to win her father's crown? Her father's crown, said I? no, it is mine own. Aye, but I love her, and must crave her; nay, I love her and will have her.

Enter Lady Katherine and her Ladies.

But here she comes: how now, fair lady, Katherine of France, what news?

Katherine. And it please your majesty, my father sent me to know if you will debate any of these unreasonable demands which you require.

Henry. Now trust me, Kate, I commend thy father's wit greatly in this; for none in the world could sooner have made me debate if it were possible. But tell me, sweet Kate, canst thou tell how to love?

Katherine. I cannot hate, my good lord; therefore far unfit were it for me to love.

Henry. Tush, Kate: but tell me in plain terms, canst thou love the king of England? I cannot do as these courtiers do, that spend half their time in wooing; tush, wench! I am none such; but wilt thou go over to England?

Kate. I would to God that I had your majesty as fast in love as you have my father in wars; I would not vouchsafe so much as one look, until you had related all these unreasonable demands.

Henry. Tush, Kate! I know thou wouldst not use me so hardly. But tell me, canst thou love the king of England?

Katherine. How should I love him that hath dealt so hardly with my father?

Henry. But I'll deal as easily with thee, as thy heart can imagine, or tongue can require. How sayest thou? what will it be?

Katherine. If I were of my own direction I could give you answer; but seeing I stand at my father's direction, I must first know his will.

Henry. But shall I have thy good will in the mean season?

Katherine. Whereas I can put your grace in no assurance, I would be loth to put you in any despair.

Henry. Now, before God, it is a sweet wench!

Katherine. [*goes aside, and speaks*] I may think myself the happiest in the world, that is beloved of the mighty king of England. . . .

Enter Derrick, with his girdle full of shoes.

Derrick. How now? Zounds! it did me good to see how I did triumph over the Frenchmen!

Enter John Cobbler, with a pack full of apparel.

John. Whoop, Derrick! how dost thou?

Derrick. What, John, comedevales, alive yet?

John. I promise thee, Derrick, I 'scaped hardly, for I was within half a mile when one was killed.

Derrick. Were you so?

John. Aye, trust me, I had like been slain.

Derrick. But once killed, why, 'tis nothing. I was four or five times slain.

John. Four or five times slain! Why, how couldst thou have been alive now?

Derrick. O John, never say so; for I was called the bloody soldier amongst them all.

John. Why, what didst thou?

Derrick. Why, I will tell thee, John. Every day when I went into the field, I would take a straw and thrust it into my nose, and make my nose bleed; and then I would go into the field, and when the captain saw me, he would say, " Peace! a bloody soldier," and bid me stand aside; whereof I was glad. But mark the chance, John: I went and stood behind a tree; but mark then, John: I thought I had been safe, but on a sudden there steps to me a lusty tall Frenchman. Now he drew, and I drew; now I lay here, and he lay there; now I set this leg before, and turned this backward, and I skipped quite over a hedge, and he saw me no more there that day. And was not this well done, John?

John. Mass, Derrick, thou hast a witty head.

Derrick. Aye, John, thou mayest see, if thou hadst taken my counsel. But what hast thou there? I think thou hast been robbing the Frenchmen.

John. I'faith, Derrick, I have gotten some reparel to carry home to my wife.

Derrick. And I have got some shoes; for, I'll tell thee what I did; when they were dead I would go and take off their shoes.

John. Aye, but Derrick, how shall we get home?

Derrick. Nay, zounds, and they take thee they will hang thee. Oh, John, never do so; if it be thy fortune to be hanged, be hanged in thy own language, whatsoever thou dost.

John. Why, Derrick, the wars is done; we may go home now.

MUCH ADO ABOUT NOTHING

THE principal plot of this comedy is found in one of the Novelle of Bandello (1554), though it is not known whether Shakespeare was directly acquainted with the Italian version, which is not known to have been translated into English before the time of *Much Ado*. No source has been discovered for the secondary plot concerned with Benedick and Beatrice.

The following is a brief abstract of Bandello's tale.

THE TWENTIETH STORY OF THE NOVELS OF BANDELLO

(Signor Timbreo di Cardona and Fenicia Leonata)

A Sicilian knight of high renown, Don Timbreo di Cardona, became desperately enamoured of a young lady named Fenicia, daughter of Messer Lionato de Lionati, a gentleman of Messina, and, though her family was of less repute and fortune than his, sought her hand in marriage. Both she and her father gladly accepted, and their betrothal was accomplished. But it chanced that a friend of Don Timbreo's, Signor Girondo, had secretly loved Fenicia for a long time; and when he learned that a marriage had been arranged for her, he was so mad with disappointment that he resolved to break it off. He therefore employed a courtier to go to Don Timbreo and tell him that Fenicia was so far from being faithful to him that a certain gentleman visited her twice or thrice weekly and was given all her love. He further offered to prove what he had said, proposing that Don Timbreo secrete himself near the garden of Lionato's house that night, and see with his own eyes what went on. Don Timbreo, torn with jealous anxiety, did as he was requested; and at the third hour of the night, being hidden opposite the windows of one quarter of Lionato's house, he saw three men come by with a ladder. Then one of them, who played the lover, said to him who bore the ladder, "Look thou set it carefully to the window, so it make no noise, for when we were last here my lady Fenicia told me that thou lettest it fall over heavily." Then they set the ladder softly against the house, and he who played the lover climbed it and went in. Then the love of Don Timbreo for Fenicia was not only quenched but turned to hatred, and he went away in despair. Whereupon the three plotters removed the ladder, and, going to Signor Girondo, told them what they had done.

On the morrow Don Timbreo sent a friend to Lionato and his daughter, with this message: that the love he had borne Fenicia had not deserved such requital as she had made him, and that she would do well to marry the lover with whom she had provided herself. Then Lionato believed that Don Timbreo, repenting of having agreed to a marriage beneath his own estate, had taken this means of withdrawing from it. But Fenicia fell into a swoon, so that she was as one dead. When she had revived a little she said to her mother and sisters that she had no desire to live, since her name had been brought to shame before all Messina, but that they might live comforted by the assurance of her innocence. And she prayed God to open the eyes of Don Timbreo, that he might know that she had been faithful to him, even when he should take another lady to wife. Then, crossing her hands upon her breast, she seemed to give up the ghost; so that the physicians went their ways, and the women prepared her body for burial. But when she had been thus lifeless for seven hours, her limbs and eyes began to show manifest signs of life, and soon she came to herself saying, "Alas, where am I?" And her mother, rejoicing, called Lionato to see her restored. Then Lionato determined not to make known the fact that Fenicia had not died, but kept her secretly, and presently sent her to a country house of his brother's. Meantime the coffin which had been prepared for her was sealed up, and the funeral was carried on at the church with all ceremony, and an epitaph graved upon Fenicia's monument, declaring that she had died of grief over the slander uttered against her faith.

Now Signor Girondo, hearing of Fenicia's death and feeling himself to have been her murderer, could not contain himself for remorse, but went to Don Timbreo and confessed what he had done, praying his friend to slay him instantly for his treachery. Don Timbreo, feeling himself equally guilty for having believed the false charge without due cause, forgave Girondo, and they went together to Lionato, and revealed the whole truth of the matter; moreover, Don Timbreo protested that he would still count himself Lionato's son, and ever be willing to do anything in the world at his behest. Then Lionato said to him that he would ask but a single favor, namely that Don Timbreo, when he felt himself desirous again of taking a wife, would permit Lionato to propose to him a young lady that he should marry if she proved pleasing to him. To this Don Timbreo readily agreed.

After about a year's time, when Fenicia had always remained hidden in the country, and meantime grown so much more beautiful that one would scarcely know her to be the same maiden that had been betrothed to Don Timbreo, Lionato determined to carry out his design. He therefore sent for Don Timbreo, and besought him to come to a dinner at a village in the country, where he should meet the damsel whom Lionato thought he might gladly take to wife. And so it was done. It happened, then, that Don Timbreo was so much pleased with the beautiful damsel to whom Lionato presented him, that he gladly requested her hand in marriage, and a priest was sent for at once to accomplish the espousal. At the feast which followed one of the company asked the bridegroom if he had never yet had a wife; and he, with tears filling his eyes, related the sad story of his betrothal to Fenicia and his remorse for having doubted her faith to him. Then they asked him, "If, before this damsel had been given to you, you could have recalled your beloved Fenicia, to life, what would have done to bring it about?" And he swore that he would have given half his life to do so.

Then Lionato, unable longer to restrain himself, cried out that Don Timbreo's acts belied his words, since he had already espoused his Fenicia and remained all the morning beside her without recognizing her. Thereupon the bridegroom's eyes were opened, and he cast himself on Fenicia's neck, kissing her a thousand times, and all the time weeping because of his blindness. And Lionato related all that had happened, to the great wonder and joy of the whole company. Moreover, Girondo, who was present among the guests, not only sought and obtained the forgiveness of Fenicia, but was presently betrothed to her sister Belfiore, who was scarcely less beautiful than she.

As You Like It

THIS comedy is a re-telling, by Shakespeare, of the story of Thomas Lodge's *Rosalynde*, a euphuistic pastoral romance which had been published in 1590. The main plot goes back to a medieval story, the Tale of Gamelyn, formerly attributed to Chaucer. In the following pages the plot of Lodge's romance is given in brief outline, followed by certain passages from the text *verbatim,* of special interest for comparison with particular scenes in the Shakespearean version.

ROSALYNDE

Sir John of Bordeaux, dying, left three sons, of whom the oldest, Saladyne, conspired against the life and property of the youngest, Rosader, because his father had shown special affection for Rosader and left him the larger share of the estate. At length when a Norman wrestler was to appear before Torismond, King of France, Saladyne encouraged Rosader to compete in the tournament, and secretly bribed the Norman to slay him if possible. A great company of the court witnessed the tournament, among them the princess Alinda, and Rosalynde, daughter of the late king Gerismond, whom Torismond had dispossessed and banished from his kingdom. Rosader fought so valiantly that he slew the Norman, and won the admiration of the king and all the nobles. Meantime he had fallen in love at first sight with Rosalynde, who in turn so favored him that she sent him a jewel by a page. Returning to his brother's house, he was treated harshly by Saladyne, but for a time was reconciled to him through the offices of Adam Spencer the old serving man; Saladyne " concealing a poisoned hate in a peaceable countenance."

Meantime Rosalynde, while meditating on her love for Rosader, was banished from the court by King Torismond, fearful of her great charm and popularity. His daughter Alinda, failing to alter his purpose, incurred the same sentence, and they determined to set out for exile together. Rosalynde, being of tall stature, assumed the guise of a page and the name of Ganymede; Alinda, as her mistress, the name Aliena. Passing into Arden forest, they met two shepherds, Montanus and Corydon, and listened to an eclogue recited between them, wherein Montanus declared his love for Phoebe. Revealing themselves presently, Ganymede and Aliena asked for a place of shelter, and the latter declared her intention to buy a farm and a flock of sheep. Corydon took them to his cottage, and on the following day Aliena purchased the place and the sheep from his landlord.

Now Saladyne, at length unable to restrain his hatred for his brother, seized Rosader and put him in chains. He was released, however, by the faithful Adam Spencer; and they two broke through the company of men whom Saladyne had brought to his aid, fled from the sheriff and his officers (whom Saladyne had stirred up against them), and made their way into the forest of Arden. Here they wandered about until faint for want of food, and at length the old man, unable to go further, desired to put an end to himself to save Rosader; but the younger encouraged him, and went by himself to seek for food. Chance brought him to a spot where Gerismond, the banished king, was celebrating his birthday with a feast among his friends. Breaking in among them, Rosader prayed for food, but would not receive it for himself till he had brought Adam thither. Then, when the king had heard his story, and knew him to be the son of his old friend Sir John, he fell on his neck, and presently made him one of his foresters. But the king was greatly saddened to hear from Rosader of the banishment of his daughter Rosalynde.

Meantime King Torismond, hearing that Saladyne was now possessed of all the estates of Sir John of Bordeaux, made excuse to send for him and put him into prison; and there, meditating his past life, he repented of his ill treatment of his brother. At length the king, taking him from prison, banished him from France, and Saladyne set forth alone, resolved to find Rosader and prove his penitence.

In the forest Rosader every day wrote songs and sonnets on his love for Rosalynde, sometimes carving them upon the trees. On a certain day Ganymede and Aliena came upon him as he was calling upon his lady's name, and Ganymede boldly entered into conversation and asked him about Rosalynde. Thereafter they had no little discourse about love, and Rosader recited many of his poems.

All this while Saladyne wandered in the forest; and at length, weary with fasting, fell asleep. A hungry lion stood by, ready to attack him as soon as he should move, when Rosader came that way and saw his brother's peril. At first he purposed to steal away and leave Saladyne to his fate; but then, reflecting whose son he was and on the honor of a gentleman, he stood by, and presently attacked the lion so valiantly that he slew it, though not without wounds on his own part. Saladyne, awaking, did not know his brother, but gave thanks to the stranger for his aid, and presently told him his story, confessing his sins to his younger brother and declaring his intention to live a life of penitence. Rosader thereupon revealed himself, and, after much show of affection between them, brought him to King Gerismond. It happened some days later that certain rascally outlaws of the forest made an attack upon Aliena and Ganymede, and Rosader was hardly able alone to defend them; but his brother coming that way to look for him, helped him to put the villains to flight. The ladies now tended the wounds of Rosader; and meantime Aliena and Saladyne fell in love. The next day she confessed her passion to Ganymede, and together they " sate in their dumps," talking of their loves.

So doing, they were visited by Corydon, who brought them to see Montanus wooing the hard-hearted Phoebe. At length Ganymede broke in and remonstrated with Phoebe, who thereupon fell in love with the beautiful page. Presently came Saladyne, bringing news of Rosader's wounds, and confessed his love to Aliena; she promised him either to marry him or remain a virgin.

At length Phoebe, burning with her passion for Ganymede, sent her a letter declaring it, by the hand of the faithful Montanus; whose love for Phoebe was such that, when he knew her desires, he urged Ganymede to yield to them. Thereupon Ganymede visited Phoebe, telling her that he could not marry her, and at length bringing her to say that if her love for Ganymede could be quenched, she would favor Montanas. To which Ganymede replied, promising never to wed any other woman than Phoebe.

Plans were now afoot for the marriage of Aliena to Saladyne, and Ganymede promised Rosader to invoke the agency of magic to bring in Rosalynde in time for the wedding. So the house was made festive, and the king and his foresters came to frolic with the shepherds. Then the king met Ganymede, noting his resemblance to his daughter; and at length she revealed herself, in her own woman's attire. Then he gave her to Rosader; and Phoebe accepted the hand of Montanus. So the three marriages were performed, and Corydon played and sang them " a fit of mirth." Whereupon there was announced the second son of John of Bordeaux, brother of Saladyne and Rosader, who had lived as a scholar at Paris, and now brought news that the twelve peers of France were rising against the tyrant Torismond, who was giving them battle near the edge of the forest. So the king Gerismond leaped to horse, and Saladyne and Rosader followed him to the battle; where presently Torismond was slain. Then Gerismond resumed his throne, made Rosader his heir, Saladyne Duke of Nameurs, Montanus lord of the Forest of Arden, Adam Spencer captain of the King's Guard, and Corydon master of Alinda's flocks.

ALIENA AND GANYMEDE

"No doubt," quoth Aliena, "this poesy is the passion of some perplexed shepherd, that being enamoured of some fair and beautiful shepherdess, suffered some sharp repulse, and therefore complained of the cruelty of his mistress."

"You may see," quoth Ganymede, "what mad cattle you women be, whose hearts sometimes are made of adamant that will touch with no impression, and sometime of wax that is fit for every form: they delight to be courted, and then they glory to seem coy, and when they are most desired then they freeze with disdain: and this fault is so common to the sex, that you see it painted out in the shepherd's passions, who found his mistress as froward as he was enamoured."

"And I pray you," quoth Aliena, "if your robes were off, what mettle are you made of that you are so satirical against women? Is it not a foul bird defiles the own nest?

Beware, Ganymede, that Rosader hear you not; if he do, perchance you will make him leap so far from love, that he will anger every vein in your heart."

"Thus," quoth Ganymede, "I keep decorum: I speak now as I am Aliena's page, not as I am Gerismond's daughter; for put me but into a petticoat, and I will stand in defiance to the uttermost, that women are courteous, constant, virtuous, and what not."

GANYMEDE AND ROSADER

Reading the sonnet over, and hearing him name Rosalynde, Aliena looked on Ganymede and laughed, and Ganymede looking back on the forester, and seeing it was Rosader, blushed; yet thinking to shroud all under her page's apparel, she boldly returned to Rosader, and began thus:

"I pray thee tell me, forester, what is this Rosalynde for whom thou pinest away in such passions? Is she some nymph that waits upon Diana's train, whose chastity thou has deciphered in such epithets? Or is she some shepherdess that haunts these plains whose beauty hath so bewitched thy fancy, whose name thou shadowest in covert under the figure of Rosalynde, as Ovid did Julia under the name of Corinna? Or say me forsooth, is it that Rosalynde, of whom we shepherds have heard talk, she, forester, that is the daughter of Gerismond, that once was king, and now an outlaw in the forest of Arden?"

At this Rosader fetched a deep sigh, and said:

"It is she, O gentle swain, it is she; that saint it is whom I serve, that goddess at whose shrine I do bend all my devotions; the most fairest of all fairs, the phoenix of all that sex, and the purity of all earthly perfection."

"And why, gentle forester, if she be so beautiful, and thou so amorous, is there such a disagreement in thy thoughts? Happily she resembleth a rose, that is sweet but full of prickles? or the serpent Regius that hath scales as glorious as the sun and a breath as infectious as the aconitum is deadly? So thy Rosalynde may be most amiable and yet unkind; full of favor and yet froward, coy without wit, and disdainful without reason."

"O shepherd," quoth Rosader, "knewest thou her personage, graced with the excellence of all perfection, being a harbor wherein the graces shroud their virtues, thou wouldest not breathe out such blasphemy against the beauteous Rosalynde. She is a diamond, bright but not hard, yet of most chaste operation; a pearl so orient, that it can be stained with no blemish; a rose without prickles, and a princess absolute as well in beauty as in virtue. But I, unhappy I, have let mine eye soar with the eagle against so bright a sun that I am quite blind; I have with Apollo enamoured myself of a Daphne, not, as she, disdainful, but far more chaste than Daphne: I have with Ixion laid my love on Juno, and shall, I fear, embrace nought but a cloud. Ah, shepherd, I have reached at a star: my desires have mounted above my degree, and my thoughts above my fortunes. I being a peasant, have ventured to gaze on a princess, whose honors are too high to vouchsafe such base loves."

"Why, forester," quoth Ganymede, "comfort thyself; be blithe and frolic, man. Love souseth as low as she soareth high: Cupid shoots at a rag as soon as at a robe; and

Venus' eye that was so curious, sparkled favor on pole-footed Vulcan. Fear not, women's looks are not tied to dignity's feathers, nor make they curious esteem where the stone is found, but what is the virtue. Fear not, forester; faint heart never won fair lady. But where lives Rosalynde now? at the court?"

"Oh, no," quoth Rosader, "she lives I know not where, and that is my sorrow; banished by Torismond, and that is my hell."

[Here Rosader reads his description of his mistress' excellence in the poem beginning:]

> Like to the clear in highest sphere,
> Where all imperial glory shines,
> Of selfsame color is her hair,
> Whether unfolded or in twines:
>   Heigh ho, fair Rosalynde!

. . . "Believe me," quoth Ganymede, "either the forester is an exquisite painter, or Rosalynde far above wonder; so it makes me blush to hear how women should be so excellent, and pages so imperfect."

Rosader, beholding her earnestly, answered thus:

"Truly, gentle page, thou hast cause to complain thee wert thou the substance, but resembling the shadow content thyself; for it is excellence enough to be like the excellence of nature."

"He hath answered you, Ganymede," quoth Aliena, "it is enough for pages to wait on beautiful ladies, and not to be beautiful themselves."

"O mistress," quoth Ganymede, "hold you your peace, for you are partial. Who knows not, but that all women have desire to tie sovereignty to their petticoats, and ascribe beauty to themselves, where, if boys might put on their garments, perhaps they would prove as comely; if not as comely, it may be more courteous." . . .

As soon as they had taken their repast, Rosader, giving them thanks for his good cheer, would have been gone: but Ganymede, that was loath to let him pass out of her presence, began thus:

"Nay, forester," quoth he, "if thy business be not the greater, seeing thou sayest thou art so deeply in love, let me see how thou canst woo: I will represent Rosalynde, and thou shalt be as thou art, Rosader. See in some amorous eclogue, how if Rosalynde were present, how thou couldest court her; and while we sing of love, Aliena shall tune her pipe and play us melody."

"Content," quoth Rosader, and Aliena, she, to show her willingness, drew forth a recorder, and began to wind it. Then the loving forester began thus:

The wooing Eclogue betwixt Rosalynde and Rosader

ROSADER

I pray thee, nymph, by all the working words,
By all the tears and sighs that lovers know,
Or what or thoughts or faltering tongue affords,
I crave for mine in ripping up my woe.
Sweet Rosalynde, my love (would God, my love!)
My life (would God, my life) aye, pity me!
Thy lips are kind, and humble like the dove,
And but with beauty, pity will not be.
Look on mine eyes, made red with rueful tears,

From whence the rain of true remorse descendeth,
All pale in looks am I though young in years,
And nought but love or death my days befriendeth.
Oh let no stormy rigor knit thy brows,
Which love appointed for his mercy seat:
The tallest tree by Boreas' breath it bows;
The iron yields with hammer, and to heat.
O Rosalynde, then be thou pitiful,
For Rosalynde is only beautiful.

ROSALYNDE

Love's wantons arm their trait'rous suits with tears,
With vows, with oaths, with looks, with showers of gold;
But when the fruit of their affects appears,
The simple heart by subtle sleights is sold.
Thus sucks the yielding ear the poisoned bait,
Thus feeds the heart upon his endless harms,
Thus gluts the thoughts themselves on self-deceit,
Thus blind the eyes their sight by subtle charms.
The lovely looks, the sighs that storm no sore,
The dew of deep-dissembled doubleness,
These may attempt, but are of power no more
Where beauty leans to wit and soothfastness.
O Rosader, then be thou wittiful,
For Rosalynde scorns foolish pitiful. . . .

[The eclogue continues for fifty more lines.]

When thus they had finished their courting eclogue in such a familiar clause, Ganymede, as augur of some good fortunes to light upon their affections, began to be thus pleasant:

"How now, forester, have I not fitted your turn? have I not played the woman handsomely, and showed myself as coy in grants as courteous in desires, and been as full of suspicion as men of flattery? and yet to salve all, jumped I not all up with the sweet union of love? Did not Rosalynde content her Rosader?"

The forester at this smiling, shook his head, and folding his arms made this merry reply:

"Truth, gentle swain, Rosader hath his Rosalynde; but as Ixion had Juno, who, thinking to possess a goddess, only embraced a cloud: in these imaginary fruitions of fancy I resemble the birds that fed themselves with Zeuxis' painted grapes; but they grew so lean with pecking at shadows, that they were glad, with Aesop's cock, to scrape for a barley cornel. So fareth it with me, who to feed myself with the hope of my mistress' favors, soothe myself in thy suits, and only in conceit reap a wished-for content; but if my food be no better than such amorous dreams, Venus at the year's end shall find me but a lean lover. Yet do I take these follies for high fortunes, and hope these feigned affections do devine some unfeigned end of ensuing fancies."

"And thereupon," quoth Aliena, "I'll play the priest: from this day forth Ganymede shall call thee husband, and thou shall call Ganymede wife, and so we'll have a marriage."

"Content," quoth Rosader, and laughed.

"Content," quoth Ganymede, and changed as red as a rose: and so with a smile and a blush, they made up this jesting match, that after proved to be a marriage in earnest, Rosader full little thinking he had wooed and won his Rosalynde.

GANYMEDE AND PHOEBE

Ganymede, overhearing all these passions of Montanus, could not brook the cruelty of Phoebe, but starting from behind the bush said:

"And if, damsel, you fled from me, I would transform you as Daphne to a bay, and then in contempt trample your branches under my feet."

Phoebe at this sudden reply was amazed, especially when she saw so fair a swain as Ganymede; blushing therefore, she would have been gone, but that he held her by the hand, and prosecuted his reply thus:

"What, shepherdess, so fair and so cruel? Disdain beseems not cottages, nor coyness maids; for either they be condemned to be too proud, or too froward. Take heed, fair nymph, that in despising love, you be not overreached with love, and in shaking off all, shape yourself to your own shadow, and so with Narcissus prove passionate and yet unpitied. Oft have I heard, and sometimes have I seen, high disdain turned to hot desires. Because thou art beautiful be not so coy: as there is nothing more fair, so there is nothing more fading; as momentary as the shadows which grows from a cloudy sun. Such, my fair shepherdess, as disdain in youth desire in age, and then are they hated in the winter, that might have been loved in the prime. A wrinkled maid is like to a parched rose, that is cast up in coffers to please the smell, not worn in the hand to content the eye. There is no folly in love to *had I wist*, and therefore be ruled by me. Love while thou art young, lest thou be disdained when thou art old. Beauty nor time cannot be recalled, and if thou love, like of Montanus; for if his desires are many, so his deserts are great."

Phoebe all this while gazed on the perfection of Ganymede, as deeply enamoured on his perfection as Montanus inveigled with hers; for her eye made survey of his excellent feature, which she found so rare, that she thought the ghost of Adonis had been leaped from Elysium in the shape of a swain. When she blushed at her own folly to look so long on a stranger, she mildly made answer to Ganymede thus:

"I cannot deny, sir, but I have heard of love, though I never felt love; and have read of such a goddess as Venus, though I never saw any but her picture; and, perhaps" —and with that she waxed red and bashful, and withal silent; which Ganymede perceiving, commended in herself the bashfulness of the maid, and desired her to go forward.

"And perhaps, sir, mine eye hath been more prodigal today than ever before"—and with that she stayed again, as one greatly passionate and perplexed.

Aliena seeing the hare through the maze, bade her forward with her prattle, but in vain; for at this abrupt period she broke off, and with her eyes full of tears, and her face covered with a vermilion dye, she sate down and sighed. Whereupon Aliena and Ganymede, seeing the shepherdess in such a strange plight, left Phoebe with her Montanus, wishing her friendly that she would be more pliant to love, lest in penance Venus joined her to some sharp repentance. Phoebe made no reply, but fetched such a sigh, that Echo made relation of her plaint, giving Ganymede such an adieu with a piercing glance, that the amorous girl-boy perceived Phoebe was pinched by the heel.

JULIUS CAESAR

THOUGH there had been a number of earlier plays on the subject of Caesar, Shakespeare drew his material for this tragedy chiefly from Sir Thomas North's version of Plutarch's *Lives of the Noble Grecians and Romans,* which had appeared in 1579 and again in 1595. The passages that follow represent the essential elements of his drama, but by no means all that he may be supposed to have drawn upon; for example, he consulted the parallel passages in the Life of Mark Antony, as well as the Lives of Caesar and Brutus.

FROM THE LIFE OF CAESAR

The chiefest cause that made him mortally hated was the covetous desire he had to be called king: which first gave the people just cause and next his secret enemies honest color, to bear him ill will. . . . Caesar returning to Rome from the city of Alba, when they came to salute him, they called him king. But the people being offended and Caesar also angry, he said he was not called king, but Caesar. Then, every man keeping silence, he went his way heavy and sorrowful. . . .

At that time the feast Lupercalia was celebrated. . . . Caesar sat to behold that sport upon the pulpit for orations, in a chair of gold, apparelled in triumphing manner. Antonius, who was consul at that time, was one of them that ran this holy course. So, when he came into the market-place, the people made a lane for him to run at liberty, and he came to Caesar, and presented him with a diadem wreathed about with laurel. Whereupon there rose a certain cry of rejoicing, not very great, done only by a few appointed for the purpose. But when Caesar refused the diadem, then all the people together made an outcry of joy. Then, Antonius offering it him again, there was a second shout of joy, but yet of a few. But when Caesar refused it again the second time, then all the whole people shouted. Caesar having made this proof found that the people did not like of it, and thereupon rose out of his chair, and commanded the crown to be carried unto Jupiter in the Capitol. After that, there were set up images of Caesar in the city with diadems upon their heads, like kings. Those the two tribunes, Flavius and Marullus, went and pulled down. . . .

Now they that desired change and wished Brutus only their prince and governor above all other, they durst not come to him themselves to tell him what they would have him to do, but in the night did cast sundry papers into the praetor's seat where he gave audience, and the most of them to this effect: "Thou sleepest, Brutus, and art not Brutus indeed." . . . Caesar also had Cassius in great jealousy and suspected him much: whereupon he said on a time to his friends, "What will Cassius do, think ye? I like not his pale looks." Another time, when Caesar's friends complained unto him of Antonius and Dolabella, that they pretended some mischief towards him: he answered them again, "As for those fat men and smoothcombed heads," quoth he, "I never reckon of them: but these pale-visaged and carrion lean people, I fear them most": meaning Brutus and Cassius.

Certainly, destiny may easier be foreseen than avoided: considering the strange and wonderful signs that were said to be seen before Caesar's death. For, touching the fires in the element and spirits running up and down in the night, and also the solitary birds to be seen at noon-days sitting in the great market-place: are not all these signs perhaps worth the noting in such a wonderful chance as happened? But Strabo the philosopher writeth that divers men were seen going up and down in fire: and furthermore, that there was a slave of the soldiers, that did cast a marvelous burning flame out of his hand, insomuch as they that saw it thought he had been burnt, but when the fire was out, it was found he had no hurt. Caesar self also, doing sacrifice unto the gods, found that one of the beasts which was sacrificed had no heart: and that was a strange thing in nature, how a beast could live without a heart. Furthermore, there was a certain soothsayer that had given Caesar warning long time afore, to take heed of the day of the Ides of March (which is the fifteenth of the month), for on that day he should be in great danger. That day being come, Caesar going unto the senate-house, and speaking merrily to the soothsayer, told him, "the Ides of March be come." "So be they," softly answered the soothsayer, "but yet are they not past." . . . Then going to bed the same night as his manner was, and lying with his wife Calpurnia, all the windows and doors of his chamber flying open, the noise awoke him, and made him afraid when he saw such light: but more, when he heard his wife Calpurnia, being fast asleep, weep and sigh, and put forth many fumbling lamentable speeches. For she dreamed that Caesar was slain, and that she had him in her arms. . . . Caesar rising in the morning, she prayed him if it were possible not to go out of the doors that day, but to adjourn the session of the Senate until another day. And if that he made no reckoning of her dream, yet that he would search further of the soothsayers by their sacrifices, to know what should happen him that day. Thereby it seemed that Caesar likewise did fear and suspect somewhat, because his wife Calpurnia until that time was never given to any fear or superstition: and then, for that he saw her so troubled in mind with this dream she had. But much more afterwards, when the soothsayers, having sacrificed many beasts one after another, told him that none did like them: then he determined to send Antonius to adjourn the session of the Senate. But in the meantime came Decius Brutus, surnamed Albinus: . . . he, fearing that if Caesar did adjourn the session that day the conspiracy would out, laughed the soothsayers to scorn, and reproved Caesar, saying: that he gave the Senate occasion to mislike with him, and that they might think he mocked them, considering that by his commandment they were assembled, and that they were ready willingly to grant him all things, and to proclaim him king of all the provinces of the empire of Rome out of Italy, and that he should wear his diadem in all other places both by sea and land. . . . Therewithal he took Caesar by the hand, and brought him out of his house. . . .

And one Artemidorus also, born in the Isle of Gnidos, a doctor of rhetoric in the Greek tongue, who by means of his profession was very familiar with certain of Brutus' confederates, and therefore knew the most part of all their practices against Caesar, came and brought him a little bill written with his own hand, of all that he meant to tell him. He, marking how Caesar received all the supplications that were offered him, and that he gave them straight to his men that were about him, pressed nearer to him, and said: "Caesar, read this memorial to yourself, and that quickly, for they be matters of great weight, and touch you nearly." Caesar took it of him, but could never read it, though he many times attempted it, for the number of people that did salute him: but holding it still in his hand, keeping it to himself, went on withal into the senate-house. . . . So, Caesar coming into the house, all the Senate stood up on their feet to do him honor. Then part of Brutus' company and confederates stood round about Caesar's chair, and part of them also came towards them, as though they made suit with Metellus Cimber, to call home his brother again from banishment: and thus, prosecuting still their suit, they followed Caesar, till he was set in his chair. Who denying their petitions, and being offended with them one after another, because the more they were denied, the more they pressed upon him, and were the earnester with him: Metellus at length, taking his gown with both his hands, pulled it over his neck, which was the sign given the confederates to set upon him. Then Casca behind him strake him in the neck with his sword: howbeit the wound was not great nor mortal. . . . At the beginning of this stir, they that were present, not knowing of the conspiracy, were so amazed with the horrible sight they saw, that they had no power to fly, neither to help him, not so much as once to make any outcry. They on th' other side that had conspired his death compassed him in on every side with their swords drawn in their hands, that Caesar turned him nowhere but he was stricken at by some, and still had naked swords in his face, and was hacked and mangled among them, as wild beast taken of hunters. . . . Men report also that Caesar did still defend himself against the rest, running every way with his body: but when he saw Brutus with his sword drawn in his hand, then he pulled his gown over his head, and made no more resistance, and was driven either casually or purposedly by the counsel of the conspirators against the base whereupon Pompey's image stood, which ran all of a gore-blood till he was slain. Thus it seemed that the image took just revenge of Pompey's enemy, being thrown down on the ground at his feet, and yielding up his ghost there for the number of wounds he had upon him. For it is reported that he had three-and-twenty wounds upon his body: and divers of the conspirators did hurt themselves, striking one body with so many blows. When Caesar was slain, the Senate (though Brutus stood in the midst among them, as though he would have said somewhat touching this fact) presently ran out of the house, and flying filled all the city with marvelous fear and tumult. . . .

Caesar died at six-and-fifty years of age: and Pompey also lived not passing four more years than he. So he reaped no other fruit of all his reign and dominion, which he had so vehemently desired all his life, and pursued with such extreme danger, but a vain name only, and a superficial glory that procured him the envy and hatred of his country. But his great prosperity and good fortune, that favored him all his lifetime, did continue afterwards in the revenge of his death, pursuing the murtherers both by sea and land, till they had not left a man more to be executed, of all them that were actors or counsellors in the conspiracy of his death. . . . But, above all, the ghost that appeared unto Brutus shewed plainly that the gods were offended with the murther of Caesar. The vision was thus. Brutus, being ready to pass over his army from the city of Abydos to the other coast lying directly against it, slept every night (as his manner was) in his tent, and being yet awake thinking of his affairs (for by report he was as careful a captain, and lived with as little sleep, as ever man did), he thought he heard a noise at his tent door, and, looking towards the light of the lamp that waxed very dim he saw a horrible vision of a man, of a wonderful greatness, and dreadful look, which at the first made him marvelously afraid. But when he saw that it did him no hurt, but stood by his bedside and said nothing, at length he asked him what he was. The image answered him: "I am thy ill angel, Brutus, and thou shalt see me by the city of Philippi." Then Brutus replied again, and said: "Well, I shall see thee then." Therewithal the spirit presently vanished from him. After that time Brutus being in battle near unto the city of Philippi against Antonius and Octavius Caesar, at the first battle he won the victory, and, overthrowing all them that withstood him, he drave them into young Caesar's camp, which he took. The second battle being at hand, this spirit appeared again unto him, but spake never a word.

FROM THE LIFE OF MARCUS BRUTUS

Now when Cassius felt his friends, and did stir them up against Caesar, they all agreed and promised to take part with him, so Brutus were the chief of their conspiracy. For they told him, that so high an enterprise and attempt as that did not so much require men of manhood and courage to draw their swords, as it stood them upon to have a man of such estimation as Brutus, to make every man boldly think that by his only presence the fact were holy and just. If he took not this course, then that they should go to it with fainter hearts, and when they had done it they should be more fearful: because every man would think that Brutus would not have refused to have made one with them, if the cause had been good and honest. Therefore Cassius, considering this matter with himself, did first of all speak to Brutus. . . .

Now amongst Pompey's friends there was one called Caius Ligarius, who had been accused unto Caesar for taking part with Pompey, and Caesar discharged him. But Ligarius thanked not Caesar so much for his discharge, as he was offended with him for that he was brought in danger by his tyrannical power. And therefore in his heart he was alway his mortal enemy, and was besides very familiar with Brutus, who went to see him being sick in his bed, and said unto him: "O Ligarius, in what a time art thou sick?" Ligarius rising up in his bed, and taking him by the right hand, said unto him: "Brutus," said he, "if thou hast any great enterprise in hand worthy of thyself, I am whole." After that time they began to feel all their acquaintance whom they trusted, and laid their heads together consulting upon it. . . . The only name and great calling of Brutus did bring on the most of them to give consent to this conspiracy. Who having never taken oaths together, nor taken or given any caution or assurance, nor binding themselves one to another by any religious oaths: they all kept the matter so secret to themselves, and could so cunningly handle it, that notwithstanding the gods did reveal it by manifest signs and tokens from above, and by predictions of sacrifices, yet all this would not be believed.

Now Brutus, who knew very well that for his sake all the noblest, valiantest, and most courageous men of Rome did venture their lives, weighing with himself the greatness of the danger: when he was out of his house, he did so frame and fashion his countenance and looks, that no man could discern he had anything to trouble his mind. But when night came that he was in his own house, then he was clean changed. For either care did wake him against his will when he would have slept, or else oftentimes of himself he fell into such deep thoughts of this enterprise, casting in his mind all the dangers that might happen, that his wife, lying by him, found that there was some marvelous great matter that troubled his mind. . . .

All the conspirators but Brutus, determining upon this matter, thought it good also to kill Antonius, because he was a wicked man, and that in nature favoured tyranny: besides also, for that he was in great estimation with soldiers, having been conversant of long time amongst them: and specially having a mind bent to great enterprises, he was also of great authority at that time, being consul with Caesar. But Brutus would not agree to it. First, for that he said it was not honest: secondly, because he told them there was hope of change in him. For he did not mistrust, but that Antonius, being a noble-minded and courageous man (when he should know that Caesar was dead), would willingly help his country to recover her liberty. . . .

Now at the first time when the murther was newly done, there were sudden outcries of people that ran up and down the city, the which indeed did the more increase the fear and tumult. But when they saw they slew no man, neither did spoil or make havoc of anything, then certain of the senators and many of the people, emboldening themselves, went to the Capitol unto them. There a great number of men being assembled together one after another, Brutus made an oration unto them to win the favour of the people, and to justify that they had done. All those that were by said they had done well, and cried unto them that they should boldly come down from the Capitol. Whereupon, Brutus and his companions came boldly down into the market-place. The rest followed in troop, but Brutus went foremost, very honourably compassed in round about with the noblest men of the city, which brought him from the Capitol, through the market-place, to the pulpit for orations. When the people saw him in the pulpit, although they were a multitude of rakeshells of all sorts, and had a good will to make some stir: yet being ashamed to do it for the reverence they bare unto Brutus, they kept silence, to hear what he would say. When Brutus began to speak, they gave him quiet audience: howbeit immediately after, they showed that they were not all contented with the murther. . . .

The next day following, the Senate . . . came to talk of Caesar's will and testament, and of his funerals and tomb. Then Antonius thinking good his testament should be read openly, and also that his body should be honourably buried, and not in hugger mugger, lest the people might thereby take occasion to be worse offended if they did otherwise: Cassius stoutly spake against it. But Brutus went with the motion, and agreed unto it: wherein it seemeth he committed a second fault. For the first fault he did was when he would not consent to his fellow-conspirators, that Antonius should be slain: and therefore he was justly accused, that thereby he had saved and strengthened a strong and grievous enemy of their conspiracy. The second fault was when he agreed that Caesar's funerals should be as Antonius would have them: the which indeed marred all. For first of all, when Caesar's testament was openly read among them, whereby it appeared that he bequeathed unto every citizen of Rome 75 drachmas a man, and that he left his gardens and arbours unto the people, which he had on this side of the river of Tiber, in the place where now the temple of Fortune is built: the people then loved him, and were marvelous sorry for him. Afterwards, when Caesar's body was brought into the market-place, Antonius making his funeral oration in praise of the dead, according to the ancient custom of Rome, and perceiving that his words moved the common people to compassion: he framed his eloquence to make their hearts yearn the more, and, taking Caesar's gown all bloody in his hand, he laid it open to the sight of them all, showing what a number of cuts and holes it had upon it. . . . Therewithal the people fell presently into such a rage and mutiny, that there was no more order kept among the common people. For some of them cried out, "Kill the murtherers" : others plucked up forms, tables, and stalls about the market-place, as they had done before at the funerals of Clodius, and having laid them all on a heap together they set them on fire, and thereupon did put the body of Caesar, and burnt it in the midst of the most holy places. And furthermore, when the fire was thoroughly kindled, some here, some there, took burning firebrands, and ran with them to the murtherers' houses that had killed him, to set them afire. Howbeit the conspirators, foreseeing the danger before, had wisely provided for themselves, and fled. . . .

Brutus preparing to go into Asia, news came unto him of the great change at Rome. For Octavius Caesar was in arms, by commandment and authority from the Senate, against Marcus Antonius. But after that he had driven Antonius out of Italy, the Senate then began to be afraid of him; because he sued to be consul, which was contrary to the law, and kept a great army about him, when the empire of Rome had no need of them. . . . Then coming on with his army near to Rome, he made himself to be chosen consul, whether the Senate would or not, when he was yet but a stripling or springal of twenty year old. . . . After that, these three, Octavius Caesar, Antonius, and Lepidus, made an agreement between themselves, and did set up bills of proscription and outlawry, condemning two hundred of the noblest men of Rome to suffer death, and among that number Cicero was one. . . .

Now Cassius would have done Brutus as much honour as Brutus did unto him: but Brutus most commonly prevented him, and went first unto him, both because he was the elder man, as also for that he was sickly of body. And men reputed him commonly to be very skilful in wars, but otherwise marvelous, choleric and cruel, who sought to rule men by fear, rather than with lenity: and on the other side he was too familiar with his friends, and would jest too broadly with them. But Brutus in contrary manner, for his virtue and valiantness, was well-beloved of the people and his own, esteemed of noble men, and hated of no man, not so much as of his enemies: because he was a marvelous lowly and gentle person, noble-minded, and would never be in any rage, nor carried away with pleasure and covetousness, but had ever an upright mind with him, and would never yield to any wrong or injustice, the which was the chiefest cause of his fame. . . .

[Before the battle of Philippi] both the chieftains spake together in the midst of their armies. There Cassius began to speak first, and said: "The gods grant us, O Brutus, that this day we may win the field, and ever after to live all the rest of our life quietly, one with another. But sith the gods have so ordained it, that the greatest and chiefest things amongst men are most uncertain, and that if the battle fall out otherwise today than we wish or look for, we shall hardly meet again: what art thou then determined to do, to fly, or die?" Brutus answered him, "Being yet but a young man, and not over greatly experienced in the world, I trust (I know not how) a certain rule of philosophy, by the which I did greatly blame and reprove Cato for killing of himself, as being no lawful nor godly acts, touching the gods, nor, concerning men, valiant; not to give place and yield to divine providence, and not constantly and patiently to take whatsoever it pleaseth him to send us, but to draw back and fly: but, being now in the midst of the danger, I am of a contrary mind. For if it be not the will of God that this battle fall out fortunate for us, I will look no more for hope, neither seek to make any new supply for war again, but will rid me of this miserable world, and content me with my fortune. For I gave up my life for my country on the Ides of March, for the which I shall live in another more glorious world." . . .

Now the night being far spent, Brutus as he sate bowed towards Clitus, one of his men, and told him somewhat in his ear: the other answered him not, but fell a-weeping. Thereupon he proved Dardanus, and said somewhat also to him: at length he came to Volumnius himself, and speaking to him in Greek, prayed him for the study's sake which brought them acquainted together, that he would help him to put his hand to the sword, to thrust it in him to kill him. Volumnius denied his request, and so did many others: and amongst the rest, one of them said, there was no tarrying for them there, but that they must needs fly. Then Brutus rising up, "We must fly indeed," said he, "but it must be with our hands, not with our feet." Then taking every man by the hand, he said these words unto them with a cheerful countenance. "It rejoiceth my heart that not one of my friends hath failed as at my need, and I do not complain of my fortune, but only for my country's sake: for, as for me, I think myself happier than they that have overcome, considering that I leave a perpetual fame of our courage and manhood, the which our enemies the conquerors shall never attain unto by force nor money, neither can let their posterity to say that they, being naughty and unjust men, have slain good men, to usurp tyrannical power not pertaining to them." Having said so, he prayed every man to shift for themselves, and then he went a little aside with two or three only, among the which Strato was one, with whom he came first acquainted by the study of rhetoric. He came as near to him as he could, and taking his sword by the hilts with both his hands, and falling down upon the point of it, ran himself through. Others say that not he, but Strato (at his request) held the sword in his hand, and turned his head aside, and that Brutus fell down upon it: and so ran himself through, and died presently.

TWELFTH NIGHT

THE plot of this comedy appeared in an Italian drama of 1531, called *Gl' Ingannati* (The Deceived), of which a Latin version was acted at Queen's College, Cambridge, in 1595, but not printed in Shakespeare's time. Bandello the Italian novelist retold the story in his collection of 1554, whence it passed into a French version by Belleforest, and through Belleforest into the English version by Barnabe Riche in 1581. This may be thought to have been Shakespeare's principal direct source, although, as in several other instances, it is possible that a lost English play intervened. The following is a brief outline of Riche's version.

OF APOLONIUS AND SILLA

(The " Second Historie " in *Riche his Farewell to Militarie Profession,* 1581)

The story is described at the outset as one in which Dame Error plays her part " with a leash of lovers, a male and two females: . . . the first neglecting the love of a noble dame, young, beautiful, and fair, who only for his goodwill played the part of a serving-man, contented to abide any manner of pain only to behold him; he again setting his love of a dame that, despising him (being a noble duke), gave herself to a serving-man (as she had thought)."

Apolonius, a noble young duke, spent some time at Pontus while on his way from the wars to his home in Constantinople; and there Silla, the beautiful daughter of the governor, fell irrecoverably in love with him, though he gave her no heed. When he had departed, the fervency of her love led her to set forth toward Constantinople in order to be near him, taking with her as companion a servant Pedro. On the voyage they were shipwrecked, Pedro was drowned, and Silla was washed ashore. Finding a chest containing the captain's clothing, she disguised herself as a young man, and resolved to take the name of her brother Silvio as a protection. Then, seeking the palace of Apolonius at Constantinople, she was received into the duke's service, soon becoming his favorite personal attendant.

Now the duke was at this time wooing a wealthy young widow by the name of Julina; and presently he chose Silvio to be the messenger to carry letters and love tokens to this lady. Silla, notwithstanding the fact that her heart was afflicted by such an errand, "followed his business with so good a will as if it had been in her own preferment." And Julina, perceiving the duke's messenger "to be of such excellent perfect grace, was so entangled with the often sight of this sweet temptation, that she fell into as great a liking with the man as the master was with herself." So that, as Silvio was soliciting her love on his master's behalf, Julina answered: "It is enough that you have said for your master; from henceforth either speak for yourself, or say nothing."

Meantime the true Silvio, Silla's brother, had returned from the wars to his father's court; where, learning of the seeming elopement of his sister with the servant Pedro, he vowed to take revenge upon the villain, and departed to seek them both. At last he arrived at Constantinople. Now it happened as he was walking outside the city one evening he chanced to meet with the lady Julina, who instantly took him to be the duke's serving-man; for Silvio and his sister were so alike that no one had ever been able to tell them from each other save by their apparel. Julina therefore approached the youth, and with appealing words counseled him not to despise her love because it was freely offered him. Silvio, much amazed to hear such words, and to be called by his right name, but perceiving her beauty and high position, replied, "If before this time I have seemed to forget myself, in neglecting your courtesy which so liberally you have meant unto me, please it you to pardon what is past, and from this day forwards Silvio remaineth ready to make such reasonable amends as his ability may any ways permit." Thereupon Julina invited him to supper at her house the following night, and he, learning from a stranger where she dwelt, came at the appointed time, and enjoyed her love. But the next day he thought it prudent, to avoid difficulties thereafter, to leave the city and pursue his journey.

When next the duke Apolonius came wooing his lady, Julina told him frankly that she loved another, and he went sadly away. But soon after, through the gossip of his servants and hers, word came to him that her lover was none other than his own serving-man, and he thrust Silvio into a dungeon. When the prisoner had languished there for some time, Julina came to the duke to beg his release, telling him frankly that it was Silvio whom she loved, and that her honour demanded that he be set free in order to marry her. Then the young man was sent for, but straitly denied that he had ever wronged his master by any intrigue with the lady. At length Julina's pleas led him to ask permission to take her aside for a private conversation, wherein Silvio showed her that he was in fact a woman like herself, and was in the service of the duke only because of love for Apolonius. And she said, " My love being pure, my travail continual, and my griefs endless, I trust, madam, you will not only excuse me of crime, but also pity my distress, the which, I protest, I would still have kept secret if my fortune would so have permitted."

Then Julina related to the duke what the disguised Silla had told her; and he, when he saw in truth that Silvio was a beautiful maiden, embraced her and said: " Oh, the branch of all virtue, and the flower of courtesy itself! Pardon me, I beseech you, of all such discourtesies as I have ignorantly committed towards you, desiring you that without further memory of ancient griefs you will accept of me, who is more joyful and better contented with your presence than if the whole world were at my commandment." Then he provided her with sumptuous apparel, and the marriage day was appointed.

The story of the duke's marriage now having been spread widely abroad, it came to the hearing of Silvio, the bride's brother, who was now seeking her through all the parts of

Greece; and he hastened to Constantinople, where he was joyfully received both by his sister and her lord. Then it happened that Apolonius told him the story of the lady Julina, and Silvio, blushing to think he had deserted so noble a lady, confessed that it was he who had accepted her love. So the duke led him to her house, where Julina was ravished with joy to see him again; and soon their marriage was accomplished with great joy and content to all.

HAMLET

THE story of Hamlet is of ancient Icelandic origin, the earliest known version being that found in the *Historia Danica* of Saxo Grammaticus, written at the end of the twelfth century. A French translation of Saxo's story appeared in Belleforest's *Histoires Tragiques,* 1570, and it is thought that on this version was based a lost English play about Hamlet, probably written by Thomas Kyd about 1589. Shakespeare's version was probably a rewriting of Kyd's, but the precise respective contributions of the two men can only be conjectured.[5] The following is an outline of Belleforest's Hamlet story; but, noticing what has been said above, the student will not think of it as a direct source for Shakespeare.

[5] A German tragedy on Hamlet, dating in its present form from the early eighteenth century, is believed by many scholars to have been drawn from Kyd's, and therefore to give us a fairly accurate means of estimating the differences between that play and Shakespeare's. In Professor Lewis's *The Genesis of Hamlet* (see Bibliography, page 214) the comparison is fully and suggestively worked out. According to this view, it was Kyd who introduced the story of the revelation of the murder by the dead king's ghost, and the madness of Ophelia.

FROM BELLEFOREST'S HISTOIRES TRAGIQUES

Two brothers, Horvendile and Fengon, served jointly as rulers of a province of Denmark under King Roderick; and Horvendile, having slain the king of Norway in single combat, was rewarded by being given the king's daughter Geruthe in marriage. From this marriage was born a son Amleth or Hamblet. Now Fengon, after first winning the illicit love of his brother's wife, resolved to kill Horvendile and become the sole governor. So he suddenly set upon his brother at a banquet, and slew him, affirming before the people that he had done so in order to save Geruthe, whom her husband had been on the point of putting to death. This tale being supported by false witnesses, the courtiers and the people believed Fengon and honoured him; and presently he married the widow of his murdered brother. The young prince Hamblet, perceiving that Fengon would soon send him the same way as his father, and that he could not hope for help from his mother, determined to deceive the tyrant by counterfeiting madness; and every day he rent his clothes, wallowed in the mire, ran through the streets with his face all filthy, and spoke no word save such as seemed to proceed from his frenzy. At the same time he constantly noted all that went on in the court, and planned one day to take his revenge. Often, too, he "did divers actions of great and deep consideration, and often made such and so fit answers that a wise man would soon have judged from what spirit so fine an invention might proceed." Some therefore perceived that under color of rudeness he showed craft and policy, and they counseled the king to discover Hamblet's intent. First, then, they set a beautiful woman to whom he was affectionately inclined, to meet with him in a secret place and seduce him; but both she herself, and a faithful friend of the prince's, warned him of the plot; whereupon he so conducted himself that the courtiers were the more convinced of his insanity. Thereafter one of Fengon's chief friends, who still disbelieved in Hamblet's practices, proposed that the prince should be shut up in a chamber with his mother, and that one should hide behind the arras and hear their speeches; and he offered himself to be the man that should so stand and harken. So the counsellor hid himself; but Hamblet, "as soon as he was within the chamber, doubting some treason, . . . used his ordinary manner of dissimulation, and began to come like a cock beating with his arms (in such manner as cocks use to strike with their wings) upon the hangings of the chamber; whereby, feeling something stirring under them, he cried, 'A rat, a rat!' and presently drawing his sword thrust it into the hangings; which done, pulled the counsellor, half dead, out by the heels, made an end of killing him, and being slain, cut his body in pieces." Then he came to his mother, whose conscience now pricked her for her incestuous marriage, and spoke to her soberly, saying, "Is this the part of a queen, and daughter to a king? to live like a brute beast, . . . to follow the pleasure of an abominable king that hath murdered a far more honester and better man than himself? . . . Be not offended, I pray you, Madam, if transported with dolour and grief I speak so boldly unto you, and that I respect you less than duty requireth; for you, having forgotten me, and wholly rejected the memory of the deceased king my father, must not be abashed if I also surpass the bounds and limits of due consideration." And he further told her of his reasons for professing madness, and of his intention to take revenge upon his uncle. "Although the queen perceived herself nearly touched, and that Hamblet moved her to the quick, where she felt herself interested, nevertheless she forgot all disdain and wrath . . . for the joy she then conceived to behold the gallant spirit of her son," and how he represented the proud and haughty heart of his dead father. "So, overcome and vanquished with this honest passion, and weeping most bitterly," she confessed her sin to Hamblet, and prayed him to be discreet and not over-hasty in his enterprise. And he on his part promised to meddle no further with her affairs, beseeching her to have no more to do with the tyrant whom he surely purposed to slay.

In the next place Fengon resolved to be rid of Hamblet by sending him to England with letters requesting the king of that country to put the prince to death. But Hamblet, suspecting the occasion of the voyage, confided his belief to the queen, requesting her to consent gladly to his departure, and in the following year to celebrate his funeral; at the same time assuring her that he would return in safety. Then, while at sea, as the companions sent with him by Fengon were asleep, he erased his name from the letter addressed to the English king, and put theirs in its place, adding also a request that the king should give Hamblet his daughter in marriage. Arrived at the English court, the prince displayed strange powers of divination, revealing hidden secrets concerning the birth of both the king and the queen; and the king, impressed by his wisdom, gladly gave him his daughter as had been requested in the letter. In like manner he put the two companions to death. Thereafter Hamblet returned to Denmark, arriving at his uncle's palace on the very day on which his funeral was being celebrated, to the great astonishment of all. And as the feast continued (for the northern nations are much given to the vice of drinking) he himself took the part of a cupbearer, to encourage the courtiers to make themselves drunk. When they were all helpless from their excess, he caused the hangings of the walls to fall upon them, and so fastened them to the floor that those underneath could not loose themselves; whereupon he set fire to the four corners of the hall, and destroyed his enemies. But the king had withdrawn into his own chamber. Thither Hamblet pursued him, laying his hand upon the king's own sword, and giving him such a blow that he cut his head clean from the shoulders; and he cried, "When thou comest in hell, see thou forget not to tell thy brother, whom thou traitorously slewest, that it was his son that sent thee thither with the message, to the end that, being comforted thereby, his soul may rest among the blessed spirits, and quit me of the obligation that bound me to pursue his vengeance upon mine own blood."

Thereafter the people came together to see the meaning of the great fire, and Hamblet made them an oration over the dead body of Fengon, saying, "I pray you remember this body is not the body of a king, but of an execrable tyrant, and a parricide most detestable." With much more to the same effect. And of his mother he said, "Take pity upon the queen, sometime your sovereign lady, and my right honourable mother, forced by the tyrant, and rejoice to see the end and extinguishing of the object of her dishonour, which constrained her to be less pitiful to her own blood, so far as to embrace the murderer of her own dear spouse, charging herself with a double burden of infamy and incest, together with injuring and disannulling of her house, and the ruin of her race. This hath been the occasion that made me counterfeit folly, and cover my intents under a veil of mere madness, which hath wisdom and policy thereby to enclose the fruit of this vengeance." Then the Danes were moved with both pity and joy by the gallant spirit of the prince, and with one consent proclaimed him king.

OTHELLO

THE story of this tragedy was taken, apparently, from one of the stories in Geraldi Cinthio's collection called *The Hundred Tales* (*Hecatommithi*), an Italian work of 1566. No English version of Shakespeare's time is known. Owing to the unusually close connection between the source and the dramatic masterpiece which Shakespeare made of it, and at the same time to the important elements of characterization which he added, a study of Cinthio's story is peculiarly significant for students of Shakespeare. A translation, only slightly abbreviated, follows.

THE MOOR OF VENICE

(From the *Hecatommithi* of Giraldi Cinthio)

There once lived in Venice a Moor, who was very valiant and of a handsome person; and having given proofs in war of great skill and prudence, he was highly esteemed by the signoria of the republic, who in rewarding deeds of valour advanced the interests of the state. It happened that a virtuous lady of marvelous beauty, named Disdemona, fell in love with the Moor, moved thereto by his valour; and he, vanquished by the beauty and the noble character of Disdemona, returned her love; and their affection was so mutual that, although the parents of the lady strove all they could to induce her to take another husband, she consented to marry the Moor; and they lived in such harmony and peace in Venice that no word ever passed between them that was not affectionate and kind.

Now it happened at this time that the signoria of Venice made a change in the troops whom they used to maintain in Cyprus, and they appointed the Moor commander of the soldiers whom they dispatched thither. Joyful as was the Moor at the honour preferred him, such dignity being only conferred on men of noble rank and well-tried faith, and who had displayed bravery in arms, — yet his pleasure was lessened when he reflected on the length and dangers of the voyage, fearing that Disdemona would be pained at his absence. But Disdemona, who had no other happiness in the world than the Moor, and who rejoiced to witness the testimony of his valour her husband had received from so powerful and noble a republic, was all impatient that he should embark with his troops, and longed to accompany him to so honourable a post. . . . [And she said:] " I will accompany you whithersoe'er you go, were it to pass through fire, as now to cross the water in a safe and well-provided ship; if indeed there are toils and perils to encounter, I will share them with you. And in truth I should think you loved me little were you to leave me here in Venice, denying me to bear you company, or could believe that I would liefer bide in safety here than share the dangers that await you. Prepare then for the voyage with all the readiness which the dignity of the post you hold deserves."

The Moor, in the fulness of his joy, threw his arms around his wife's neck, and with an affectionate and tender kiss exclaimed, "God keep you long in such love, dear wife!" Then speedily donning his armour, and having prepared everything for his expedition, he embarked on board the galley with his wife and all his troops, and, setting sail, they pursued their voyage, and with a perfectly tranquil sea arrived safely at Cyprus.

Now amongst the soldiery there was an ensign, a man of handsome figure, but of the most depraved nature in the world. This man was in great favour with the Moor, who had not the slightest idea of his wickedness; for, despite the malice lurking in his heart, he cloaked with proud and valourous speech and with a specious presence the villainy of his soul with such art that he was to all outward show another Hector or Achilles. This man had likewise taken with him his wife to Cyprus, a young, and fair, and virtuous lady; and being of Italian birth she was much loved by Disdemona, who spent the greater part of every day with her.

In the same company there was a certain captain of a troop, to whom the Moor was much affectioned. And Disdemona, for this cause, knowing how much her husband valued him, showed him proofs of the greatest kindness, which was all very grateful to the Moor. Now the wicked ensign, regardless of the faith that he had pledged his wife, no less than of the friendship, fidelity, and obligation which he owed the Moor, fell passionately in love with Disdemona, and bent all his thoughts to achieve his conquest; yet he dared not to declare his passion openly, fearing that, should the Moor perceive it, he would at once kill him. He therefore sought in various ways, and with secret guile, to betray his passion to the lady; but she, whose every wish was centred in the Moor, had no thought for this ensign more than for any other man; and all the means he tried to gain her love had no more effect than if he had not tried them. But the ensign imagined that the cause of his ill success was that Disdemona loved the captain of the troop; and he pondered how to remove him from her sight. The love which he had borne the lady now changed into the bitterest hate, and, having failed in his purposes, he devoted all his thoughts to plot the death of the captain of the troop and to divert the affection of the Moor from Disdemona. After revolving in his mind various schemes, all alike wicked, he at length resolved to accuse her of unfaithfulness to her husband, and to represent the captain as her paramour. But knowing the singular love the Moor bore to Disdemona, and the friendship which he had for the captain, he was well aware that, unless he practised an artful fraud upon the Moor, it were impossible to make him give ear to either accusation; wherefore he resolved to wait until time and circumstance should open a path for him to engage in his foul project.

Not long afterwards it happened that the captain, having drawn his sword upon a soldier of the guard, and struck him, the Moor deprived him of his rank; whereat

Disdemona was deeply grieved, and endeavoured again and again to reconcile her husband to the man. This the Moor told to the wicked ensign, and how his wife importuned him so much about the captain that he feared he should be forced at last to receive him back to service. Upon this hint the ensign resolved to act, and began to work his web of intrigue. "Perchance," said he, "the lady Disdemona may have good reason to look kindly on him."

"And wherefore?" said the Moor.

"Nay, I would not step 'twixt man and wife," replied the ensign, "but let your eyes be witness to themselves."

In vain the Moor went on to question the officer, — he would proceed no further; nevertheless, his words left a sharp, stinging thorn in the Moor's heart, who could think of nothing else, trying to guess their meaning and lost in melancholy. And one day, when his wife had been endeavouring to pacify his anger toward the captain and praying him not to be unmindful of ancient services and friendship for one small fault, especially since peace had been made between the captain and the soldier he had struck, the Moor was angered, and exclaimed, "Great cause have you, Disdemona, to care so anxiously about this man! Is he a brother, or your kinsman, that he should be so near your heart?"

The lady, with all gentleness and humility, replied, "Be not angered, my dear lord; I have no other cause to bid me speak than sorrow that I see you lose so dear a friend as, by your own words, this captain has been to you; nor has he done so grave a fault that you should bear him so much enmity. Nay, but you Moors are of so hot a nature that every little trifle moves you to anger and revenge."

Still more enraged at these words, the Moor replied, "I could bring proofs — by heaven, it mocks belief! but for the wrongs I have endured revenge must satisfy my wrath."

Disdemona, in astonishment and fright, seeing her husband's anger kindled against her, so contrary to his wont, said humbly and with timidness, "None save a good intent has led me thus to speak with you, my lord; but to give cause no longer for offence, I'll never speak a word more on the subject."

The Moor, observing the earnestness with which his wife again pleaded for the captain, began to guess the meaning of the ensign's words; and in deep melancholy he went to seek that villain and induce him to speak more openly of what he knew. Then the ensign, who was bent upon injuring the unhappy lady, after feigning at first great reluctance to say aught that might displease the Moor, at length pretended to yield to his entreaties, and said, "I can't deny it pains me to the soul to be thus forced to say what needs must be more hard to hear than any other grief; but since you will it so, and that the regard I owe your honour compels me to confess the truth, I will no longer refuse to satisfy your questions and my duty. Know, then, that for no other reason is your lady vexed to see the captain in disfavour than the pleasure that she has in his company whenever he comes to your house, and all the more since she had taken an aversion to your blackness."

These words went straight to the Moor's heart; but in order to hear more (now that he believed true all that the ensign had told him) he replied, with a fierce glance, "By heavens, I scarce can hold this hand from plucking out that tongue of thine, so bold, which dares to speak such slander of my wife!"

"Captain," replied the ensign, "I looked for such reward for these my faithful offices,—none else; but since my duty, and the jealous care I bear your honour, have carried me thus far, I do repeat, so stands the truth, as you have heard it from these lips; and if the lady Disdemona hath, with a false show of love for you, blinded your eyes to what you should have seen, this is no argument but that I speak the truth. Nay, this same captain told it me himself, like one whose happiness is incomplete until he can declare it to another; and, but that I feared your anger, I should have given him, when he told it me, his merited reward, and slain him. But since informing you of what concerns you more than any other man brings me so undeserved a recompense, would I had held my peace, since silence might have spared me your displeasure."

Then the Moor, burning with indignation and anguish, said, "Make thou these eyes self-witnesses of what thou tell'st, or on thy life I'll make thee wish thou hadst been born without a tongue."

"An easy task it would have been," replied the villain, "when he was used to visit at your house; but now that you have banished him, not for just cause, but for mere frivolous pretext, it will be hard to prove the truth. Still, I do not forego the hope to make you witness of that which you will not credit from my lips."

. . . Disdemona often used to go, as I have already said, to visit the ensign's wife, and remained with her a good part of the day. Now the ensign observed that she carried about with her a handkerchief, which he knew the Moor had given her, finely embroidered in the Moorish fashion, and which was precious to Disdemona, nor less so to the Moor. Then he conceived the plan of taking this kerchief from her secretly, and thus laying the snare for her final ruin. The ensign had a little daughter, a child three years of age, who was much loved by Disdemona, and one day, when the unhappy lady had gone to pay a visit at the house of this vile man, he took the little child up in his arms and carried her to Disdemona, who took her and pressed her to her bosom; whilst at the same instant this traitor, who had extreme dexterity of hand, drew the kerchief from her sash so cunningly that she did not notice him, and overjoyed he took his leave of her. Disdemona, ignorant of what had happened, returned home, and, busy with other thoughts, forgot the handkerchief. But a few days afterwards, looking for it and not finding it, she was in alarm, lest the Moor should ask her for it, as he oft was wont to do. Meanwhile the wicked ensign, seizing a fit opportunity, went to the captain of the troop, and with crafty malice left the handkerchief at the head of his bed without his discovering the trick, until the following morning, when, on his getting out of bed, the handkerchief fell upon the floor, and he set his foot upon it. And not being able to imagine how it had come into his house, knowing that it belonged to Disdemona, he resolved to give it to her; and waiting until the Moor had gone from home, he went to the back door and knocked. It seemed as if fate conspired with the ensign to work the death of the unhappy Disdemona. Just at that time the Moor returned home, and hearing a knocking at the back door, he went to the window, and in a rage exclaimed, "Who knocks there?" The captain, hearing the Moor's voice, and fearing lest he should come down stairs and attack him, took to flight without answering a word. The Moor went down, and opening the door hastened into the street and looked about, but in vain. Then, returning to the house in great anger, he demanded of his wife who it was that had knocked at the door. Disdemona replied, as was true, that she did not know; but the Moor said, "It seemed to me the captain." "I know not," answered Disdemona, "whether it was he or another person."

The Moor restrained his fury, great as it was, wishing to do nothing before consulting the ensign, to whom he hastened instantly and told him all that had passed, praying him to gather from the captain all that he could respecting the affair. The ensign, overjoyed at the occurrence, promised the Moor to do as he requested, and one day he took occasion to speak with the captain when the Moor was so placed that he could see and hear them as they conversed. And whilst talking to him of every other subject than of Disdemona, he kept laughing all the time aloud, and, feigning astonishment, he made various movements with his head and hands, as if listening to some tale of marvel. As soon as the Moor saw the captain depart, he went up to the ensign to hear what he had said to him. And the ensign, after long entreaty, at length said, "He has hidden from me nothing, and has told me that he has been used to visit your wife whenever you went from home, and that on the last occasion she gave him this handkerchief which you presented to her when you married her."

The Moor thanked the ensign, and it seemed now clear to him that, should he find Disdemona not to have the handkerchief, it was all true that the ensign had told him. One day, therefore, after dinner, in conversation with his wife on various subjects, he asked her for the kerchief. The unhappy lady, who had been in great fear of this, grew red as fire at this demand; and to hide the scarlet of her cheeks, which was closely noted by the Moor, she ran to a chest and pretended to seek the handkerchief, and after hunting for it a long time, she said, "I know not how it is — I cannot find it; can you, perchance, have taken it?" "If I had taken it," said the Moor, "why should I ask it of you? But you will look better another time."

On leaving the room, the Moor fell to meditating how he should put his wife to death, and likewise the captain of the troop, so that their death should not be laid to his charge. As he ruminated over this day and night, he could not prevent his wife's observing that he was not the same towards her as he had been wont. . . . Although conscious that she had given the Moor no cause, by act or deed, to be so troubled, yet she feared that he might have grown wearied of her; and she would say to the ensign's wife, "I know not what to say of the Moor; he used to be all love towards me; but within these few days he has become another man; and much I fear that I shall prove a warning to young girls not to marry against the wishes of their parents, and that the Italian ladies may learn from me not to wed a man whom nature and habitude of life estrange from us. But as I know the Moor is on such terms of friendship with your husband, and communicates to him all his affairs, I pray you, if you have heard from him aught that you may tell me of, fail not to befriend me." And as she said this, she wept bitterly.

The ensign's wife, who knew the whole truth (her husband wishing to make use of her to compass the death of Disdemona), but could never consent to such a project, dared not, from fear of her husband, disclose a single circumstance: all she said was, "Beware lest you give any cause of suspicion to your husband, and show to him by every means of your fidelity and love." "Indeed I do so," replied Disdemona, "but it is all of no avail."

Meanwhile the Moor sought in every way to convince himself of what he fain would have found untrue, and he prayed the ensign to contrive that he might see the handkerchief in possession of the captain. . . . Now the captain had a wife at home who worked the most marvelous embroidery upon lawn, and seeing the handkerchief, which belonged to the Moor's wife, she resolved, before it was returned to her, to work one like it. As she was engaged in this task, the ensign observed her standing at a window, where she could be seen by all the passers-by in the street, and he pointed her out to the Moor, who was now perfectly convinced of his wife's guilt. Then he arranged with the ensign to slay Disdemona and the captain of the troop, treating them as it seemed they both deserved. And the Moor prayed the ensign that he would kill the captain, promising eternal gratitude to him. But the ensign at first refused to undertake so dangerous a task, the captain being a man of equal skill and courage; until at length, after much entreating and being richly paid, the Moor prevailed on him to promise to attempt the deed.

Having formed this resolution, the ensign, going out one

dark night, sword in hand, met the captain on his way to visit a courtesan, and struck him a blow on his right thigh, which cut off his leg and felled him to the earth. Then the ensign was on the point of putting an end to his life, when the captain, who was a courageous man and used to the sight of blood and death, drew his sword, and, wounded as he was, kept on his defence, exclaiming with a loud voice, "I'm murdered!" Thereupon the ensign, hearing the people come running up, with some of the soldiers who were lodged thereabouts, took to his heels to escape being caught; then turning about again, he joined the crowd, pretending to have been attracted by the noise. And when he saw the captain's leg cut off, he judged that, if not already dead, the blow must, at all events, end his life; and whilst in his heart he was rejoiced at this he yet feigned to compassionate the captain as he had been his brother.

The next morning the tidings of this affair spread through the whole city, and reached the ears of Disdemona; whereat she, who was kind-hearted and little dreamed that any ill would betide her, evinced the greatest grief at the calamity.

This served but to confirm the Moor's suspicions, and he went to seek for the ensign, and said to him, "Do you know that my wife is in such grief at the captain's accident that she is well nigh gone mad." "And what could you expect, seeing he is her very soul?" replied the ensign. "Ay, soul forsooth!" exclaimed the Moor. "I'll draw the soul from out her body; call me no man if that I fail to shut the world upon this wretch."

Then they consulted of one means and another — poison and daggers — to kill poor Disdemona, but could resolve on nothing. At length the ensign said, "A plan comes to my mind, which will give you satisfaction, and raise cause for no suspicion. It is this: the house in which you live is very old, and the ceiling of your chamber has many cracks; I propose we take a stocking, filled with sand, and beat Disdemona with it till she dies; thus will her body bear no signs of violence. When she is dead we can pull down a portion of the ceiling, and thus make it seem as if a rafter falling on her head had killed the lady. Suspicion cannot rest on you, since all men will impute her death to accident."

This cruel counsel pleased the Moor, and he only waited for a fitting time to execute the plot. One night, when he and Disdemona had retired to bed, the ensign, whom the Moor had concealed in a closet which opened into the chamber, raised a noise in the closet, according to a concerted plan; whereat the Moor said to his wife, "Did you not hear that noise?" "Indeed I heard it," she replied. "Rise," said the Moor, "and see what 'tis."

The unhappy Disdemona rose from bed, and the instant she approached the closet, out rushed the ensign and being strong and of stout nerve, he beat her cruelly with the bag of sand across her back; upon which Disdemona fell to the ground, scarce able to draw her breath; but with the little voice she had left, she called upon the Moor for aid. But the Moor, leaping from bed, exclaimed, "Thou wickedest of women, thus has thy falseness found its just reward, the recompense to wives who, counterfeiting love, place horns upon their husbands' brows."

The wretched lady, hearing these words, and feeling that she was near her end (for the ensign had given her another blow), appealed to the justice of heaven, since justice here had failed her, in proof of her fidelity and truth; and as she was thus calling heaven to witeness, the wicked ensign inflicted a third blow, under which she sank lifeless on the floor. Then the ensign and the Moor, laying Disdemona on the bed and wounding her head, pulled down part of the ceiling of the chamber, as they had arranged; whereupon the Moor began to call aloud for help, exclaiming that the house was falling. Hearing this uproar, the neighbours all came running up, and there found Disdemona lying dead beneath a rafter, — a sight which, from the good life of that poor lady, did fill all hearts with sorrow.

On the following day Disdemona was buried, followed to the grave by the universal grief of the people. But heaven, the just regarder of all hearts, willed not that so wicked a deed should go unpunished. Ere long the Moor, whom Disdemona had loved more than her own life, began to feel such sorrow at her loss that he went wandering about as one bereft of reason, searching in every part of the house. And reflecting in his thoughts that the ensign had been the cause that he had lost, with Disdemona, all joy in life, he conceived so deep a hatred to that wicked man he could not bear to set eyes on him, and had it not been for his fear of the inviolable justice of the signoria of Venice, he would have slain him openly. But being unable to do this with safety, he deprived him of his rank, and would not allow him to remain in his company; whereat such an enmity arose between the two that no greater or more deadly can be imagined. The ensign, that wickedest of all bad men, now turned his thoughts to injuring the Moor; and seeking out the captain, whose wound was by this time healed, and who went about with a wooden leg in place of the one that had been cut off, he said to him, " 'Tis time you should be avenged for your lost limb; and if you will come with me to Venice, I'll tell you who the malefactor is, whom I dare not mention to you here for many reasons; and I will bring you proofs."

The captain of the troop, whose anger returned fiercely, but without knowing why, thanked the ensign, and went with him to Venice. On arriving there the ensign told him that it was the Moor who had cut off his leg, on account of the suspicion he had formed of Disdemona's conduct with him; and for that reason he had slain her, and then spread the report that the ceiling had fallen and killed her. Upon hearing which the captain accused the Moor to the signoria. . . . The signoria of Venice, when they heard of the cruelty inflicted by a barbarian upon a lady of their city, commanded that the Moor's arms should be pinioned in Cyprus, and he be brought to Venice, where, with many tortures, they sought to draw from him the truth. But the Moor, bearing with unyielding courage all the torment, denied the whole charge so resolutely that no confession could be drawn from him. But, although by his constancy and firmness he escaped death, he was, after being confined for several days in prison, condemned to perpetual banishment, in which he was eventually slain by the kinsfolk of Disdemona, as he merited. The ensign returned to his own country, and, following up his wonted villainy, he accused one of his companions of having sought to persuade him to kill an enemy of his, who was a man of noble rank; whereupon this person was arrested and put to the torture; but when he denied the truth of what his accuser had declared, the ensign himself was likewise tortured to make him prove the truth of his accusations; and he was tortured so that his body ruptured, upon which he was removed from prison and taken home, where he died a miserable death. Thus did heaven avenge the innocence of Disdemona; and all these events were narrated by the ensign's wife, who was privy to the whole, after his death, as I have told them here.

KING LEAR

THE primary sources of the story of Lear and his daughters are in the ancient chronicles of Britain; thus it appears as early as the work of Geoffrey of Monmouth, in the twelfth century. Shakespeare doubtless read it in Holinshed's Chronicle (see above, page 120), and also in the brief version given by Spenser in the *Faerie Queene* (1590) as well as in other Elizabethan poems. But there was already a play on the subject, called *The True Chronicle History of King Leir and his Three Daughters,* written some time before 1605, when it was printed; it may have been the work of George Peele. There follow the essential passages in Holinshed's account together with an outline of the old play.

FROM HOLINSHED'S CHRONICLES OF ENGLAND

Leir the son of Bladud was admitted ruler over the Britons in the year of the world 3105. . . . It is written that he had by his wife three daughters, without other issue, whose names were Gonorilla, Regan, and Cordeilla, which daughters he greatly loved, but specially Cordeilla the youngest far above the two elder. When this Leir therefore was come to great years, and began to wax unwieldy through age, he thought to understand the affections of his daughters towards him, and prefer her whom he best loved to the succession over the kingdom. Wherefore he first asked Gonorilla, the eldest, how well she loved him; who calling her gods to record, protested that she loved him more than her own life, which by right and reason should be most dear unto her. With which answer the father being well pleased, turned to the second, and demanded of her how well she loved him; who answered, confirming her sayings with great oaths, that she loved him more than tongue could express, and far above all other creatures of the world. Then called he his youngest daughter Cordeilla before him, and asked of her what account she made of him; unto whom she made this answer as followeth: "Knowing the great love and fatherly zeal that you have always borne towards me, for the which I may not answer you otherwise than I think, and as my conscience leadeth me, I protest unto you that I have loved you ever, and will continually, while I live, love you as my natural father. And if you would more understand of the love that I bear you, ascertain yourself that so much as you have so much you are worth, and so much I love you, and no more." The father, being nothing content with this answer, married his two eldest daughters, the one unto Henninus, the Duke of Cornwall, and the other unto Maglanus, the Duke of Albania, betwixt whom he willed and ordained that his land should be divided after his death, and the one half thereof immediately should be assigned to them in hand; but for the third daughter Cordeilla he reserved nothing.

Nevertheless it fortuned that one of the princes of Gallia (which now is called France), whose name was Aganippus, hearing of the beauty, womanhood, and good conditions of the said Cordeilla, desired to have her in marriage, and sent over to her father, requiring that he might have her to wife; to whom answer was made that he might have his daughter, but as for any dower he could have none, for all was promised and assured to her other sisters already. Aganippus, notwithstanding this answer of denial to receive anything by way of dower with Cordeilla, took her to wife, only moved thereto (I say) for respect of her person and amiable virtues. . . .

After that Leir was fallen into age, the two dukes that had married his two eldest daughters, thinking long ere the government of the land did come to their hands, arose against him in armour, and reft from him the governance of the land, upon conditions to be continued for term of life; by the which he was put to his portion, that is, to live after a rate assigned to him for the maintenance of his estate, which in process of time was diminished as well by Maglanus as by Henninus. But the greatest grief that Leir took was to see the unkindness of his daughters, which seemed to think that all was too much that their father had, the same being never so little; in so much that, going from the one to the other, he was brought to that misery that scarcely they would allow him one servant to wait upon him.

In the end, such was the unkindness, or, as I may say, the unnaturalness which he found in his two daughters, notwithstanding their fair and pleasant words uttered in time past, that being constrained of necessity, he fled the land, and sailed into Gallia, there to seek some comfort of his youngest daughter Cordeilla, whom beforetime he hated. The lady Cordeilla, hearing that he was arrived in poor estate, she first sent to him privily a certain sum of money to apparel himself withal, and to retain a certain number of servants that might attend upon him in honourable wise, as appertained to the estate which he had borne; and then so accompanied, she appointed him to come to the court, which he did and was so joyfully, honourably, and lovingly received, both by his son-in-law Aganippus and also by his daughter Cordeilla, that his heart was greatly comforted; for he was no less honoured than if he had been king of the whole country himself.

Now when he had informed his son-in-law and his daughter in what sort he had been used by his other daughters, Aganippus caused a mighty army to be put in readiness, and likewise a great navy of ships to be rigged, to pass over into Britain with Leir his father-in-law, to see him again restored to his kingdom. It was accorded that Cordeilla should also go with him to take possession of the land, the which he promised to leave unto her, as the rightful inheritor after his decease, notwithstanding any former grant made to her sisters or to their husbands in any manner of wise. Hereupon, when this army and navy of ships were ready, Leir and his daughter Cordeilla, with her husband, took the sea, and arriving in Britain, fought with their enemies, and discomfited them in battle, in the which Maglanus and Henninus were slain; and then was Leir restored to his kingdom, which he ruled after this by the space of two years, and then died, forty years after he first began to reign. . . .

This Cordeilla, after her father's decease, ruled the land

of Britain right worthily during the space of five years, in which meantime her husband died; and then, about the end of those five years, her two nephews Margan and Cunedag, sons to her aforesaid sisters, disdaining to be under the government of a woman, levied war against her, and destroyed a great part of the land, and finally took her prisoner, and laid her fast in ward; wherewith she took such grief, being a woman of a manly courage, and despairing to recover liberty, there she slew herself.

THE TRUE CHRONICLE HISTORY OF KING LEIR AND HIS THREE DAUGHTERS

ACT I. King Leir declares his wish to obtain sons by the marriage of his daughters, and in particular for his favorite Cordella, who has thus far refused to choose a husband.

"Even now my mind
Doth meditate a sudden stratagem,
To try which of my daughters loves me best:
Which till I know, I cannot be in rest,
This granted, when they jointly shall contend,
Each to exceed the other in their love,
Then at the vantage will I take Cordella,
Even as she doth protest she loves me best,
I'll say, Then, daughter, grant me one request,
To show thou lovest me as thy sisters do:
Accept a husband, whom myself will woo."

Gonorill and Ragan are heard expressing their hatred for their sister, who is

so nice and so demure,
So sober, courteous, modest, and precise,
That all the court hath work enough to do
To talk how she exceedeth me and you.

They resolve to convert her father's love to hate. The following scene presents the test, in which Gonorill and Ragan protest their willingness to make any sacrifice for their father's love; meantime Cordella, in an aside, exclaims, "O how I do abhor this flattery!" When it is her turn to protest her love, she says only:

"I cannot paint my duty forth in words;
I hope my deeds shall make report for me;
But look what love the child doth owe the father,
The same to you I bear, my gracious lord."

Accordingly Leir rejects her, announcing his intention to divide his kingdom into two parts instead of three. Perillus, a faithful courtier, alone expresses his grief at the king's decision.

ACT II. The Gallian king, in his palace, resolves to go to Brittany to find a queen from among the celebrated daughters of King Leir. In the second scene the kings of Cornwall and Cambria, who have been promised Gonorill and Ragan respectively in marriage, meet on their road to Leir's palace, and discuss the rejection of Cordella. In the third scene they are welcomed by Leir and their brides, the king declaring:

"And here I do freely dispossess my self,
And make you two my true adopted heirs:

> My self will sojourn with my son of Cornwall,
> And take me to my prayers and my beads.
> I know my daughter Ragan will be sorry,
> Because I do not spend my days with her."

Perillus protests against the disinheriting of Cordella, but in vain. In the fourth scene the Gallian king, disguised as a pilgrim, meets Cordella, and falls instantly in love with her. Notwithstanding her declaration that she is without a dowry, he tells her that his king has sent to ask her in marriage. She replies that she will wed only for love, and intimates that she would prefer his hand to his master's; thereupon he reveals himself, and they are betrothed.

ACT III. Perillus soliloquizes, revealing the fact that Gonorill is shamefully mistreating her father; she has already withdrawn half his allowance, and will soon cut off the remainder.

> But he, the mirror of wild patience,
> Puts up all wrongs, and never gives reply.

In the second scene Gonorill consults with a courtier regarding the means of crushing her father and ridding herself of him. In the third scene she abuses him before her husband, who has treated him with all courtesy but weakly leaves the matter to her. Perillus consoles the anguished king, and bids him seek his remaining daughters. In the fourth scene Ragan, in the palace at Cambria, soliloquizes, rejoicing that she is mistress of her husband and is not troubled, like Gonorill, with her father's presence. In the fifth scene Gonorill intercepts a friendly letter which her husband has sent after Leir, and substitutes a message to Ragan, making false charges against him and intimating that it would be well to put him to death.

ACT IV. Cordella soliloquizes, longing for reconciliation with her father. In the second scene Leir and Perillus approach the palace of Cambria; Ragan greets her father with dissembled affection, but when left alone reveals her intention to refuse to give him a home. In the third scene the messenger from Gonorill arrives, and Ragan employs him to " act a stratagem, and give a stab or two, if need require." In the fourth scene the king of Gallia, perceiving Cordella's sadness, promises to send an embassy to Britain inviting Leir to visit them. In the fifth scene Ragan plots definitely with the messenger for the slaying of her father. In the sixth the king of Cornwall receives the embassy from the king of Gallia, but is obliged to reply that Leir has left his court; Gonorill learns of Cordella's mingled prosperity and unhappiness, and shows her scorn. In the seventh scene Leir and Perillus, wandering in the open country, are met by the armed messenger. He reveals his intention to slay them, and presently exhibits Gonorill's letter showing under whose authority he came to Cambria. Leir and Perillus each plead for the life of the other. Meantime a storm has come up, and eventually the messenger, frightened by the thunder-claps, drops his weapons and flees. Perillus now persuades his master to attempt to find refuge with Cordella in France. In the eighth scene the Gallian ambassador is seen leaving Cornwall for Cambria to seek King Leir.

ACT V. The king of Gallia, Cordella, and the king's attendant, plan a visit to the seaside, disguised as country folk. In the second scene the Gallian ambassador presents himself to Ragan and her husband, and is insulted by the former. In the third scene Leir and Perillus are discovered, arrived on the coast of Gallia, worn and penniless. Leir discourses:

" Can kindness spring out of ingratitude?
Or love be reaped, where hatred hath been sown?
Can henbane join in league with mithridate?
Or sugar grow in wormwood's bitter stalk?
It cannot be, they are too opposite:
And so am I to any kindness here.
I have thrown wormwood on the sugared youth,
And like to henbane poisonèd the fount
Whence flowed the mithridate of a child's good will.
I, like an envious thorn, have pricked the heart,
And turned sweet grapes to sour unrelished sloes.
The causeless ire of my respectless breast
Hath soured the sweet milk of dame Nature's paps;
My bitter words have galled her honey thoughts,
And weeds of rancor choked the flower of grace."

In the fourth scene the king and Cordella come upon the wanderers, now almost perished with hunger. They overhear Leir saying:

" Ah, poor Cordella, did I give thee nought,
Nor never shall be able for to give?
Oh, let me warn all ages that ensueth,
How they trust flattery and reject the truth.
Well, unkind girls, I here forgive you both,
Yet the just heavens will hardly do the like;
And only crave forgiveness at the end
Of good Cordella, and of thee my friend,

Of God, whose majesty I have offended
By my transgression many thousand ways:
Of her, dear heart, whom I for no occasion
Turned out of all, through flatterers' persuasion;
Of thee, kind friend, who but for me, I know,
Hadst never come unto this place of woe."

He and Perillus now beg for food from the party of seeming country folk, and are graciously received and fed. Leir is encouraged to tell his story, revealing the fact that he is seeking aid at last from the daughter whom he had wronged. He concludes:

"But if she show a loving daughter's part,
It comes of God and her, nor my desert.
CORDELLA. No doubt she will, I dare be sworn she will.
LEIR. How know you that, not knowing what she is?
CORDELLA. Myself a father have a great way hence,
Used me as ill as ever you did her;
Yet, that his reverend age I once might see,
I'd creep along to meet him on my knee.
LEIR. Oh, no men's children are unkind but mine.
CORDELLA. Condemn not all, because of others' crime:
But look, dear father, look! behold and see;
Thy loving daughter speaketh unto thee.
[*Kneels.*
LEIR. Oh, stand thou up, it is my part to kneel,
And ask forgiveness for my former faults.
[*Kneels.*
CORDELLA. Oh, if you wish I should enjoy my breath,
Dear father, rise, or I receive my death.
[*He rises.*

LEIR. Then I will rise to satisfy your mind,
But kneel again, till pardon be resigned.
[*Kneels.*

CORDELLA. I pardon you: the word beseems not me;
But I do say so, for to ease your knee. . . .
KING. Good father, rise, she is your loving daughter,
And honours you with as respective duty
As if you were the monarch of the world.
CORDELLA. But I will never rise from off my knee,
Until I have your blessing, and your pardon
Of all my faults committed any way,
From my first birth unto this present day.
LEIR. The blessing which the God of Abraham gave
Unto the tribe of Judah, light on thee,
And multiply thy days, that thou may'st see
Thy children's children prosper after thee."

The Gallian king now takes oath to take arms and punish the " viperous sect " who have so maltreated King Leir. In the fifth scene Ragan soliloquizes, first saying " I feel a hell of conscience in my breast; " but she fears only that her plot to murder her father will be discovered.

" O God, that I had been but made a man,
Or that my strength were equal with my will!
These foolish men are nothing but mere pity,
And melt as butter doth against the sun."

In the sixth scene a French army is discovered embarking for Britain; in the seventh the watchmen at Dover guard the seacoast; in the eighth the French approach Dover; in the ninth fighting begins; in the tenth the Gallian king and

Leir offer terms to the conquered town, whose citizens renew their allegiance to Leir. Meantime the armies of Cornwall and Cambria arrive, and Gonorill and Ragan engage in violent controversy with the invaders. In the eleventh and twelfth scenes victory is fully attained by the Gallian army, and Leir formally thanks his son-in-law for restoring to him his kingdom.

MACBETH

SHAKESPEARE found the story of Macbeth in the portion of Holinshed's Chronicle (see above, page 120) dealing with Scotland; it goes back to earlier Scottish chronicles of the fourteenth and fifteenth centuries. The following are the essential portions of Holinshed's narrative, but its full form is abbreviated, not including minor details of which Shakespeare made some use.

FROM HOLINSHED'S HISTORY OF SCOTLAND

Shortly after [the conclusion of the war between the Scots and the Danes] happened a strange and uncouth wonder, which afterward was the cause of much trouble in the realm of Scotland, as ye shall after hear. It fortuned as Macbeth and Banquo journeyed towards Fores, where the king then lay, they went sporting by the way together without other company, save only themselves, passing through the woods and fields, when suddenly in the midst of a land there met them three women in strange and wild apparel, resembling creatures of elder world, whom when they attentively beheld, wondering much at the sight, the first of them spake and said: " All hail, Macbeth, thane of Glamis! " (for he had lately entered into that dignity and office by the death of his father Sinell). The second of them said: " Hail, Macbeth, thane of Cawdor! " But the third said: " All hail, Macbeth, that hereafter shalt be king of Scotland! " Then Banquo, " What manner of women " (saith he) " are you, that seem so little favorable unto me, whereas to my fellow here, besides high offices, ye assign also the kingdom, appointing forth nothing for me at all? " " Yes," saith the first of them, " we promise greater benefits unto thee than unto him; for he shall reign, indeed, but with an unlucky end; neither shall he leave any issue behind him to succeed in his place; where contrarily thou indeed shalt not reign at all, but of thee those shall be born which shall govern the Scottish kingdom by long order of continual descent." Herewith the foresaid women vanished immediately out of their sight.

This was reputed at the first but some vain fantastical illusion by Macbeth and Banquo, insomuch that Banquo would call Macbeth in jest " king of Scotland," and Macbeth again would call him in sport likewise " the father of many kings." But afterwards the common opinion was, that these women were either the weird sisters, that is (as ye would say) the goddesses of destiny, or else some nymphs or fairies, endued with knowledge of prophecy by their necromantical science, because everything came to pass as they had spoken. For shortly after, the thane of Cawdor being condemned at Fores of treason against the king committed, his lands, livings, and offices were given of the king's liberality to Macbeth.

The same night after, at supper, Banquo jested with him

and said: "Now, Macbeth, thou hast obtained those things which the two former sisters prophesied, there remaineth only for thee to purchase that which the third said should come to pass." Whereupon Macbeth, revolving the thing in his mind, began even then to devise how he might attain to the kingdom; but yet he thought with himself that he must tarry a time, which should advance him thereto, by the divine providence, as it had come to pass in his former preferment. . . .

The words of the three weird sisters also (of whom before ye have heard) greatly encouraged him hereunto; but specially his wife lay sore upon him to attempt the thing, as she that was very ambitious, burning in unquenchable desire to bear the name of a queen. At length therefore, communicating his purposed intent with his trusty friends, amongst whom Banquo was the chiefest, upon confidence of their promised aid, he slew the king at Enverns, or (as some say) at Botgosuane, in the sixth year of his reign. Then, having a company about him of such as he had made privy to his enterprise, he caused himself to be proclaimed king. . . . Malcolm Cammore and Donald Bane, the sons of the king Duncan, for fear of their lives (which they might well know that Macbeth would seek to bring to end for his more sure confirmation in the estate) fled into Cumberland, where Malcolm remained till time that Saint Edward the son of Etheldred recovered the dominion of England from the Danish power, . . . but Donald passed over into Ireland. Macbeth, after the departure thus of Duncan's sons, used great liberality towards the nobles of the realm, thereby to win their favor; and when he saw that no man went about to trouble him, he set his whole intention to maintain justice. . . . To be brief, such were the worthy doings and princely acts of this Macbeth in the administration of the realm, that if he had attained thereunto by rightful means, and continued in uprightness of justice as he began, till the end of his reign, he might well have been numbered amongst the most noble princes that anywhere had reigned. . . . But this was but a counterfeit zeal of equity showed by him, partly against his natural inclination, to purchase thereby the favor of the people. Shortly after, he began to show what he was, instead of equity practicing cruelty. . . . The words also of the three weird sisters would not out of his mind, which as they promised him the kingdom, so likewise did they promise it at the same time unto the posterity of Banquo. . . . He arranged therefore that Banquo with his son Fleance should come to a supper, and devised a present death for both at the hands of certain murderers whom he had hired to execute this deed, appointing them to meet Banquo and Fleance as they were returning to their lodgings, and slay them in such wise that Macbeth's house should not be slandered, and that he himself might be clear if anything were laid to his charge on any suspicion that might arise. It chanced yet by the benefit of the dark night, that though the father were slain, the son yet, by the help of almighty God, reserving him to better fortune, escaped that danger; and afterwards, having some inkling (by the admonition of some friends which he had in the court) how his life was sought no less than his father's, who was slain not by chance-medley, as by the handling of the matter Macbeth would have had it to appear, but even upon a prepensed device; whereupon to avoid further peril he fled into Wales. . . .

After the contrived slaughter of Banquo, nothing prospered with the foresaid Macbeth; for in manner every man began to doubt his own life, and durst unneath [6] appear in the king's presence; and even as there were many that stood in fear of him, so likewise stood he in fear of many, in such sort that he began to make those away, by one surmised cavillation [7] or other, whom he thought most able to work him any displeasure. At length he found such sweetness by putting his nobles thus to death, that his earnest thirst after blood in this behalf might in no wise be satisfied; for ye must consider he won double profits (as he thought) hereby: for first they were rid out of the way whom he feared, and then again his coffers were enriched by their goods which were forfeited to his use, whereby he might the better maintain a guard of armed men about him, to defend his person from injury of them whom he had in any suspicion. Further, to the end he might the more creully oppress his subjects with all tyrantlike wrongs, he builded a strong castle on the top of an high hill called Dunsinane, situate in Gowrie, ten miles from Perth, on such a proud height that, standing there aloft, a man might behold well near all the countries of Angus, Fife, Stermond, and Ernedale, as it were lying underneath him. [Macduff, alone of all the thanes of the realm, did not come himself to aid with the building of the castle, lest the king would lay violent hands upon him. This enraged Macbeth;] neither could he afterwards abide to look upon the said Macduff, either for that he thought his puissance over-great, either else for that he had learned of certain wizards, in whose words he put great confidence (for

[6] Scarcely. [7] Accusation.

that the prophecy had happened so right, which the three fairies or weird sisters had declared unto him) that he ought to take heed of Macduff, who in time to come should seek to destroy him. And surely hereupon had he put Macduff to death, but that a certain witch, whom he had in great trust, had told that he should never be slain with man born of any woman, nor vanquished till the wood of Bernane came to the castle of Dunsinane. . . .

Macduff, to avoid peril of life, purposed with himself to pass into England, to procure Malcolm Cammore to claim the crown of Scotland. . . . Immediately then, being advised whereabout Macduff went, [Macbeth] came hastily with a great power into Fife, and forthwith besieged the castle where Macduff dwelled, trusting to have found him therein. They that kept the house without any resistance opened the gates, and suffered him to enter, mistrusting none evil. But nevertheless Macbeth most cruelly caused the wife and children of Macduff, with all other whom he found in that castle, to be slain. . . .

[Macduff, coming to Malcolm, besought his aid in delivering Scotland from the tyrant; but Malcolm, not certain whether he came as a friend or sent by Macbeth to betray him, "thought to have some further trial, and thereupon, dissembling his mind at the first, he answered" as in Act IV, sc. iii. After they had come to an agreement,] Malcolm purchased such favor at King Edward's hands, that old Siward, earl of Northumberland, was appointed, with ten thousand men, to go with him into Scotland to support him in this enterprise for recovery of his right. . . . Malcolm following hastily after Macbeth, came the night before the battle unto Birnane wood, and when his army had rested awhile there to refresh them, he commanded every man to get a bough of some tree or other of that wood in his hand, as big as he might bear, and to march forth therewith in such wise that on the next morrow they might come closely and without sight in this manner within view of his enemies. On the morrow, when Macbeth beheld them coming in this sort, he first marvelled what the matter meant, but in the end remembered himself that the prophecy which he had heard long before that time, of the coming of Birnane wood to Dunsinane castle, was likely to be now fulfilled. Nevertheless he brought his men in order of battle, and exhorted them to do valiantly; howbeit his enemies had scarcely cast from them their boughs when Macbeth, perceiving their numbers, betook him straight to flight, whom Macduff pursued with great hatred even till he came unto Lunfanain; where Macbeth, perceiving that Macduff was hard at his back, leaped beside his horse, saying, "Thou traitor! what meaneth it that thou shouldst thus in vain follow me, that am not appointed to be slain by any creature that is born of a woman? Come on, therefore, and receive thy reward which thou hast deserved for thy pains." And therewithal he lifted up his sword, thinking to have slain him. But Macduff, quickly avoiding from his horse, ere he came at him, answered, with his naked sword in his hand, saying: "It is true, Macbeth; and now shall thine insatiable cruelty have an end; for I am even he that thy wizards have told thee of, who was never borne of my mother, but ripped out of her womb." Therewithal he stepped unto him, and slew him in the place. Then, cutting his head from his shoulders, he set it upon a pole, and brought it unto Malcolm. This was the end of Macbeth, after he had reigned seventeen years over the Scottishmen. In the beginning of his reign he accomplished many worthy acts, very profitable to the commonwealth, as ye have heard, but afterward, by illusion of the devil, he defamed the same with most terrible cruelty.

[Certain other passages, from an earlier portion of the Chronicle, concerning the murder of king Duff by Donwald, are supposed to have suggested to Shakespeare certain details in the story of Macbeth:]

[Donwald's wife] counseled him, sith the king oftentimes used to lodge in his house without any guard about him, other than the garrison of the castle, which was wholly at his commandment, to make him away, and showed him the means whereby he might soonest accomplish it. Donwald, thus being the more kindled in wrath by the words of his wife, determined to follow her advice in the execution of so heinous an act. . . . It chanced that the king, upon the day before he purposed to depart forth of the castle, was long in his oratory at his prayers, and there continued till it was late in the night. At the last, coming forth, he called such afore him as had faithfully served him in pursuit and apprehension of the rebels, and giving them hearty thanks, he bestowed sundry honourable gifts among them, of the which number Donwald was one. . . . Then Donwald, though he abhorred the act greatly in his heart, yet through instigation of his wife, he called four of his servants unto him, whom he had made privy to his wicked intent before, and framed to his purpose with large gifts, and now declaring unto them after what sort they should work the feat, they gladly obeyed his instructions, and speedily going about the murder, they enter the chamber in which the king lay a little before cock's crow, where they secretly cut his throat as he lay sleeping. . . . In the morning when the noise was raised in the king's chamber how the king was slain, his body conveyed away, and the bed all berayed with blood, [Donwald] with the watch ran thither, as though he had known nothing of the matter, and breaking into the chamber, and finding cakes of blood in the bed and on the floor about the sides of it, he forthwith slew the chamberlains, as guilty of that heinous murder, and then like a madman running to and fro, he ransacked every corner within the castle, as though it had been to have seen if he might have found either the body or any of the murderers hid in any privy place.

ANTONY AND CLEOPATRA

THE materials for this tragedy Shakespeare found in Plutarch's *Lives* (see above, page 174). The essential portions of North's version of the "Life of Antony" (not including, however, all which is pertinent to Shakespeare's play) are here reproduced.

FROM THE LIFE OF MARCUS ANTONIUS

[Antonius] had a noble mind, as well to punish offenders, as to reward well-doers: and yet he did exceed more in giving than in punishing. Now for his outrageous manner of railing he commonly used, mocking and flouting of every man, that was remedied by itself. For a man might as boldly exchange a mock with him, and he was as well contented to be mocked as to mock others. But yet it oftentimes marred all. For he thought that those which told him so plainly and truly in mirth would never flatter him in good earnest in any manner of weight. But thus he was easily abused by the praises they gave him, not finding how these flatterers mingled their flattery, under this familiar and plain manner of speech unto him. . . .

Antonius being thus inclined, the last and extremest mischief of all other (to wit, the love of Cleopatra) lighted on him, who did waken and stir up many vices yet hidden in him, and were never seen to any: and if any spark of goodness or hope of rising were left him, Cleopatra quenched it straight, and made it worse than before. The manner how he fell in love with her was this. Antonius, going to make war with the Parthians, sent to command Cleopatra to appear personally before him, when he came into Cilicia, to answer unto such accusations as were laid against her. . . . Cleopatra, . . . guessing by the former access and credit she had with Julius Caesar and Cneius Pompey (the son of Pompey the Great) only for her beauty: she began to have good hope that she might more easily win Antonius. For Caesar and Pompey knew her when she was but a young thing, and knew not then what the world meant: but now she went to Antonius at the age when a woman's beauty is at the prime, and she also of best judgment. So, she furnished herself with a world of gifts, store of gold and silver, and of riches and other sumptuous ornaments as is credible enough she might bring from so great a house, and from so wealthy and rich a realm as Egypt was. But yet she carried nothing with her wherein she trusted more than in herself, and in the charms and enchantment of her passing beauty and grace. Therefore when she was sent unto by divers letters, both from Antonius himself, and also from his friends, she made so light of it and mocked Antonius so much, that she disdained to set forward otherwise, but to take her barge in the river of Cydnus, the poop whereof was of gold, the sails of purple, and the oars of silver, which kept stroke in rowing after the sound of the music of flutes, hautboys, citherns, viols, and such other instruments as they played upon in the barge. And now for the person of herself: she was laid under a pavilion of cloth of gold of tissue, apparelled and attired like the goddess Venus commonly drawn in picture: and hard by her, on either hand of her, pretty fair boys apparelled as painters do set forth god Cupid, with little fans in their hands, with the which they fanned wind upon her. Her ladies and gentlewomen also, the fairest of them were apparelled like the nymphs Nereides (which are the mermaids of the waters) and like the Graces, some steering the helm, others tending the tackle and ropes of the barge, out of the which there came a wonderful passing sweet savour of perfumes, that perfumed the wharf's side, pestered with innumerable multitudes of people. Some of them followed the barge all along the river's side: others also ran out of the city to see her coming in. So that in th' end, there ran such multitudes of people one after another to see her, that Antonius was left post alone in the market-place in his imperial seat to give audience: and there went a rumour in the people's mouths, that the goddess Venus was come to play with the god Bacchus, for the general good of all Asia. When Cleopatra landed, Antonius sent to invite her to supper to him. But she sent him word again, he should do better rather to come and sup with her. Antonius therefore, to shew himself courteous unto her at her arrival, was contented to obey her, and went to supper to her: where he found such passing sumptuous fare, that no tongue can express it. . . . The next night, Antonius feasting her contended to pass her in magnificence and fineness: but she overcame him in both. So that he himself began to scorn the gross service of his house, in respect of Cleopatra's sumptuousness and fineness. And when Cleopatra found Antonius' jests and slents to be but gross and soldierlike in plain manner, she gave it him finely, and without fear taunted him throughly. Now her beauty (as it is reported) was not so passing, as unmatchable of other women, nor yet such as upon present view did enamour men with her: but so sweet was her company and conversation, that a man could not possibly but be taken. And besides her beauty, the good grace she had to talk and discourse, her courteous nature that tempered her words and deeds, was a spur that pricked to the quick. . . . Now Antonius was so ravished with the love of Cleopatra, that though his wife Fulvia had great wars, and much ado with Caesar for his affairs, and that the army of the Parthians (the which the king's lieutenants had given to the only leading of Labienus) was now assembled in Mesopotamia ready to invade Syria: yet, as though all this had nothing touched him, he yielded himself to go with Cleopatra to Alexandria, where he spent and lost in childish sports (as a man might say) and idle pastimes the most precious thing a man can spend, as Antiphon saith: and that is, time. For they made an order between them, which they called *Amimetobion* (as much as to say, no life comparable and matchable with it) one feasting each other by turns, and in cost exceeding all measure and reason. . . . Plato writeth that there are four kinds of flattery: but Cleopatra divided it into many kinds. For she, were it in sport or in matter of earnest, still devised sundry new delights to have Antonius at commandment, never leaving him night nor day, nor once letting him go out of her sight. For she would play at dice with him, drink with him, and hunt commonly with him, and also be with him when he went to any exercise or activity of body. And sometime also, when he would go up and down the city disguised like a slave in the night, and would peer into poor men's windows and their shops, and scold and brawl with them within the house: Cleopatra would be also in a chambermaid's array, and amble up and down the streets with him, so that oftentimes Antonius bare away both mocks and blows. . . .

Now Antonius delighting in these fond and childish pastimes, very ill news were brought him from two places. The first from Rome, that his brother Lucius and Fulvia his wife fell out first between themselves, and afterwards fell to open war with Caesar, and had brought all to nought, that they were both driven to fly out of Italy. The second news, as bad as the first: that Labienus had conquered all Asia with the army of the Parthians, from the river of Euphrates, and from Syria, unto the countries of Lydia and Ionia. Then began Antonius with much ado a little to rouse himself, as if he had been wakened out of a deep sleep, and as a man may say, coming out of a great drunkenness. . . .

It is reported that [Caesar] dearly loved his sister Octavia, for indeed she was a noble lady, and left the widow of her first husband Caius Marcellus, who died not long before: and it seemed also that Antonius had been widower ever since the death of his wife Fulvia. For he denied not that he kept Cleopatra, but so did not confess that he had her as his wife: and so with reason he did defend the love he bare unto this Egyptian Cleopatra. Thereupon every man did set forward this marriage, hoping thereby that this lady Octavia, having an excellent grace, wisdom, and honesty, joined unto so rare a beauty, that when she were with Antonius (he loving her as so worthy a lady deserveth) she should be a good mean to keep good love and amity betwixt her brother and him. So, when Caesar and he had made the match between them, they both went to Rome about this marriage. . . .

Sextus Pompeius at that time kept in Sicilia, and so made many an inroad into Italy with a great number of pinnaces and other pirates' ships, of the which were captains two notable pirates, Menas and Menecrates, who so scoured all the sea thereabouts, that none durst peep out with a sail. Furthermore, Sextus Pompeius had dealt very friendly with Antonius, for he had courteously received his mother, when she fled out of Italy with Fulvia: and therefore they thought good to make peace with him. So they met all three together by the mount of Misenum, upon a hill that runneth far into sea: Pompey having his ships riding hard by at anchor, and Antonius and Caesar their armies upon the shore side, directly over against him. Now, after they had agreed that Sextus Pompeius should have Sicile and Sardinia, with this condition, that he should rid the sea of all thieves and pirates, and make it safe for passengers, and withal that he should send a certain of wheat to Rome: one of them did feast another, and drew cuts who should begin. It was Pompeius' chance to invite them first. Whereupon Antonius asked him: "And where shall we sup?" "There," said Pompey, and shewed him his admiral galley which had six banks of oars: "That" (said he) "is my father's house they have left me." He spake it to taunt Antonius, because he had his father's house, that was Pompey the Great. So he cast anchors enow into the sea to make his galley fast, and then built a bridge of wood to convey them to his galley from the head of mount Misenum: and there he welcomed them, and made them great cheer. Now in the midst of the feast, when they fell to be merry with Antonius' love unto Cleopatra, Menas the pirate came to Pompey, and, whispering in his ear, said unto him: "Shall I not cut the cables of the anchors, and make thee lord not only of Sicile and Sardinia, but of the whole empire of Rome besides?" Pompey, having paused awhile upon it, at length answered him: "Thou shouldst have done it, and never have told it me, but now we must content us with that we have. As for myself, I was never taught to break my faith, nor to be counted a traitor." The other two also did likewise feast him in their camp, and then he returned into Sicile. . . .

With Antonius there was a soothsayer or astronomer of Egypt, that could cast a figure, and judge of men's nativities, to tell them what should happen to them. He, either to please Cleopatra, or else for that he found it so by his art, told Antonius plainly, that his fortune (which of itself was excellent good, and very great) was altogether blemished and obscured by Caesar's fortune: and therefore he counselled him utterly to leave his company, and to get him as far from him as he could. "For thy demon," said he, "(that is to say, the good angel and spirit that keepeth thee), is afraid of his: and being courageous and high when he is alone, becometh fearful and timorous when he cometh near unto the other." Howsoever it was, the events ensuing proved the Egyptian's words true. For it is said that as often as they two drew cuts for pastime, who should have anything or whether they played at dice, Antonius always lost. . . .

Antonius also, leaving his wife Octavia and little children begotten of her with Caesar, and his other children which he had by Fulvia, he went directly into Asia. Then began this pestilent plague and mischief of Cleopatra's love (which had slept a long time, and seemed to have been utterly forgotten, and that Antonius had given place to better counsel) again to kindle, and to be in force, so soon as Antonius came near unto Syria. And in the end, the horse of the mind, as Plato termeth it, that is so hard of rein (I mean the unreined lust of concupiscence), did put out of Antonius' head all honest and commendable thoughts: for he sent Fonteius Capito to bring Cleopatra into Syria, Unto whom, to welcome her, he gave no trifling things: but unto that she had already he added the provinces of Phoenicia, those of the nethermost Syria, the Isle of Cyprus, and a great part of Cilicia, and that country of Jewry where the true balm is, and that part of Arabia where the Nabathaeans do dwell, which stretcheth out towards the ocean. These great gifts much misliked the Romans. . . .

Now whilst Antonius was busy in this preparation [against the Parthians], Octavia his wife, whom he had left at Rome, would needs take sea to come unto him.

Her brother Octavius Caesar was willing unto it, not for his respect at all (as most authors do report), as for that he might have an honest colour to make war with Antonius if he did misuse her, and not esteem of her as she ought to be. . . . When Niger, one of Antonius' friends whom he had sent unto Athens, had brought these news from his wife Octavia, and withal did greatly praise her, as she was worthy, and well deserved: Cleopatra knowing that Octavia would have Antonius from her, and fearing also that if with her virtue and honest behaviour (besides the great power of her brother Caesar) she did add thereunto her modest kind love to please her husband, that she would then be too strong for her, and in the end win him away: she subtly seemed to languish for the love of Antonius, pining her body for lack of meat. Furthermore, she every way so framed her countenance that, when Antonius came to see her, she cast her eyes upon him like a woman ravished for joy. Straight again, when he went from her, she fell a-weeping and blubbering, looked ruefully of the matter, and still found the means that Antonius should oftentimes find her weeping: and then, when he came suddenly upon her, she made as though she dried her eyes, and turned her face away, as if she were unwilling that he should see her weep. . . .

Now, after that Caesar had made sufficient preparation, he proclaimed open war against Cleopatra, and made the people to abolish the power and empire of Antonius, because he had before given it up unto a woman. And Caesar said furthermore, that Antonius was not master of himself, but that Cleopatra had brought him beside himself by her charms and amorous poisons: and that they that should make war with them should be Mardian the eunuch, Pothinus, and Iras, a woman of Cleopatra's bedchamber, that frizzled her hair and dressed her head, and Charmion, the which were those that ruled all the affairs of Antonius' empire.

Now Antonius was made so subject to a woman's will, that though he was a great deal the stronger by land, yet for Cleopatra's sake he would needs have this battle tried by sea: though he saw before his eyes that, for lack of watermen, his captains did press by force all sorts of men out of Greece that they could take up in the field, as travelers, muleteers, reapers, harvest men, and young boys, and yet could they not sufficiently furnish his galleys: so that the most part of them were empty, and could scant row, because they lacked watermen enow. But on the contrary Caesar's ships were not built for pomp, high and great, only for a sight and bravery: but they were light of yarage, armed and furnished with watermen as many as they needed, and had them all in readiness at the havens of Tarentum and Burndusium. . . . Notwithstanding all these good persuasions, Cleopatra forced him to put all to the hazard of battle by sea: considering with herself how she might fly and provide for her safety, not to help him to win the victory, but to fly more easily after the battle lost. . . .

Howbeit the battle was yet of even hand, and the victory doubtful, being indifferent to both: when suddenly they saw the three score ships of Cleopatra busy about their yard masts, and hoisting sail to fly. So they fled through the midst of them that were in fight, for they had been placed behind the great ships, and did marvelously disorder the other ships. For the enemies themselves wondered much to see them sail in that sort, with full sail towards Peloponnesus. There Antonius shewed plainly, that he had not only lost the courage and heart of an emperor, but also of a valiant man, and that he was not his own man (proving that true which an old man spake in mirth, that the soul of a lover lived in another body, and not in his own): he was so carried away with the vain love of this woman, as if he had been glued unto her, and that she could not have removed without moving of him also. For when he saw Cleopatra's ship under sail, he forgot, forsook, and betrayed them that fought for him, and embarked upon a galley with five banks of oars, to follow her that had already begun to overthrow him, and would in the end be his utter destruction. When she knew this galley afar off, she lift up a sign in the poop of her ship, and so Antonius coming to it was plucked up where Cleopatra was: howbeit he saw her not at his first coming, nor she him, but went and sate down alone in the prow of his ships, and said never a word, clapping his head between both his hands. . . .

Cleopatra in the meantime was very careful in gathering all sorts of poisons together to destroy men. Now, to make proof of those poisons which made men die with least pain, she tried it upon condemned men in prison. For, when she saw the poisons that were sudden and vehement, and brought speedy death with grievous torments, and, in contrary manner, that such as were more mild and gentle had not that quick speed and force to make one die suddenly: she afterwards went about to prove the stinging of snakes and adders, and made some to be applied to men in her sight, some in one sort and some in another. So, when she had daily made divers and sundry proofs, she found none of all them she had proved so fit as the biting of an aspic, the which only causeth a heaviness of the head, without swounding or complaining, and bringeth a great desire also to sleep, with a little sweat in the face, and so by little and little taketh away the senses and vital powers. . . .

Caesar would not grant unto Antonius' requests: but for Cleopatra he made her answer that he would deny her nothing reasonable, so that she would either put Antonius to death, or drive him out of her country. Therewithal he sent Thyreus one of his men unto her, a very wise and discreet man, who, bringing letters of credit from a young lord unto a noble lady, and that besides greatly liked her beauty, might easily by his eloquence have persuaded her. He was longer in talk with her than any man else was, and the queen herself also did him great honour: insomuch as he made Antonius jealous of him. Whereupon Antonius caused him to be taken and well-favouredly whipped, and so sent him unto Caesar: and bade him tell him that he made him angry with him. . . . From thenceforth Cleopatra, to clear herself of the suspicion he had of her, she made more of him than ever she did. For first of all, where she did solemnize the day of her birth very meanly and sparingly, she now in contrary manner did keep it with such solemnity, that she exceeded all measure of sumptuousness and magnificence: so that the guests that were bidden to the feasts, and came poor, went away rich. . . .

Then Antonius, seeing there was no way more honourable for him to die than fighting valiantly, he determined to set up his rest, both by sea and land. So, being at supper (as it is reported), he commanded his officers and household servants that waited on him at his board, that they should fill his cups full, and make as much of him as they could: "For," said he, "you know not whether you shall do so much for me to-morrow or not, or whether you shall serve another master: and it may be you shall see me no more, but a dead body." This notwithstanding, perceiving that his friends and men fell a-weeping to hear him say so: to salve that he had spoken, he added this more unto it, that he would not lead them to battle, where he thought not rather safely to return with victory, than valiantly to die with honour. Furthermore, the self same night within little of midnight, when all the city was quiet, full of fear and sorrow, thinking what would be the issue and end of this war: it is said that suddenly they heard a marvelous sweet harmony of sundry sorts of instruments of music, with the cry of a multitude of people, as they had been dancing, and had sung as they use in Bacchus' feasts, with movings and turnings after the manner of the satyrs: and it seemed that this dance went through the city unto the gate that opened to the enemies, and that all the troop that made this noise they heard went out of the city at that gate. Now, such as in reason sought the depth of the interpretation of this wonder, thought that it was the god unto whom Antonius bare singular devotion to counterfeit and resemble him, that did forsake them. . . .

When Antonius saw that his men did forsake him, and yielded unto Caesar, and that his footmen were broken and overthrown: he then fled into the city, crying out that Cleopatra had betrayed him unto them, with whom he had made war for her sake. Then she, being afraid of his fury, fled into the tomb which she had caused to be made, and there locked the doors unto her, and shut all the springs of the locks with great bolts, and in the meantime sent unto Antonius to tell him that she was dead. Antonius, believing it, said unto himself: "What dost thou look for further, Antonius, sith spiteful fortune hath taken from thee the only joy thou hadst, for whom thou yet reservedst thy life?" When he had said these words, he went into a chamber and unarmed himself, and being naked said thus: "O Cleopatra, it grieveth me not that I have lost thy company, for I will not be long from thee: but I am sorry that, having been so great a captain and emperor, I am indeed condemned to be judged of less courage and noble mind than a woman." Now he had a man of his called Eros, whom he loved and trusted much, and whom he had long before caused to swear unto him, that he should kill him when he did command him: and then he willed him to keep his promise. His man drawing his sword lift it up as though he had meant to have stricken his master: but turning his head at one side he thrust his sword into himself, and fell down dead at his master's foot. Then said Antonius, "O noble Eros, I thank thee for this, and it is valiantly done of thee, to shew me what I should do to myself, which thou couldst not do for me." Therewithal he took his sword, and thrust it into his belly, and so fell down upon a little bed. The wound he had killed him not presently, for the blood stinted a little when he was laid: and when he came somewhat to himself again, he prayed them that were about him to dispatch him. But they all fled out of the chamber, and left him crying out and tormenting himself: until as last there came a secretary unto him called Diomedes, who was commanded to bring him into the tomb or monument where Cleopatra was. When he heard that she was alive, he very earnestly prayed his men to carry his body thither, and so he was carried in his men's arms into the entry of the monument. Notwithstanding, Cleopatra would not open the gates, but came to the high windows, and cast out certain chains and ropes, in which Antonius was trussed: and Cleopatra her own self, with two women only, which she had suffered to come with her into these monuments, triced Antonius up. They that were present to behold it said they never saw so pitiful a sight. For they plucked up poor Antonius all bloody as he was, and drawing on with pangs of death, who holding up his hands to Cleopatra raised up himself as well as he could. It was a hard thing for these women to do, to lift him up: but Cleopatra stooping down with her head, putting to all her strength to her uttermost power, did lift him up with much ado, and never let go her hold, with the help of the women beneath that bade her be of good courage, and were as sorry to see her labour so, as she herself. So when she had gotten him in after that sort, and laid him on a bed, she rent her garments upon him, clapping her breast, and scratching her face and stomach. Then she dried up his blood that had berayed his face, and called him her lord, her husband, and emperor, forgetting her own misery and calamity, for the pity and compassion she took of him. Antonius made her cease her lamenting, and called for wine, either because he was athirst, or else for that he thought thereby to hasten his death. When he had drunk, he earnestly prayed her, and persuaded her, that she would seek to save her life, if she could possible, without reproach and dishonour: and that chiefly she should trust Proculeius above any man else about Caesar. And, as for himself, that she should not lament nor sorrow for the miserable change of fortune at the end of his days: but rather that she should think him the more fortunate for the former triumphs and honours he had received, considering that while he lived he was the noblest and greatest prince of the world, and that now he was overcome not cowardly, but valiantly, a Roman by another Roman. As Antonius gave the last gasp, Proculeius came that was sent from Caesar. . . .

Caesar hearing these news straight withdrew himself into a secret place of his tent, and then burst out with tears, lamenting his hard and miserable fortune that had been his friend and brother-in-law, his equal in the empire, and companion with him in sundry great exploits and battles. Then he called for all his friends, and shewed them the letters Antonius had written to him, and his answers also sent him again, during their quarrel and strife: and how fiercely and proudly the other answered him to all just and reasonable matters he wrote unto him. After this, he sent Proculeius, and commanded him to do what he could possible to get Cleopatra alive, fearing lest otherwise all the treasure would be lost: and furthermore, he thought that if he could take Cleopatra, and bring her alive to Rome, she would marvelously beautify and set out his triumph. . . .

[Cleopatra] requested Caesar that it would please him to suffer her to offer the last oblations of the dead unto the soul of Antonius. This being granted her, she was carried to the place where his tomb was, and there falling down on her knees, embracing the tomb with her women, the tears running down her cheeks, she began to speak in this sort. "O my dear lord Antonius, not long sithence I buried thee here, being a freewoman: and now I offer unto thee the funeral sprinklings and oblations, being a captive and prisoner, and yet I am forbidden and kept from tearing and murdering this captive body of mine with blows, which they carefully guard and keep, only to triumph of thee: look therefore henceforth for no other honours, offerings, nor sacrifices from me, for these are the last which Cleopatra can give thee, sith now they carry her away. Whilst we lived together, nothing could sever our companies: but now at our death I fear me they will make us change our countries. For as thou, being a Roman, hast been buried in Egypt: even so wretched creature I, an Egyptian, shall be buried in Italy. If therefore the gods where thou art now have any power and authority, sith our gods here have forsaken us, suffer not thy true friend and lover to be carried away alive, that in me they triumph of thee: but receive me with thee, and let me be buried in one self tomb with thee. For though my griefs and miseries be infinite, yet none hath grieved me more, nor that I could less bear withal, than this small time which I have been given to live alone without thee." Then, having ended these doleful plaints, and crowned the tomb with garlands and sundry nosegays, and marvelous lovingly embraced the same, she commanded they should prepare her bath, and when she had bathed and washed herself she fell to her meat, and was sumptuously served. Now whilst she was at dinner, there came a countryman, and brought her a basket. The soldiers that warded at the gates asked him straight what he had in his basket. He opened the basket, and took out the leaves that covered the figs, and shewed them that they were figs he brought. They all of them marvelled to see so goodly figs. The countryman laughed to hear them, and bade them take some if they would. They believed he told them truly, and so bade him carry them in. After Cleopatra had dined, she sent a certain table written and sealed unto Caesar, and commanded them all to go out of the tombs where she was, but the two women: then she shut the doors to her. Caesar, when he received this table, and began to read her lamentation and petition, requesting him that he would let her be buried with Antonius, found straight what she meant, and thought to have gone thither himself: howbeit he sent one before in all haste that might be, to see what it was. Her death was very sudden. For those whom Caesar sent unto her ran thither in all haste possible, and found the soldiers standing at the gate, mistrusting nothing, nor understanding of her death. But when they had opened the doors, they found Cleopatra stark dead, laid upon a bed of gold, attired and arrayed in her royal robes, and one of her two women, which was called Iras, dead at her feet; and her other woman called Charmion half dead, and trembling, trimming the diadem which Cleopatra ware upon her head. One of the soldiers, seeing her angrily said unto her: "Is that well done, Charmion?" "Very well," said she again, "and meet for a princess descended from the race of so many noble kings." She said no more, but fell down dead hard by the bed. . . . Now Caesar, though he was marvelous sorry for the death of Cleopatra, yet he wondered at her noble mind and courage, and therefore commanded she should be nobly buried, and laid by Antonius.

CORIOLANUS

AGAIN Shakespeare based his tragedy on North's translation of Plutarch's Lives (see above, page 174), bringing into the drama an unusual amount of the original historical material. The essential portions of the source, but by no means all the details used for the play, are reproduced here.

FROM THE LIFE OF CAIUS MARTIUS CORIOLANUS

The house of the Martians at Rome was of the number of the patricians, out of the which had sprung many noble personages: whereof Ancus Martius was one, King Numa's daughter's son, who was King of Rome after Tullus Hostilius. . . . Caius Martius, whose life we now intend to write, being left an orphan by his father, was brought up under his mother, a widow, who taught us by experience that orphanage bringeth many discommodities to a child, but doth not hinder him to become an honest man, and to excel in virtue above the common sort. . . . This man also is a good proof to confirm some men's opinions, that a rare and excellent wit untaught doth bring forth many good and evil things together, like as a fat soil bringeth forth herbs and weeds that lieth unmanured. For this Martius' natural wit and great heart did marvelously stir up his courage to do and attempt notable acts. But on the other side, for lack of education, he was so choleric and impatient, that he would yield to no living creature: which made him churlish, uncivil, and altogether unfit for any man's conversation. Yet men marvelling much at his constancy, that he was never overcome with pleasure, nor money, and how he would endure easily all manner of pains and travails: thereupon they well liked and commended his stoutness and temperancy. But for all that, they could not be acquainted with him, as one citizen useth to be with another in the city; his behaviour was so unpleasant to them by reason of a certain insolent and stern manner he had, which, because it was too lordly, was disliked. . . .

The Romans having many wars and battles in those days, Coriolanus was at them all: and there was not a battle fought, from whence he returned not without some reward of honour. And as for other, the only respect that made them valiant was they hoped to have honour: but touching Martius, the only thing that made him to love honour was the joy he saw his mother did take of him. For he thought nothing made him so happy and honourable, as that his mother might hear everybody praise and commend him, that she might always see him return with a crown upon his head, and that she might still embrace him with tears running down her cheeks for joy. . . .

In the country of the Volsces, against whom the Romans made war at that time, there was a principal city and of most fame, that was called Corioli, before the which the consul Cominius did lay siege. Wherefore all the other Volsces fearing lest that city should be taken by assault, they came from all parts of the country to save it, intending to give the Romans battle before the city, and to give an onset on them in two several places. The consul Cominius, understanding this, divided his army also in two parts, and taking the one part with himself, he marched towards them that were drawing to the city out of the country: and the other part of his army he left in the camp with Titus Lartius (one of the valiantest men the Romans had at that time) to resist those that would make any sally out of the city upon them. So the Coriolans, making small accompt of them that lay in camp before the city, made a sally out upon them, in the which at the first the Coriolans had the better, and drave the Romans back again into the trenches of their camp. But Martius being there at that time, running out of the camp with a few men with him, he slew the first enemies he met withal, and made the rest of them stay upon a sudden, crying out to the Romans that had turned their backs, and calling them again to fight with a loud voice. For he was even such another as Cato would have a soldier and a captain to be, not only terrible and fierce to lay about him, but to make the enemy afeard with the sound of his voice and grimness of his countenance. Then there flocked about him immediately a great number of Romans: whereat the enemies were so afeared, that they gave back presently. But Martius, not staying so, did chase and follow them to their own gates, that fled for life. . . . The city being taken in this sort, the most part of the soldiers began incontinently to spoil, to carry away, and to lock up the booty they had won. But Martius was marvelous angry with them, and cried out on them, that it was no time now to look after spoil, and to run straggling here and there to enrich themselves, whilst the other consul and their fellow citizens peradventure were fighting with their enemies. . . .

The consul Cominius, going up to his chair of state, in the presence of the whole army, gave thanks to the gods for so great, glorious, and prosperous a victory: then he spake to Martius, whose valiantness he commended beyond the moon, both for that he himself saw him do with his eyes, as also for that Martius had reported unto him. So in the end he willed Martius that he should choose out of all the horses they had taken of their enemies, and of all the goods they had won (whereof there was great store) ten of every sort which he liked best, before any distribution should be made to other. Besides this great honourable offer he had made him, he gave him, in testimony that he had won that day the price of prowess above all other, a goodly horse with a caparison, and all furniture to him: which the whole army beholding did marvelously praise and commend. But Martius, stepping forth, told the consul he most thankfully accepted the gift of his horse, and was a glad man besides, that his service had deserved his general's commendation: and as for his other offer, which was rather a mercenary reward, he would none of it, but was contented to have his equal part with other soldiers. "Only this grace" (said he) "I crave and beseech you to grant me. Among the Volsces there is an old friend and host of mine, an honest wealthy man, and now a prisoner, who, living before in great wealth in his own country, liveth now a poor prisoner in the hands of his enemies: and yet, notwithstanding all this his misery and misfortune, it would do me great pleasure if I could save him from this one danger: to keep him from being sold as a slave." The soldiers, hearing Martius' words, made a marvelous great shout among them: and they were moe that wondered at his great contentation and abstinence, when they saw so little coveteousness in him, than they were that highly praised and extolled his valiantness. . . . After this shout and noise of the assembly was somewhat appeased, the consul Cominius began to speak in this sort: "We cannot compel Martius to take these gifts we offer him, if he will not receive them: but we will give him such a reward for the noble service he hath done, as he cannot refuse. Therefore we do order and decree, that henceforth he be called Coriolanus, unless his valiant acts have won him that name before our nomination." And so ever since he still bare the third name of Coriolanus. . . .

Shortly after this, Martius stood for the consulship: and the common people favoured his suit, thinking it would be a shame to them to deny and refuse the chiefest nobleman of blood, and most worthy person of Rome, and specially him that had done so great service and good to the commonwealth. For the custom at Rome was at that time, that such as did sue for any office should for certain days before be in the market-place, only with a poor gown on their backs and without any coat underneath, to pray the citizens to remember them at the day of election: which was thus devised, either to move the people the more by requesting them in such mean apparel, or else because they might shew them their wounds they had gotten in the wars in the service of the commonwealth, as manifest marks and testimony of their valiantness. . . . Now Martius, following this custom, shewed many wounds and cuts upon his body, which he had received in seventeen years' service at the wars, and in many sundry battles, being ever the foremost man that did set out feet to fight. So that there was not a man among the people, but was ashamed of himself, to refuse so valiant a man: and one of them said to another, "We must needs choose him consul, there is no remedy." But when the day of election was come, and that Martius came to the market-place with great pomp, accompanied with all the senate, and the whole nobility of the city about him, who sought to make him consul, with the greatest instance and entreaty they could, or ever attempted for any man or matter: then the love and good will of the common people turned straight to an hate and envy toward him, fearing to put this office of sovereign authority into his hands, being a man somewhat partial toward the nobility, and of great credit and authority amongst the patricians, and as one they might doubt would take away altogether the liberty from the people. Whereupon, for these considerations, they refused Martius in the end, and made two other that were suitors, consuls. The senate, being marvelously offended with the people, did accompt the shame of this refusal rather to redound to themselves, than to Martius: but Martius took it in far worse part than the senate, and was out of all patience. For he was a man too full of passion and choler, and too much given to over self-will and opinion, as one of a high mind and great courage, that lacked the gravity and affability that is gotten with judgment of learning and reason, which only is to be looked for in a governor of state: and that remembered not how wilfulness is the thing of the world, which a governor of a commonwealth for pleasing should shun, being that which Plato called solitariness. As in the end, all men that are wilfully given to a self-opinion and obstinate mind, and who will never yield to others' reason but to their own, remain without company, and forsaken of all men. For a man that will live in the world must needs have patience, which lusty bloods make but a mock at. So Martius . . . went to his house full freighted with spite and malice against the people, being accompanied with all the lustiest young gentlemen, whose minds were nobly bent as those that came of noble race, and commonly used for to follow and honour him. But then specially they flocked about him and kept him company, to his much harm: for they did but kindle and inflame his choler more and more. . . .

In the mean season there came great plenty of corn to Rome; . . . [and] the common people [persuaded themselves] that the corn they had bought should be sold good cheap, and that which was given should be divided by the poll without paying any penny, and the rather, because certain of the senators amongst them did so wish and persuade the same. But Martius, standing up on his feet, did somewhat sharply take up those who went about to gratify the people therein: and called them people-pleasers, and traitors to the nobility. Moreover, he said, they nourished against themselves the naughty seed and cockle of insolency and sedition, which had been sowed and scattered abroad amongst the people, whom they should have cut off, if they had been wise, and have prevented their greatness. . . . "For they will not think it is done in recompense of their service past, sithence they know well enough they have so oft refused to go to the wars, when they were commanded: neither for their mutinies when they went with us, whereby they have rebelled and forsaken their country: neither for their accusations which their flatterers have preferred unto them, and they have received, and made good against the Senate: but they will rather judge, we give and grant them this, as abasing ourselves, and standing in fear of them, and glad to flatter them every way. By this means their disobedience will still grow worse and worse: and they will never leave to practise new sedition and uproars.". . .

Hereupon the people ran on head in tumult together, before whom the words that Martius spake in the Senate were openly reported: which the people so stomached, that even in that fury they were ready to fly upon the whole Senate. But the tribunes laid all the fault and burden wholly upon Martius, and sent their sergeants forthwith to arrest him, presently to appear in person before the people, to answer the words he had spoken in the Senate. Martius stoutly withstood these officers that came to arrest him. Then the tribunes in their own persons, accompanied with the aediles, went to fetch him by force, and so laid violent hands upon him. . . .

To conclude, when they came to tell the voices of the tribes, there were three voices odd, which condemned him to be banished for life. After declaration of the sentence, the people made such joy, as they never rejoiced more for any battle they had won upon their enemies, they were so brave and lively, and went home so jocundly from the assembly, for triumph of this sentence. The Senate again in contrary manner were as sad and heavy. . . . Saving Martius alone, who neither in his countenance, nor in his gait, did ever show himself abashed, or once let fall his great courage: but he only of all other gentlemen that were angry at his fortune did outwardly show no manner of passion, nor care at all of himself. Not that he did patiently bear and temper his good hap, in respect of any reason he had, or by his quiet condition: but because he was so carried away with the vehemency of anger, and desire of revenge, that he had no sense or feeling of the hard state he was in. . . . When he was come home to his house again, and had taken his leave of his mother and wife, finding them weeping and shrieking out for sorrow, and had also comforted and persuaded them to be content with his chance; he went immediately to the gate of the city, accompanied with a great number of patricians that brought him thither, from whence he went on his way with three or four of his friends only, taking nothing with him, nor requesting anything of any man. . . . In the end, seeing he could resolve no way to take a profitable or honourable course, but only was pricked forward still to be revenged of the Romans: he thought to raise up some great wars against them, by their nearest neighbours. Whereupon he thought it his best way first to stir up the Volsces against them. . . .

[Volumnia] took her daughter-in-law and Martius' children with her, and being accompanied with all the other Roman ladies, they went in troop together unto the Volsces' camp: whom when they saw, they of themselves did both pity and reverence her, and there was not a man among them that once durst say a word unto her. Now was Martius set then in his chair of state, with all the honours of a general, and, when he had spied the women coming afar off, he marveled what the matter meant: but afterwards, knowing his wife which came foremost, he determined at the first to persist in his obstinate and inflexible rancour. But overcome in the end with natural affection, and being altogether altered to see them, his heart would not serve him to tarry their coming to his chair, but coming down in haste, he went to meet them, and first he kissed his mother, and embraced her a pretty while, then his wife and little children. And nature so wrought with him, that the tears fell from his eyes, and he could not keep himself from making much of them, but yielded to the affection of his blood, as if he had been violently carried with the fury of a most swift-running stream. After he had thus lovingly received them, and perceiving that his mother Volumnia would begin to speak to him, he called the chiefest of the council of the Volsces to hear what she would say. Then she spake in this sort: "If we held our peace (my son) and determined not to speak, the state of our poor bodies and present sight of our raiment would easily bewray to thee what life we have led at home, since thy exile and abode abroad. But think now with thyself, how much more unfortunately than all the women living we are come hither, considering that the sight which should be most pleasant to all other to behold, spiteful fortune hath made most fearful to us: making myself to see my son, and my daughter here, her husband besieging the walls of his native country. So as that which is th' only comfort to all other in their adversity and misery, to pray unto the gods, and to call to them for aid, is the only thing which plungeth us into most deep perplexity. For we cannot (alas) together pray, both for victory for our country, and for safety of thy life also: but a world of grievous curses, yea more than any mortal enemy can heap upon us, are forcibly wrapped up in our prayers. For the bitter sop of most hard choice is offered thy wife and children, to forgo the one of the two: either to lose the person of thy self, or the nurse of their native country. For my self (my son) I am determined not to tarry till fortune in my lifetime to make an end of this war. For if I cannot persuade thee, rather to do good unto both parties, than to overthrow and destroy the one, preferring love and nature before the malice and calamity of wars: thou shalt see, my son, and trust unto it, thou shalt no sooner march forward to assault thy country, but thy foot shall tread upon thy mother's womb, that brought thee first into the world. . . . Dost thou think it good altogether to give place unto thy choler and desire of revenge, and thinkest thou it not honesty for thee to grant thy mother's request, in so weighty a cause? Dost thou take it honourable for a noble man to remember the wrongs and injuries done him, and dost not in like case think it an honest noble man's part to be thankful for the goodness that parents do shew their children, acknowledging the duty and reverence they ought to bear unto them? No man living is more bound to shew himself thankful in all parts and respects, than thyself: who so unnaturally sheweth all ingratitude. Moreover (my son) thou hast sorely taken of thy country, exacting grievous payments upon them, in revenge of the injuries offered thee: besides, thou hast not hitherto shewed thy poor mother any courtesy. And therefore, it is not only honest, but due unto me, that without compulsion

I should obtain my so just and reasonable request of thee. But since by reason I cannot persuade thee to it, to what purpose do I defer my last hope? " And with these words, her self, his wife, and children fell down upon their knees before him. Martius, seeing that, could refrain no longer, but went straight and lift her up, crying out: " O mother, what have you done to me? " And holding her hard by the right hand, " O mother," said he, " you have won a happy victory for your country, but mortal and unhappy for your son: for I see myself vanquished by you alone."

These words being spoken openly, he spake a little apart with his mother and wife, and then let them return again to Rome, for so they did request him: and so, remaining in camp that night, the next morning he dislodged, and marched homeward into the Volsces' country again. . . .

Now when Martius was returned again into the city of Antium from his voyage, Tullus, that hated and could no longer abide him for fear he had of his authority, sought divers means to make him out of the way, thinking that if he let slip that present time, he should never recover the like and fit occasion again. Wherefore Tullus, having procured many other of his confederacy, required Martius might be deposed from his estate, to render up accompt to the Volsces of his charge and government. . . . The people hereupon called a common council, in which assembly there were certain orators appointed, that stirred up the common people against him: and when they had told their tales, Martius rose up to make them answer. Now, notwithstanding the mutinous people made a marvelous great noise, yet when they saw him, for the reverence they bare unto his valiantness, they quieted themselves, and gave still audience to allege with leisure what he could for his purgation. Moreover, the honestest men of the Antiates, and who most rejoiced in peace, shewed by their countenance that they would hear him willingly, and judge also according to their conscience. . . . Wherefore those that were of the conspiracy began to cry out that he was not to be heard, nor that they would not suffer a traitor to usurp tyrannical power over the tribe of the Volsces, who would not yield up his estate and authority. And in saying these words, they fell upon him, and killed him in the market-place, none of the people once offering to rescue him. Howbeit it is a clear case, that this murder was not generally consented unto of the most part of the Volsces: for men came out of all parts to honour his body, and did honourably bury him, setting out his tomb with great store of armour and spoils, as the tomb of a worthy person and great captain.

THE WINTER'S TALE

FOR this play, as he had done in the case of *As You Like It,* Shakespeare remade a popular Elizabethan novel, Robert Greene's *Pandosto,* first published in 1588 and thereafter in many other editions. The following is an outline of Greene's story, with certain *verbatim* extracts from passages of special significance for the play.

THE HISTORY OF DORASTUS AND FAWNIA

Pandosto, king of Bohemia, was linked in perfect love with his queen Bellaria, by whom he had a young son named Garinter. His boyhood friend Egistus, now king of

Sicilia, came to pay a royal visit, and was received with every honor and courtesy by Pandosto and his queen.

"Bellaria, who in her time was the flower of courtesy, willing to shew how unfeignedly she loved her husband by his friend's entertainment, used him likewise so familiarly that her countenance bewrayed how her mind was affected towards him, oftentimes coming herself into his bed-chamber to see that nothing should be amiss to mislike him. This honest familiarity increased daily more and more betwixt them; for Bellaria, noting in Egistus a princely and bountiful mind, adorned with sundry and excellent qualities, and Egistus, finding in her a virtuous and courteous disposition, there grew such a secret uniting of their affections, that the one could not well be without the company of the other: in so much, that when Pandosto was busied with such urgent affairs that he could not be present with his friend Egistus, Bellaria would walk with him into the garden, where they two in private and pleasant devices would pass away the time to both their contents. This custom still continuing betwixt them, a certain melancholy passion entering the mind of Pandosto drave him into sundry and doubtful thoughts. First, he called to mind the beauty of his wife Bellaria, the comeliness and bravery of his friend Egistus, thinking that love was above all laws and, therefore, to be stayed with no law; that it was hard to put fire and flax together without burning; that their open pleasures might breed his secret displeasures. He considered with himself that Egistus was a man and must needs love, that his wife was a woman, and therefore, subject unto love, and that where fancy forced friendship was of no force.

"These and such like doubtful thoughts, a long time smothering in his stomach, began at last to kindle in his mind a secret mistrust, which, increased by suspicion, grew at last to a flaming jealousy that so tormented him as he could take no rest. He then began to measure all their actions, and to misconstrue of their too private familiarity, judging that it was not honest affection, but for disordinate fancy, so that he began to watch them more narrowly to see if he could get any true or certain proof to confirm his doubtful suspicion. While thus he noted their looks and gestures and suspected their thoughts and meanings, they two silly souls, who doubted nothing of this his treacherous intent, frequented daily each other's company, which drave him into such a frantic passion, that he began to bear a secret hate to Egistus and a lowering countenance to Bellaria; who marveling at such unaccustomed frowns, began to cast beyond the moon, and to enter into a thousand sundry thoughts, which way she should offend her husband: but finding in herself a clear conscience ceased to muse, until such time as she might find fit opportunity to demand the cause of his dumps."

Pandosto now determined to make an end of Egistus, and bribed his cupbearer to poison his guest. Franion the cupbearer, after having vainly tried to dissuade his master, at length confessed the plan to Egistus, who speedily fled homeward to Sicilia, Franion accompanying him. This Pandosto conceived to be a final proof of his friend's guilt, and made a general proclamation that Egistus had committed adultery; his queen he imprisoned, refusing her even a hearing. When, some time afterward, Bellaria gave birth to a child, the king commanded that it be exposed in an open boat, and set adrift on the sea; and this was done. At length Pandosto, purposing to punish his wife still further, brought her to an open trial.

"Bellaria, who standing like a prisoner at the bar, feeling in herself a clear conscience to withstand her false accusers, seeing that no less than death could pacify her husband's wrath, waxed bold and desired that she might have law and justice, for mercy she neither craved nor hoped for; and that those perjured wretches which had falsely accused her to the king might be brought before her face to give in evidence. But Pandosto, whose rage and jealousy were such as no reason nor equity could appease, told her that, for her accusers, they were of such credit as their words were sufficient witness, and that the sudden and secret flight of Egistus and Franion confirmed that which they had confessed; and as for her, it was her part to deny such a monstrous crime, and to be impudent in forswearing the fact, since she had past all shame in committing the fault: but her stale countenance should stand for no coin, for as the bastard which she bare was served, so she should with some cruel death be requited. Bellaria, no whit dismayed with this rough reply, told her husband Pandosto that he spake upon choler and not conscience, for her virtuous life had been ever such as no spot of suspicion could ever stain. And if she had borne a friendly countenance to Egistus, it was in respect he was his friend, and not for any lusting affection; therefore, if she were condemned without any further proof it was rigour and not law.

"The noblemen, which sate in judgment, said that Bellaria spake reason, and intreated the king that the accusers might be openly examined and sworn, and if then the evidence were such as the jury might find her guilty (for seeing she was a prince she ought to be tried by her peers), then let her have such punishment as the extremity of the law will assign to such malefactors. The king presently made answer that in this case he might and would dispense with the law and that the jury being once panelled they should take his word for sufficient evidence; otherwise he would make the proudest of them repent it. The noblemen seeing the king in choler were all whist; but Bellaria, whose life then hung in the balance, fearing more perpetual infamy than momentary death, told the king if his fury might stand for a law that it were vain to have the jury yield their verdict; and, therefore, she fell down upon her knees, and desired the king that for the love he bare to his young son Garinter, whom she brought into the world, that he would grant her a request; which was this, that it would please his majesty to send six of his noblemen whom he best trusted to the Isle of Delphos, there to inquire of the oracle of Apollo whether she had committed adultery with Egistus."

This request the king could not for shame deny, and he despatched six noblemen to Delphos. There Apollo bade them take away an oracle upon a scroll of parchment, whereon were written these words:

"Suspicion is no proof: jealousy is an unequal judge: Bellaria is chaste: Egistus blameless: Franion a true subject: Pandosto treacherous: his babe an innocent: and the king shall live without an heir, if that which is lost be not found."

The court being again summoned, the king caused the indictment to be read once more.

"Bellaria hearing the contents was no whit astonished, but made this cheerful answer:

"'If the divine powers be privy to human actions — as no doubt they are — I hope my patience shall make fortune blush, and my unspotted life shall stain spiteful discredit. For although lying report hath sought to appeach mine honour, and suspicion hath intended to soil my credit with infamy, yet where virtue keepeth the fort, report and suspicion may assail, but never sack: how I have led my life before Egistus' coming, I appeal, Pandosto, to the gods and to thy conscience. What hath passed betwixt him and me, the gods only know, and I hope will presently reveal: that I loved Egistus I cannot deny; that I honoured him I shame not to confess: to the one I was forced by his virtues, to the other for his dignities. But as touching lascivious lust, I say Egistus is honest, and hope myself to be found without spot: for Franion, I can neither accuse him nor excuse him, for I was not privy to his departure: and that this is true which I have here rehearsed I refer myself to the divine oracle.'

"Bellaria had no sooner said but the king commanded that one of his dukes should read the contents of the scroll, which after the commons had heard they gave a great shout, rejoicing and clapping their hands that the queen was clear of that false accusation. But the king, whose conscience was a witness against him of his witless fury and false suspected jealousy, was so ashamed of his rash folly that he entreated his nobles to persuade Bellaria to forgive and forget these injuries; promising not only to shew himself a loyal and loving husband, but also to reconcile himself to Egistus and Franion; revealing then before them all the cause of their secret flight, and how treacherously he thought to have practised his death, if the good mind of his cupbearer had not prevented his purpose. As thus he was relating the whole matter, there was word brought to him that his young son Garinter was suddenly dead, which news so soon as Bellaria heard, surcharged before with extreme joy and now suppressed with heavy sorrow, her vital spirits were so stopped that she fell down presently dead, and could be never revived."

Thereafter Pandosto sought to slay himself, but was prevented by his lords; and he erected a great supulchre in honor of his queen and his dead son, repairing to it once a day to bewail his misfortune.

Meantime the infant that had been set adrift at sea came to land on the coast of Sicilia, driven with the tide; and a poor shepherd named Porrus, hearing the child cry, found her lying at the water's edge, wrapped in a rich mantle and having a chain about the neck; furthermore there was with her a purse full of gold. He thereupon took her home to his wife, who laid away the gold and jewels, and cared for the babe. So she grew to ripe years as the shepherd's daughter, and at the age of sixteen was of such exquisite perfection, both of body and mind, that one might have guessed her high parentage. It chanced that the king Egistus had one son, named Dorastus, now aged twenty, who one evening came upon Fawnia as he returned from hawking; and he stood in a maze because of her perfection. Talking with her, he presently became wholly a slave to love; and, despite all his efforts to reproach himself because of her lowly birth, he soon came again to woo her. When he tested her, whether she would come to the court to serve,

" 'Sir,' quoth she, 'beggars ought not to strive against fortune, nor to gaze after honour, lest either their fall be greater, or they become blind. I am born to toil for the court, not in the court, my nature unfit for their nurture: better live, then, in mean degree than in high disdain.'

" 'Well said, Fawnia,' quoth Dorastus: 'I guess at thy thoughts; thou art in love with some country shepherd.'

" 'No, sir,' quoth she: 'shepherds cannot love that are so simple, and maids may not love that are so young.'

" 'Nay, therefore,' quoth Dorastus, 'maids must love because they are young; for Cupid is a child, and Venus, though old, is painted with fresh colours.'

" 'I grant,' quoth she, 'age may be painted with new shadows, and youth may have imperfect affections; but what art concealeth in one ignorance revealeth in the other.' Dorastus, seeing Fawnia held him so hard, thought it was vain so long to beat about the bush; therefore he thought to have given her a fresh charge, but he was so prevented by certain of his men, who, missing their master, came puffing to seek him, seeing that he was gone forth all alone: yet, before they drew so nigh that they might hear their talk, he used these speeches:

" 'Why, Fawnia, perhaps I love thee, and then thou must needs yield, for thou knowest I can command and constrain.' 'Truth, sir,' quoth she, 'but not to love; for constrained love is force, not love: and know this, sir, mine honesty is such, as I had rather die than be a concubine, even to a king, and my birth is so base as I am unfit to be a wife to a poor farmer.' 'Why then,' quoth he, 'thou canst not love Dorastus.' 'Yes,' said Fawnia, 'when Dorastus becomes a shepherd.'"

On his next visit Dorastus wore shepherd's clothing, and promised to make Fawnia his wife; so she readily yielded her love. Thereupon they planned to flee to Italy; and after a time, having got gold and jewels together, Dorastus persuaded an old servant named Capnio to get a ship ready for their passage. Meantime Fawnia's foster-parents, perceiving that the prince was making love to her, decided to show him the garments and jewels which had been found with her in the boat, to prove that she was not their own child. As Porrus set out on this errand, Dorastus' servant Capnio became aware of his intent, and, that the lovers might not be hindered in their plans, enticed the old shepherd to the ship where the young people already were; and against his will they took him with them on the voyage.

Now there came up a great storm, which at length drove the ship to the coast of Bohemia. And when the voyagers came ashore, and knew that they were in the country of Pandosto, Egistus' enemy, Dorastus changed his name to Meleagrus, and professed to be a gentlemen of Trapolonia. Then it happened that the beauty of Fawnia was so noised abroad that the king sent for them to the court; and, when he had seen her, he made excuse to imprison Dorastus, that he might woo her for himself; for, though he was now aged fifty, he still had young affections. But Fawnia resisted his advances courageously. Meantime word came to Egistus that his son had been seen at the court of Bohemia, and he sent an embassy to

Pandosto, telling him that Meleagrus was in fact his son, and requesting that the king would return the boy to him and put Fawnia, Porrus, and Capnio to death. This Pandosto determined to do; but Porrus, thinking it well to show that he was not the father of Fawnia, revealed her true story, and showed the chain and the jewels which were with her in the boat wherein she had drifted to Sicilia. Then the king knew that Fawnia was his lost daughter, and there was great rejoicing that the princess had been found. Dorastus presently returned home with Fawnia, whom Egistus now gladly welcomed as his son's wife. But Pandosto, recalling how his jealousy had been the cause of his queen's death, and how he had unlawfully desired his own daughter, fell into a melancholy fit and slew himself.

BIBLIOGRAPHY

THE following list is not complete in any respect, but is intended merely to suggest to students the best editions and critical works of which they are likely to make use, with the addition of some of the more important critical articles of recent times, such as are likely to be useful for the study of particular plays.

EDITIONS

In one volume.

The Globe Edition. Edited by W. G. Clark and W. Aldis Wright. 1864.

The 'Oxford' Edition. Edited by W. J. Craig. 1904.

The Cambridge Poets Edition. Edited by W. A. Neilson. 1906. Introductions to each play and a Glossary; no notes.

Annotated editions.

The New Variorum Shakespeare. Edited by Horace Howard Furness and later by Horace Howard Furness, Jr. 1871.

Still incomplete. Full textual and critical notes summarizing the work of all earlier editions.

The Arden Shakespeare. General editor W. J. Craig. 1899.

Each play in a separate volume. Introductions and full notes, both textual and interpretative.

The Tudor Shakespeare. Edited by W. A. Neilson and A. H. Thorndike. 1913.

Each play in a separate volume, with separate editor.

Introductions, notes, and glossaries.

The Rolfe Shakespeare. Edited by W. J. Rolfe. 40 volumes. Second edition, 1903–06. Introductions and notes; the text expurgated.

The New Cambridge Shakespeare. Edited by Sir Arthur Quiller-Couch and J. Dover Wilson. 1921. In progress. Introductions, notes, both textual and interpretative, and glossaries.

BOOKS ON SHAKESPEARE'S LIFE AND WORK

Adams, Joseph Quincy. *A Life of William Shakespeare.* 1923.

Alden, Raymond Macdonald. *Shakespeare.* 1922. ("Master Spirits of Literature" series.)

Alexander, Peter. *Shakespeare's Henry VI and Richard III,* 1929.

Baker, George P. *The Development of Shakespeare as a Dramatist.* 1907.

Boas, F. S. *Shakespeare and his Predecessors.* 1896.

Brandes, George. *William Shakespeare.* Translated from the Copenhagen edition by William Archer and others. 2 vols. 1898. New edition, 1924.

Chambers, Sir Edmund K. *William Shakespeare.* A Study of facts and problems. 2 vols. 1930.

Croce, Benedetto. *Ariosto, Shakespeare and Corneille.* 1920.

Dowden, Edward. *Shakspere:* a Critical Study of his Mind and Art. 1875.

Halliwell-Phillipps, J. O. *Outlines of the Life of Shakespeare.* 11th edition. 1907.

Harris, Frank. *The Man Shakespeare and his Tragic Story.* 1909.

Lee, Sir Sidney. *A Life of William Shakespeare.* 1898. New edition. 1925.

Masefield, John. *William Shakespeare.* 1911. (Home University Library.)

Matthews, Brander. *Shakespeare as a Playwright,* 1913.

Raleigh, Sir Walter. *Shakespeare.* 1907. ("Men of Letters" series.)

Rolfe, W. J. *Life of Shakespeare.* 1904.

Stopes, C. C. *Shakespeare's Warwickshire Contemporaries.* 1907.

Wendell, Barrett. *Shakspere.* 1894.

SPECIAL PROBLEMS, LARGELY BIOGRAPHICAL

Abbott, E. A. *A Shakespearean Grammar.* Third Edition. London, 1870.

Anders, H. R. D. *Shakespeare's Books.* 1904.

Barton, Sir D. P. *Links between Shakespeare and the Law.* 1929.

Boas, F. S. *Shakespeare and the Universities.* 1923.

Boswell-Stone, W. G. *Shakspere's Holinshed.* 1896. (Reprints all those passages from Holinshed's *Chronicle* which appear to have been used by Shakespeare in the historical plays.)

Brooke, C. F. Tucker. *Shakespeare's Plutarch.* 1909. (Reprints the Lives by Plutarch which Shakespeare used for his Roman plays.)

Gordon, G. S. *Shakespeare's English.* 1928.

Gray, J. W. *Shakespeare's Marriage and Departure from Stratford.* 1905.

Hotson, J. Leslie. *Shakespeare versus Shallow.* 1931.

Onions, C. T., editor. *Shakespeare Glossary.* 1911. New edition, 1922.

Pollard, A. W. *Shakespeare Folios and Quartos:* A study in the Bibliography of Shakespeare's Plays, 1594–1685. 1909.

Root, R. K. *Classical Mythology in Shakespeare.* 1913.

Simpson, Percy. *Shakespearean Punctuation.* 1911.

BOOKS ON THE ELIZABETHAN AGE AND THEATRE

Adams, J. Q. *Shakespearean Playhouses.* 1917.

Albright, E. M. *Dramatic Publication in England, 1580–1640.* 1927.

Baldwin, T. W. *The Organization and Personnel of the Shakespearean Company.* 1927.

Bartlett, Henrietta C. *Mr. William Shakespeare.* Original and Early editions of his Quartos and Folios, his Source Books and those containing Contemporary Notices. 1922.

Brooke, C. F. Tucker. *The Tudor Drama.* 1911.

Campbell, Lily Bess. *Scenes and Machines in the English Stage During the Renaissance.* 1923.

Chambers, Sir Edmund K. *The Elizabethan Stage*. 4 vols. 1923.

Craig, Hardin. *Shakespeare: A Historical and Critical Study with Annotated Texts of Twenty-one Plays*. 1931.

Creizenach, W. M. A. *The English Drama in the Age of Shakespeare*. 1916. (Translated from Vol. IV of *Geschichte des Neueren Dramas*.)

Fleay, C. H. *A Chronicle History of the London Stage, 1559–1642*. 1890.

Greg, W. W. Ed. *Henslow's Diary*. 2 vols. 1904–1908.

Two Elizabethan Stage Arrangements: The Battle of Alcazar and Orlando Furioso. An Essay in Critical Bibliography. 1923.

Principles of Emendation in Shakespeare, 1928.

Harrison, G. B. *England in Shakespeare's Day*. 1928. ("English in English Literature" series.)

Hillebrand, Harold N. *The Child Actors*, 1926.

Matter, T. H. Vail. *The School Drama in England*, 1929.

Munro, J. *The Shakespeare Allusion-Book, 1591–1700*. Revised with introduction. 2 vols. 1909.

Murray, J. Tucker. *English Dramatic Companies*. 1558–1642. 2 vols. 1909.

Neilson, W. A. and Thorndike, A. H. *The Facts about Shakespeare*. 1913. New edition. 1931.

Onions, C. T., editor. *Shakespeare's England. An Account of the Life and Manners of his Age*. (By various Authors.) 2 vols. 1916, 1926.

Pollard, A. W. *Shakespeare's Fight with the Pirates and the Problems of the Transmission of his Text*. 1917, 1920.

Schelling, F. E. *Elizabethan Drama, 1558–1642*. 2 vols. 1908.

Stephenson, H. T. *Shakespeare's London*. 1905.

Symons, John Addington. *Shakspere's Predecessors in the English Drama*. New Edition, 1900.

Thorndike, A. H. *Shakespeare's Theatre*. 1916.

Ward, A. W. *History of English Dramatic Literature to the Death of Queen Anne*. 2 vols. 1875; 2nd edition, 3 vols. 1899.

Wilson, F. P. *The Plague in Shakespeare's London*. 1927.

SHAKESPEARE CRITICISM

Bradley, A. C. *Shakespearean Tragedy.* 2nd edition. 1905.

Bradley, A. C. " The Rejection of Falstaff " and " Antony and Cleopatra " in *Oxford Lectures on Poetry,* 1909.

Boyer, C. V. *The Villain as Hero in Elizabethan Tragedy.* 1914.

Brooke, C. F. Tucker. Editor. *The Shakespeare Apocrypha.* 1908.

Brooke, S. A. *On Ten Plays of Shakespeare.* 1905.

Ten More Plays of Shakespeare. 1903.

Campbell, Lily Bess. *Shakespeare's Tragic Heroes, Slaves of Passion.* Cambridge, 1930.

Coleridge, S. T. *Shakespearean Criticism.* Edited by T. M. Raysor. 2 vols. 1930.

Goll, August. *Criminal Types in Shakespeare.* Translated from the Danish by Mrs. Charles Weeks. 1909.

Hazlitt, W. *Characters of Shakespeare's Plays.* 1817. Reprinted in Everyman Library, New Universal Library and Bohn's Library.

Herford, C. H. *A Sketch of Recent Shakespearean Investigation.* 1923.

Lawrence, W. W. *Shakespeare's Problem Comedies.* 1931. (Essays on *All's Well, Troilus and Cressida, Measure for Measure* and *Cymbeline.*)

Lewis, Charlton. *The Genesis of Hamlet.* 1907.

Lounsbury, T. R. *Shakespeare as a Dramatic Artist.* 1902.

MacCallum, M. W. *Shakespeare's Roman Plays and their Background.* 1910.

Moulton, Richard G. *Shakespeare as a Dramatic Artist.* 1906.

Schücking, L. L. *Character Problems in Shakespeare's Plays.* 1922.

Smith, Nichol. *Shakespeare in the Eighteenth Century.* 1928.

Stoll, E. E. *Shakespeare Studies.* 1927.

Taylor, G. C. *Shakespeare's Debt to Montaigne.* 1925.

Thorndike, A. H. *The Influence of Beaumont and Fletcher on Shakespeare.* 1901.

SIGNIFICANT MODERN CONTRIBUTIONS TO SHAKESPEARE CRITICISM

CRITICISM of Shakespeare's work during the last hundred years has borne a close relationship to the habits of thought of the age in which it was written. The attitude of the romantic critics of the early 19th century, of whom Coleridge was the most famous, was near idolatry. They regarded Shakespeare's plays as expressions of an inexplicable genius, who showed ultimate insight into human character and ultimate philosophical grasp of the forces which control human destiny. They also viewed his work as unrelated to its historical background and to the intellectual currents of his age. It was regarded as the expression of an absolute and transcendent mind.

With the growth of the scientific spirit during the nineteenth century, the character of Shakespeare criticism changed radically. The methods of historical study were applied to his work. His debt to his predecessors was discovered and his place in the development of Elizabethan drama appraised. The course of Shakespeare's own artistic growth came to be explained as due largely to contemporary fashions in the drama.

This kind of scientific criticism has yielded other significant results. It has, in the first place, led to a study of Shakespeare as a playwright adapting his art to the conditions of the Elizabethan playhouse, to the histrionic abilities of the actors composing his company, and to the character of his audiences. Such works as G. P. Baker's *The Development of Shakespeare as a Dramatist* (1907), Brander Matthews's *Shakespeare as a Playwright* (1913), and T. W. Baldwin's recent *The Organization and Personnel of the Shakespearean Company* (1927) take this point of view toward Shakespeare. Another group of critics, often called the sceptics, of whom E. E. Stoll and L. L. Schücking are the most important, relate his work so firmly to the naïve conventions of Elizabethan dramaturgy that they explain his characters almost exclusively in these terms. They ignore the timeless elements in these great imaginative creations. In their opinion Iago, for example, is a calumniator whose dramatic function is to deceive Othello and to destroy him. Therefore, attempts to discover motives for the acts of this stage villain in the subtleties of a profoundly conceived personality are merely anachronisms in criticism. Clearly related to this school is the one which seeks to explain the nature of Shakespeare's characters in terms of Elizabethan psychology and ethics. The most recent and comprehensive of the books of this sort is Miss Lily Bess Campbell's *Shakespeare's Tragic Heroes* (1930).

Two other scientific approaches to Shakespeare's work are now popular. The first is that adopted by the editors of the New Cambridge Shakespeare and by Peter Alexander in his brilliant study, *Shakespeare's Henry VI and Richard III* (1929). Through a critical scrutiny of Shakespeare's text, in the light of modern knowledge of conditions of Elizabethan printing and of the career of manuscripts in the playhouses, they have been able to throw light upon the construction of many of the dramas and to make probable Shakespeare's unaided composition of such early plays as the second and third parts of *Henry VI*.

The second of these contemporary approaches to Shakespeare is a genetic one. Critics of this school compare Shakespeare's works to their sources and to the literary and social traditions which they embody. They thus explain many apparent inconsistencies in the plays and many actions almost incomprehensible to us by reducing them to terms of the artistic preconceptions and ethical prejudices of the audiences who knew the stories dramatized. Charlton M. Lewis in his *The Genesis of Hamlet* (1907), wrote one of the first and best of such studies and Professor W. W. Lawrence, through a modification of the same method, has explained many of the puzzling parts of Shakespeare's tragi-comedies in his *Shakespeare's Problem Comedies* (1931).

In these various ways, contemporary criticism of Shakespeare has shown its relation to the scientific and critical temper of our age. Yet the most significant fact that emerges from the work of these critics, regarded as a unit, is that their essentially realistic scrutiny has established with a new security Shakespeare's supremacy as a poet and a dramatist.

GLOSSARY [1]

IN THIS Glossary no word is defined that does not occur at least five times in the text of Shakespeare, but, of course, not every meaning here given occurs so often. The reader will remember that in a great many instances these words had in the time of Shakespeare their modern meanings, while also bearing Elizabethan meanings now obsolete. Only the Elizabethan meanings are here given. In some instances, when a noun and the corresponding verb agree closely in their meanings, only one form is inserted in the list. I must acknowledge the usual debt to Schmidt's *Lexicon* and the *New English Dictionary,* and I have derived assistance from consulting the Glossary appended to Neilsen's edition of Shakespeare in the Cambridge series. —W. D. B.

A, reduced form of of, on, in.

'A, he.

ABATE, blunt; deduct, curtail, deprive.

ABHOR, reject; horrify.

ABLE, vigorous; competent; sufficient.

ABOUT, intent on; circuitously, round about. Go about, have in hand, prepare to do.

ABSOLUTE, positive, certain; highly accomplished; faultless.

ABUSE, use wrongly or badly, ill-use; offend; disgrace; corrupt; deceive.

ACCOMPLISH, equip; obtain.

ADDITION, title, denomination.

ADDRESS, direct; prepare, make ready.

[1] Perhaps it is fair to add that while this book was left by the author in a state all but complete, acknowledgment is due especially to Professor William Dinsmore Briggs, of Leland Stanford University, who has generously prepared the glossary in accordance with Doctor Alden's original design.

ADHERE, agree, suit.

ADMIRATION, wonder, astonishment.

ADMIRE, wonder at, feel both wonder and delight.

ADMIT, allow, permit; choose.

ADVANCE, lift; show.

ADVERTISE, inform; counsel.

ADVICE, consideration, reflection.

ADVISE, persuade; inform; consider.

AFFECT, like, love; purpose, aim at; imitate.

AFFECTED, disposed, inclined.

AFFECTION, disposition, inclination; emotion, passion; love; affectation.

AGAINST, toward, before, in front of; shortly before; in preparaton for or expectation of.

AIM, guess, conjecture.

ALLOW, approve; license; acknowledge.

ALONG, at one's length.

AN, if; whether.

ANCIENT, ensign; standard.

AND, see an.

ANGEL, a gold coin with the figure of an angel stamped on it (worth ten shillings).

ANNOY, pain, grief; injury.

ANON, immediately; also used as correlative with sometimes, now.

ANSWER, *sb.*, account; retaliation; *vb.*, render account; reply to a summons; correspond; atone for.

ANTIC, *adj.*, antique, ancient; fantastic, foolish; *sb.*, buffoon.

APPEAL, impeach.

APPELLANT, accuser.

APPLIANCE, cure; applied remedy.

APPLY, explain the application of; devote.

APPOINT, fix, determine; equip.

APPREHENSION, imagination; faculty of perception.

APPROBATION, proof.

APPROVE, try, experience; prove; confirm, justify; commend.

ARGOSY, a large merchant vessel.

ARGUMENT, matter, subject-matter, theme; cause, reason.

ARTICLE, clause, item.

ARTIFICIAL, produced by art, artful (not necessarily in a bad sense).

ASSOCIATE, accompany.

ASSURE, persuade, convince.

ASSURED, affianced.

ATONE, reconcile; agree.

ATTACH, seize; arrest.

ATTAINT, disgrace, stain.

ATTRIBUTE, reputation.

AVOID, get rid of; leave, withdraw.

AWFUL, filled with awe.

BAN, curse.

BANDY, beat to and fro; contend, fight.

BANE, poison; destruction.

BANQUET, dessert.

BASE, *sb.*, a rustic game; *adj.*, low. Base court, lower courtyard.

BASILISK, a fabulous, serpent-like creature, whose look was fatal; a cannon.

BASTARD, a sweet wine from Spain.

BAT, a thick stick, club.

BATE, weaken; abate; flutter.

BATTLE, an army ready for battle; a division of an army.

BAUBLE, short staff carried by a fool as one of the signs of his office.

BEAR, administer, manage; possess, own; carry away, win. Bear hard, dislike. Bear in hand, deceive, give fair words.

BEAVER, helmet, visor of a helmet.

BEDLAM, *sb.*, lunatic; madhouse; *adj.*, mad.

BEING, manner of life; residence.

BELIE, misrepresent, slander.

BEND, direct, turn.

BENT, tension; inclination; look.

BESHREW, curse (always in a mild, often in a playful sense).

BESPEAK, speak to, address; order, engage.

BEWRAY, reveal, discover.

BIAS, irregularity in the construction of a bowl, such that it does not run true; tendency; prejudice.

BIDE, endure.

BILL, a kind of pike; note, written notice; list.

BLACK, dark-complexioned.

BLANK, *sb.*, the white mark in the centre of a target; *vb.*, make pale.

BLENCH, start, be inconstant.

BLOW, bloom.

BOARD, accost, woo.

BONNY, pretty, handsome; big.

BOOT, booty; profit.

BOURN, boundary; brook.

BRACH, female dog.

BRAINSICK, mad.

BRAKE, thicket.

BRAVE, *adj.*, fine, splendid; *vb.*, defy, threaten.

BRAVERY, splendour, finery; bravado, ostentatious valour.

BRAWN, a mass of flesh; muscle (of the arm).

BREATHE, take exercise.

BREATHED, having good wind (as an athlete).

BRIEF, note, letter; abstract, summary.

BROACH, transfix; begin.

BROOCH, jewel, ornament.

BUCKLE, join in close fight.

BUCKLER, shield, defend.

BUG, bugbear.

BULK, body.

BULLY, an epithet of coarse, half-humourous praise.

CAGE, prison.

CAN, be able, be skilled in.

CAN, see gin.

CANARY, a sweet wine, a lively dance.

CANKER, a worm that eats blossoms; a corrosive evil; the dog-rose.

CAPABLE, capacious; able, gifted; susceptible.

CARBONADO, meat cut across for broiling.

CAREER, a gallop at high speed.

CARRIAGE, load; behaviour; management; import.

CASE, *sb.*, that which encloses, box, sheath; body; pair or set; *vb.*, mask; surround, cover; flay.

CAST, dismiss; discard; vomit; compute; inspect.

CEASE, cease to be.

CENSURE, *sb.*, opinion; judgment; *vb.*, judge; sentence.

CHANNEL, gutter.

CHAPS, jaws; wrinkles.

CHARACTER, *sb.*, writing; letter used in writing; handwriting; *vb.*, write.

CHARGE, load; weight; expense.

CHOUGH, jackdaw.

CIRCUMSTANCE, accident; detail; superfluous phrases; ceremony.

CITE, urge, incite; mention, recount.

CLAP, begin briskly.

CLIMATE, region.

CLIP, embrace, surround.

CLOSE, *sb.*, union, harmony; *adj.*, secret; *adv.*, secretly; *vb.*, join; enclose; come to agreement.

CLOUT, piece of cloth, centre of the target.

COAST, sail along the coast; advance hesitatingly.

COCK, corruption of God.

COG, cheat.

COIL, turmoil, confusion.

COLLECT, infer.

COLLECTION, inference.

COLOUR, pretence, excuse; standard.

COME OFF, get off, escape; acquit one's self; pay.

COMFORT, consolation; encouragement; joy.
COMFORTABLE, serviceable, benevolent; consoling.
COMMEND, commit, deliver.
COMMENT, to discourse, reason.
COMMODITY, convenience; profit, advantage; merchandize; parcel.
COMPACT, composed of.
COMPANION, fellow.
COMPASS, make circular; obtain; accomplish.
COMPETITOR, associate.
COMPLEMENT, outward show, ceremony; courtesy.
COMPLEXION, temperament, disposition; appearance, look.
COMPLICE, accomplice, confederate.
COMPT, account; reckoning.
CON, learn by heart. Con thanks, be thankful.
CONCEIT, *sb.*, imagination, thought; conception, idea; fanciful idea; *vb.*, be of importance, interest, import.
CONCLUSION, experiment.
CONDITION, contract; rank; quality; character.
CONFOUND, destroy, waste.
CONSCIENCE, consciousness, thought.
CONSIDER, pay.
CONSIST, insist.
CONSORT, company.
CONTAGIOUS, poisonous; pernicious.
CONTENT, happiness.
CONTINENT, *sb.*, that which contains or encloses; summary, abstract; *adj.*, restraining.
CONTRIVE, plan, plot.
CONVERSATION, intercourse; address, behaviour.
CONVEY, carry away secretly; do secretly; steal.
CONVEYANCE, grant, deed; trickery.
CONVINCE, prove; prove guilty; overcome.
COPE, meet, encounter.
COPY, original; example; lease, tenure.
CORPORAL, corporeal.
COSTARD, an apple; the head.
COUNTENANCE, self-assurance; appearance; authority; favor.
COUNTER, in the wrong direction.
COURTSHIP, civility, politeness.
COUSIN, relation.
COVER, lay the cloth, set the table.
COZ, cousin (*q.v.*).
COZEN, cheat, deceive.
CRACK, boast.
CROSS, a coin stamped with a

cross; *vb.*, thwart, hinder; contradict.

CRY, pack, troop; report.

CURIOSITY, exactness; fastidiousness.

CURIOUS, exact, fastidious, scrupulous; elegant; elaborate.

DANGER, power. In your danger, bound to you by a penalty.

DASH, dash to pieces, shatter.

DEAR, heartfelt; earnest; inmost.

DEEM, judge, estimate.

DEFEAT, destroy; disfigure.

DEFENCE, armament, arms; readiness for combat; skill in fencing.

DEFEND, forbid.

DEFORMED, deforming.

DELICATE, delightful, delicious; ingenious.

DELIGHTED, delightful.

DEPART, part.

DEPEND, lean; serve, attend; impend.

DEPRIVE, take away.

DEPUTATION, office of a substitute.

DESIGN, enterprise.

DESPISED, despicable.

DETECT, discover, reveal.

DETERMINE, limit; put an end to; come to an end.

DEVOTE, consecrate.

DEXTERITY, nimbleness, speed.

DIFFERENCE, a mark of distinction in heraldry; quarrel, contention.

DIRECTLY, exactly; without ambiguity, plainly, clearly.

DISCHARGE, perform.

DISCOURSE, reasoning, thought.

DISCOVER, recognize; show, reveal.

DISEASE, vexation, cause of uneasiness, trouble.

DISHONEST, dishonourable; unchaste.

DISLIKE, *sb.*, dissension; *vb.*, disapprove; displease.

DISPATCH, finish, wind up.

DISPOSE, disposal, disposition.

DISPUTE, discuss.

DISTANCE, hostility; reserve.

DISTASTE, be distasteful; make distasteful; embitter; dislike, loathe.

DISTEMPER, disturb, put out of temper, derange bodily or mentally.

DISTINCTLY, separately.

DISTRACT, divide.

DIVISION, variation, modulation.

DOGGED, cruel, malicious.

DOIT, a small coin, value half a farthing; trifle.

DOLE, sorrow.

DOOM, judgment.

DOUBT, apprehension, suspicion, fear.

DRAUGHT, privy.

DRAW, assemble, levy; withdraw; track.

DRAWER, waiter.

DRESS, put in order, prepare.

DRY, thirsty; stupid.

DUMP, melancholy; a melancholy tune.

DURANCE, imprisonment.

EAGER, sour, bitter, biting.

EAR, to plough.

EASY, slight.

ECSTASY, extreme excitement *or* passion; madness.

EFFECT, manifestation, sign, token; meaning, import.

ELEMENT, sky; one of the four elements.

EMBOSSED, swollen; foaming at the mouth.

EMPERY, empire.

ENCOUNTER, behaviour.

END, scrap of quotation.

ENDEARED, bound.

ENFORCE, urge, ply hard; demand; insist upon.

ENGAGE, pledge, enlist, bind; give as a pledge or hostage.

ENGINE, contrivance, device; instrument, implement.

ENGROSS, fatten; amass; take wholesale, take wholly, entirely.

ENLARGE, give scope to, set at liberty.

ENLARGEMENT, release, liberty.

ENTERTAIN, treat; receive; take into service; harbor, feel.

ENTITLED, having a title or claim.

ENTREAT, prevail by solicitation; invite; treat.

ENVIOUS, malicious, mischievous.

ENVY, malice, hatred.

EPITHET, phrase.

EQUAL, just, impartial.

ERR, stray, wander, roam.

ESCAPE, sally (of wit); transgression.

ESTATE, *sb.*, situation, state; affairs; rank; *vb.*, bestow, settle on.

ESTIMATE, estimation, value.

ESTIMATION, value, worth; esteem; conjecture.

EVIL, disease. King's evil, scrofula.

EXCEED, to be surpassing.

EXCEPT, object to, protest against; make an exception or reservation.

EXCLAIM, outcry.

EXCREMENT, hair, beard.

EXEMPT, far from, remote.

EXHIBITION, allowance, pension.

EXPECT, await.

EXPEDIENT, quick.

EXPENSE, spending; loss.

EXPOSTULATE, discuss; converse.

EXPRESS, exact; explicit; expressive.

EXTEND, increase; show; use; seize upon.

EXTENUATE, mitigate; undervalue.

EYE, tinge; presence.

EYNE, eyes.

FACE, brazen out; brave, bully; trim.

FACT, deed; crime.

FACTIOUS, taking sides.

FACTOR, agent.

FACULTY, power; essential quality.

FAIL, failure; deficiency; offence.

FAIN, glad; obliged.

FAIR, beauty; a beautiful person.

FALL, *sb.*, ebb; cadence; *vb.*, bring forth, be brought forth; begin; come, become; let fall; befall.

FAME, *sb.*, rumour, report; *vb.*, to make famous.

FAMILIAR, particular friend; attendant spirit.

FANCY, love; song .

FANTASTIC, imaginary; prodigious.

FANTASTICAL, fantastic; imaginary; imaginative.

FANTASY, love.

FARDEL, bundle, pack.

FAVOUR, aspect, feature; attraction, charm; present, love-token.

FEAR, *sb.*, object of fear; *vb*., frighten; fear for.

FEARFUL, causing fear, dreadful.

FEATURE, shape, form of body; general appearance.

FEE, reward, recompense. In fee, in full ownership.

FEEDER, servant, parasite.

FELLOW, comrade; equal.

FICO (fig, figo), a gesture of contempt.

FIGURE, idea, imagination.

FILE, *sb.*, list; number; *vb.*, polish; defile.

FIND, detect, discover.

FINE, sb., end, conclusion; money paid by tenant to owner of land for permission to alienate or transfer title; *vb.*, fix as the sum to be paid; refine.

FIT, ready, prepared.

FLAW, gust of wind, of passion.

FLEET, pass rapidly; float.

FLOWER-DE-LUCE, fleur-de-lis.

FOIL, *sb.*, defeat; that which serves by contrast or background to give lustre to another thing; *vb.*, mar.

FOISON, plenty, abundance.

FOLLY, wantonness.
FOND, foolish; slight, trivial.
FOOL, a term of endearment.
FOOT, kick.
FORCE, *sb.*, validity; of force, of necessity; *vb.*, reinforce; violate; urge; care for; stuff.
FORDO, destroy, undo; exhaust.
FORFEND, forbid.
FORLORN, lost; abandoned, outcast; meagre.
FORMAL, ordinary.
FOUL, ugly; wicked.
FRAME, *sb.*, form; contrivance; *vb.*, beget; devise, plan; manage; fashion.
FRANK, liberal.
FRAUGHT, load.
FREE, voluntary; unreserved; generous; noble; innocent; sound, happy.
FRENCH CROWN, baldness resulting from venereal disease.
FRESH, brisk, lively; youthful; refreshing.
FRET, eat away; variegate.
FROM, away from; differing from, opposed to.
FRUITFUL, plentiful, copious; liberal, bountiful.

GAGE, pledge; engage, bind.
GAIT, way; proceeding.
GALL, wear away; injure, annoy; scoff.
GAMESTER, a merry fellow; a prostitute.
GAN, see gin.
GAWD, bauble, pleasing trifle.
GEAR, stuff; affair, business.
GENERAL, *sb.*, the whole, total; the people; *adj.*, common, public.
GENERATION, offspring; race.
GENEROUS, of noble birth.
GENIUS, good or evil spirit supposed to direct men's actions.
GENTLE, *sb.*, person of good birth; *adj.*, of good birth; lovely, amiable.
GENTLEMAN, a man of good birth (not necessarily of noble rank).
GENTRY, rank by inheritance; courtesy.
GERMAN, germane, akin.
GILD, to make red.
GIN (pret. can, gan), begin.
GIVE, call, ascribe, represent; to show as a part of a coat-of-arms. Give out, surrender; declare, report, make public.
GLANCE, hint.
GLOZE, interpret, comment; flatter, talk idly.
GOOD, often used as an intensive.
GOOD-YEAR, used in exclamations or curses. What the good-year, what the pox!

GORGE, throat, stomach.

GOSSIP, *sb.*, sponsor at baptism; a talkative woman of the lower class, fond of drinking with her neighbours; *vb.*, to be sponsor at baptism; to make merry at a feast.

GOVERNMENT, self-control.

GRACEFUL, favourable; virtuous.

GRACIOUS, finding favour; virtuous, holy; fortunate; attractive, beautiful. Used often in addressing persons of high rank.

GRAFF, graft.

GRAMERCY, great thanks.

GRATIFY, requite, reward.

GRAVE, bury; engrave.

GROAT, a coin worth fourpence.

GROSS, palpable, easily discerned.

GROW, accrue.

GUARDS, trimmings, ornaments.

GULF, whirlpool; gullet.

GULL, *sb.*, dupe; trick, deception; *vb.*, trick, impose on.

GYVE, fetter.

HABIT, carriage, behaviour; dress.

HANGMAN, executioner.

HAPPILY, perhaps, haply.

HARDNESS, hardship.

HARLOT, a lewd person (irrespective of sex).

HATCH, a half door.

HATEFUL, full of hate, malignant.

HAVE, used with prepositions and adverbs (*e.g.*, have at) in the sense of "I'll do," "Let us do," whatever the sense of the second element suggests.

HAVING, property, possessions; quality.

'HAVIOUR, behaviour.

HAZARD, a winning opening in the wall of a court in which court-tennis is played; a game of dice.

HEALTH, welfare, prosperity.

HEAP, crowd, throng.

HEAVINESS, sorrow, drowsiness.

HEDGE, skulk, go aside from the direct way.

HENCE, henceforth.

HEST, command.

HILDING, base person, menial.

HIND, peasant, farm-labourer, menial.

HINT, occasion.

HISTORY, play; play based on history.

HIT, agree with.

HITHERTO, so far, up to this point.

HOBBY-HORSE, one of the characters in the morris-dance; a loose or foolish person.

HOLD, preserve, maintain, carry on; take; think, consider,

estimate; endure; refrain; prove true.

HOLP, helped.

HOME, to the quick, to the extreme point; effectively, completely.

HONEST, decent; respectable, honourable; chaste.

HONESTY, decency; honourableness; chastity.

HOODWINK, blindfold.

HOPE, expect.

HORN, symbol of a cuckold.

HOSE, breeches; long stockings.

HUMOUROUS, moist; capricious, whimsical.

HUMOUR, *sb.*, moisture; caprice, whim; character; trait; *vb.*, please or gain over by falling in with one's humour.

HUSBAND, *sb.*, housekeeper; husbandman; *vb.*, use with economy, manage.

HUSBANDRY, economy; care, careful management.

I, ay.

IDLE, vain, useless; frivolous, absurd, foolish.

'IELD, yield.

I'FECKS, in faith.

IGNORANT, dull, silly.

'ILD, yield.

IMAGINARY, imaginative.

IMPART, offer, give.

IMPEACH, expose to reproach.

IMPERIOUS, imperial.

IMPORTANCE, import; matter; importunity.

IMPORTANT, pressing; importunate.

IMPOSITION, order, command.

IMPRESS, press (into military service), enlist.

IMPUTATION, reputation.

IN, on; into; by means of, by; to, for.

INCAPABLE, not able to contain; not susceptible.

INCISION, blood-letting.

INDEX, table of contents, prologue, introduction.

INDIFFERENT, impartial; ordinary, not striking in any way; somewhat, tolerably.

INDIFFERENTLY, somewhat, tolerably.

INDIRECT, wrong, unjust.

INDUE, endow, fit.

INFER, allege, prove.

INGENIOUS, keenly sensitive; intellectual.

INGENUOUS, ingenious (*q.v.*).

INHERIT, possess; put in possession.

INHERITOR, possessor, owner.

INJURIOUS, insulting.

INJURY, injustice; insult.

INLAND, well-bred.

INNOCENT, simpleton, idiot.

INSINUATE, ingratiate oneself.

INSTANCE, cause, motive; proof, example; proverb, maxim.

INSULT, exult.

INTELLIGENCE, communication.

INTELLIGENT, bearing intelligence, giving information.

INTEND, tend; direct; mean; pretend.

INTO, unto, to.

INWARD, confidential.

ISSUED, descended.

IT, its.

JACK, a term of contempt, knave, rascal; a figure striking the bell in old clocks; the object-bowl in the game of bowls; the key of a virginal; a small drinking vessel.

JACK-AN-APES, monkey.

JAR, discord, quarrel.

JAY, loose woman.

JERKIN, short coat, jacket.

JET, walk proudly, strut; encroach.

JIG, a merry song, or the accompanying dance.

JOY, gladden; enjoy.

JUMP, *vb.*, agrees; hazard; *adv.*, exactly.

JUVENAL, a youth.

KEEP, guard; maintain; inhabit, dwell, remain; restrain.

KEN, *sb.*, sight, view; *vb.*, descry; know.

KERN, a light-armed Irish foot-soldier.

KIND, *sb.*, nature; *adj.*, natural, not degenerate.

KINDLE, incite; bring forth.

KINDLY, natural, suitable, seasonable.

KNAVE, boy, lad; servant.

KNOLL, ring, knell.

KNOT, company; garden-plot.

LACE, adorn.

LAP, wrap.

LARD, fatten; garnish.

LARGE, unrestrained; licentious.

LATE, *adj.*, recent; *adv.*, recently; once.

LAVISH, profuse, unrestrained, licentious.

LAY, waylay; plan.

LEADING, command; generalship.

LEAVE, cease; abandon.

LAG, bow, obeisance.

LET, hinder; cause.

LETHE, oblivion.

LEVEL, *sb.*, range, aim; *adj.*, straight; *vb.*, aim; guess; be equal.

LEWD, vile, base.

LIABLE, fit; subject.

LIBERAL, frank; licentious; accomplished; tasteful.

LIBERTY, license; licentiousness.

LIE, to be confined; dwell, lodge.

LIEF, dear.

LIGHT, merry, cheerful; frivolous, wanton.

LIGHTLY, easily, readily; usually.

LIKE, compare, liken; please. Like well, thrive.

LIKELIHOOD, sign, indication.

LIME, *sb.*, bird-lime; *vb.*, smear with bird-lime; catch with bird-lime; put lime into liquor; cement.

LIMIT, *sb.*, fixed time; district; *vb.*, appoint.

LINE, draw, paint; strengthen.

LINEAL, hereditary.

LIST, *sb.*, boundary; barrier; desire; *vb.*, desire; please; listen.

LIVELY, living; life-like; in a life-like manner, vividly.

LIVERY, the delivery of a freehold into the possession of the heir.

LIVING, life; property, income.

LODGE, *sb.*, a small house in a forest or park; *vb.*, beat down.

LONG, belong.

LOOK, seek for, search out.

LOSE, forget; cause to be lost, ruin.

LOSS, failure, ruin; desertion.

LOVER, friend; mistress, loved one.

LUXURIOUS, lustful.

LUXURY, lust, lechery.

MAIN, main point; mainland; stake in gaming.

MAKE, fasten; gather, assemble; enrich; consider as; do; move, go.

MAN, tame; furnish with a servant.

MANAGE, training (of a horse); administration, direction.

MARGENT, margin.

MARK, thirteen shillings and fourpence.

MARRY, an exclamation corrupted from by Mary (the Virgin).

MART, *sb.*, market-place; bargain; *vb.*, traffic, self.

MARTYR, maltreat, torture.

MATCH, appointment; agreement.

MATE, *sb.*, fellow; *vb.*, marry; match; confound, disable.

MATERIAL, sensible; important.

MATTER, subject-matter, meaning, contents; ground for complaint; importance.

MAW, stomach.

MEAN, that which is between; means; a middle or intermediate part in a harmonized composition, tenor.

MEASURE; a dance; a stately dance; the music accompanying a dance.

MEDICINABLE, medicinal.

MEDICINE, physician; *vb.*, cure.

MEED, merit, worth.

MEMORY, memorial.

MERCHANT, merchant ship; fellow.

MERE, unqualified, absolute.

MERELY, absolutely, entirely.

MERIT, reward.

MESS, a small quantity; a set of four persons.

MEW, confine, shut up.

MICKLE, great.

MINCE, walk, speak, or act affectedly; affect, make a show of.

MIND, attend to, care for; remind; intend.

MINION, favourite, darling; saucy person.

MISERABLE, worthless.

MISPRISION, mistake; contempt.

MISPRIZE, undervalue.

MISS, be without; be wanting, deficient.

MISTAKEN, misjudge.

MISUSE, revile; deceive.

MODEL, copy.

MODERN, commonplace, trite.

MODEST, moderate, sober.

MODESTY, moderation; decency, propriety.

MOE, more.

MOIETY, half; portion.

MOOD, grief, anger; expression.

MORAL, *sb.*, hidden meaning; *adj.*, moralizing; *vb.*, moralize.

MORTAL, deadly.

MORTIFIED, insensible; ascetic.

MOTION, motive; impulse; proposal; sense, perception; a puppet; a puppet-show.

MOTIVE, cause; instrument; agent.

MOTLEY, particolored dress of a jester; fool.

MOVE, incite, impel; make angry; influence, touch; excite, rouse; address oneself to; suggest to, urge.

MUSE, wonder.

MYSTERY, calling, trade; professional skill.

NAPKIN, handkerchief.

NATIVE, natural; hereditary, resulting from birth.

NATURAL, idiot.

NAUGHT, worthless, wicked; lost, ruined.

NAUGHTY, wicked.

NEAR, nearer.

NEEDFUL, important.

NEEDLESS, groundless; having no need.

NEPHEW, cousin; grandchild.

NERVE, sinew.

NEXT, nearest.

NICE, fine; delicate; precise; scrupulous; subtle; prudish, coy; trifling.

NOBLE, a gold coin worth six shillings and eightpence.

NOISE, music; a band of musicians.

NOT, not only.

NOTE, list; stigma; distinction, eminence; observation; information, knowledge; remark.

NUNCLE, uncle.

OBSEQUIOUS, zealous in mourning for the dead.

OBSERVANCE, observation; observance of rule or ceremony; homage.

OBSERVE, do homage; show respect.

OCCUPATION, trade.

ODDS, quarrel, discord.

O'ERLOOK, peruse; despise; bewitch.

O'ERRAUGHT, see o'erreach.

O'ERREACH, overtake; trick, cheat.

OF, from; by; during; in; on

OFFER, try, attempt; attack.

OFFICE, duty; function; act of good will; act of worship.

OFFICIOUS, busy, ready to do service.

OLD, plentiful; great.

ON, of.

ONCE, once for all; sometime.

OPINION, reputation; arrogance.

OPPOSITE, *sb.*, adversary; *adj.*, hostile, adverse.

OPPRESSION, affliction.

OR, before.

ORB, circle, orbit; the earth.

ORDER, arrangement, measure. Take order, take measures.

ORDINARY, meal at a restaurant, *table d'hôte* (where all pay alike.)

ORT, leaving, scrap, refuse.

OSTENT, external show.

OSTENTATION, spectacle.

OUT, from, out of; at an end, finished; fully; on the wrong scent; at a loss; ragged; abroad; in field.

OUTRAGE, outbreak of rage.

OVERTURE, disclosure.

OWE, own, possess.

PACE, train (a horse).

PACK, *sb.*, conspiracy; *vb.*, go in a hurry.

PAIN, punishment, penalty.

PARCEL, part, piece, item; party.

PARDON, excuse.

PARLE, parley, conference.

PARLOUS, perilous (used intensively).

PART, depart, go from.

PARTAKE, impart.

PARTICULAR, *sb.*, single person; private concern or business; *adj.*, private, personal.

PARTISAN, a kind of halberd.

PARTY, part, side.

PASS, surpass; die; happen; state, pronounce; pronounce sentence; thrust (in fencing); care for; disregard.

PASSAGE, death; occurrence; course; action.

PASSING, surpassing; exceedingly.

PASSION, any violent emotion, suffering, sorrow, disease.

PASSIONATE, expressing great emotion; sorrowful.

PATCH, paltry fellow; fool.

PATIENCE, composure, calmness.

PATTERN, exemplar, masterpiece; copy; example.

PAUCA (*pauca verba, paucas palabris*), few words.

PAWN, pledge; stake.

PAY, punish; requite.

PEDANT, schoolmaster.

PEER, appear; let appear.

PEEVISH, childish, silly; wayward, fretful.

PELTING, paltry.

PENITENT, doing penance.

PERDY, by God.

PEREMPTORY, bold, imperious.

PERFECT, *adj.*, well informed in; well-prepared, letter-perfect; *vb.*, instruct fully.

PERFORCE (force perforce), by force; of necessity.

PERIOD, limit, end.

PERPEND, consider.

PERPLEX, bewilder.

PERSEVER, persevere.

PERSUADE, advise; strive to persuade.

PICKED, refined.

PITCH, height.

PLACE, station in life; residence; room.

PLAIN, make plain; complain.

PLEACHED, interwoven.

POINT, a tagged lace; state, situation; trumpet-blast. At point, fully prepared.

POISE, weight.

POLICY, statesmanship; prudent management; cunning, stratagem.

POPULAR, vulgar.

PORPENTINE, porcupine.

PORT, bearing.

POSSESS, give possession of; inform.

POWDER, to salt.

PRACTICE, skill; artifice, stratagem, plot.

PRACTISE, contrive, plot.

PRAISE, appraise.

PRECEDENT, *sb.*, original copy; presage, sign; *adj.*, former.

PRECEPT, command; summons.

PREFER, present; recommend; promote.

PREGNANT, clever; ready; clear, evident.

PRESENCE, company; person; presence-chamber.

PRESENT, *sb.*, present time, present occasion; *vb.*, represent; accuse.

PRESENTLY, immediately.

PRESS, force into military service.

PRETENCE, purpose.

PRETEND, intend; allege as a pretext.

PREVENT, anticipate.

PRICK, *sb.*, prickle; *vb.*, mark.

PRIME, *sb.*, spring; *adj.*, first, chief.

PRINT (in print), to the letter, accurately; above criticism, faultless.

PRIVATE, privacy.

PRIZE, *sb.*, contest for a prize; privilege; estimation; *vb.*, estimate.

PROBATION, proof; test, trial.

PROCURE, bring about, cause.

PROGENY, ancestry.

PROGRESS, a king's journey through his dominions.

PROOF, *sb.*, state of having stood the test; experience, something learned from experience; *adj.*, impenetrable.

PROPER, peculiar, one's own; respectable; pretty, handsome.

PROPERTY, *sb.*, implement, tool; individuality, particular quality; *vb.*, to make a tool of, use.

PROPORTION, estimated number or amount; portion.

PROPOSE, imagine; converse.

PROTEST, declare, proclaim.

PROVISION, things provided; preparation; foresight.

PROVOKE, call forth, rouse; impel, instigate.

PURCHASE, *sb.*, acquisition, thing acquired, gain; *vb.*, acquire.

QUAIL, overpower; slacken.

QUAINT, ingenious; neat, fine.

QUALIFY, moderate, abate.

QUALITY, profession; rank; cause.

QUARREL, cause or occasion of dispute.

QUARTER, place where soldiers are lodged; concord.

QUEST, inquest.

QUESTION, *sb.*, subject of debate; discussion, conversation; *vb.*, consider; discuss, converse.

QUICK, alive; lively; fresh.

QUICKEN, make alive; become alive; refresh.

QUILLET, subtlety, quibble.

QUIT, set free, acquit, remit; requite.

QUITTANCE, discharge; requital.

QUOTE, observe; interpret.

RACE, root; breed; disposition.

RACK, to strain.

RAGGED, beggarly; rugged, rough.

RANGE; be arranged in order, be ranked; roam.

RANK, *sb.*, row, line; *adj.*, strong, luxuriant, exuberant; lustful; foul, gross; strong-smelling.

RAP, transport, enrapture.

RASCAL, *sb.*, base, worthless person; a deer not in fit condition; *adj.*, base, good for nothing.

RASH, quick, sudden.

RATE, *sb.*, estimate; *vb.*, estimate, value; scold.

RAUGHT, *pret.* of reach.

RAZE, strike; erase, blot out.

REASON, *sb.*, discourse, conversation; *vb.*, argue, discuss, converse.

RECEIPT, thing received; capacity; reception; receptacle.

RECEIVE, believe, understand; perceive.

RECORD, *sb.*, memory; memorial; *vb.*, sing.

RECOVER, get, gain.

REDEMPTION, ransom.

REFERENCE, assignment; appeal.

REFUSE, disown.

REGARD, look; view; consideration, respect.

REGION, sky, air.

REGREET, greet; greet again.

REHEARSE, recite.

RELATION, account, narrative.

RELISH, flavour.

REMAIN, stay, dwell.

REMEMBER, mention; remind.

REMORSE, pity.

REMOVED, retired; remote.

RENDER, *sb.*, account; *vb.*, report, state, describe.

RENT, rend.

REPAIR, *sb.*, restoration; a resorting, a coming; *vb.*, come, go.

REPEAL, recall.

REPROOF, refutation, contradiction.

REPROVE, disprove.

REQUIRE, ask.

RESERVE, guard, preserve.

RESOLVE, dissolve; solve; free from doubt; satisfy, inform.

RESPECT, *sb.*, deliberation, reflection, consideration; esteem; respectability; *vb.*, consider; regard.

REST, *sb.*, to set up one's rest, to be resolved; *vb.*, remain; arrest.

RESTRAIN, . withhold; draw tight.

RETIRE, retreat.

REVOLT, desert, go over to the enemy; be faithless.

RHEUM, catarrh; humid matter secreted from the eyes, mouth, or nose.

RID, destroy.
RIVAL, associate.
RIVE, split, burst.
ROAD, roadstead, port; inroad; journey.
ROUND, *sb.*, circle; dance in a circle; *adj.*, plain, plain-spoken, direct; *vb.*, surround; whisper.
ROUNDLY, without ceremony, directly.
ROUSE, a full draught; carouse.
ROUT, mob; brawl.
ROYAL, a gold coin worth ten shillings.
RUB, impediment.

SACK, a general name for white wines from Spain and the Canaries.
SACRED, consecrated.
SAD, grave, serious, sober.
SAFETY, custody.
SALLET, salad; a close-fitting headpiece.
SALT, bitter; lecherous.
SANS, without.
SAUCY, wanton.
SAVAGE, unpolished, rude.
SAW, saying, maxim.
'SBLOOD, God's blood
SCANDAL, defame, slander.
SCANT, limit; give sparingly.
SCAPE, *sb.*, escape; impropriety; escapade; *vb.*, escape.
SCONCE, fortification; the head.
SCORN, scoff, laugh at.
SEARCH, probe.
SEASON, *sb.*, seasoning; *vb.*, temper, qualify; mature, ripen.
SECT, faction; class; scion; sex.
SECURE, *adj.*, careless, confident; *vb.*, to make careless.
SECURELY, carelessly.
SECURITY, carelessness, confidence.
SEEMING, appearance; hypocrisy.
SE'NNIGHT, a week.
SENSE, perception; sensual feeling; mental power, mind.
SENSIBLE, perceiving, feeling; perceptible.
SEQUENT, successive.
SERGEANT, a sheriff's officer.
SET, stake; estimate, value.
SEVERAL, separate, particular; private.
SHADOW, shade; shady place; shelter.
SHENT, reproached, blamed.
SHIELD, forbid.
SHREWD, mischievous; wicked; artful, sly.
SHREWDLY, often used intensively.
SHRIFT, confession and absolution.
SHRIVE, confess and absolve.
SIEGE, seat; rank; stool.

SIGN, mark, set a sign on.

SILLY, harmless, innocent; plain, simple.

SIMPLE, *sb.*, an ingredient in a medicine; medicinal herb; *adj.*, ordinary, common; plain, unaffected; sincere.

SIMPLICITY, folly.

SINCE, when.

SINEW, nerve.

SIR, lord; gentleman; the title was regularly given to priests.

SITH, since.

SLACK, neglect, be remiss.

SLANDER, disgrace.

SLANDEROUS, disgraceful.

SLIP, *sb.*, leash; counterfeit coin; *vb.*, to loose from the leash.

SMOOTH, palliate; flatter.

SNUFF, resentment. To take in snuff, to take offence.

SOLACE, amuse; be happy.

SOLICIT, incite, rouse, prompt.

SOMETIME, from time to time; sometimes.

SOMETIMES, formerly.

SOOTH, truth.

SORE, grievous, heavy.

SORRY, sad; dismal.

SORT, *sb.* class, company; rank, quality; manner; *vb.*, choose; fall out, happen; befit; make fit, adapt; dispose; consort.

SOT, fool, dolt.

SPED, undone, done for.

SPEED, *sb.*, success, fortune; assisting power; *vb.*, succeed; dispatch.

SPLEEN, eagerness; hate; caprice; fit of laughter, of passion.

SPOT, stain, pollute.

SPRIGHT (sprite), spirit.

SPRING, a young shoot, sprig.

SPRITELY, lively, brisk, spirited.

SQUARE, *sb.*, rule, measure; *vb.*, quarrel.

SQUIRE, square, *q.v.*

STAGGER, make to stagger; hesitate.

STAIN, *sb.*, tincture; taint of disgrace; *vb.*, darken; deface; disgrace; pervert.

STALE, *sb.*, decoy, bait; dupe, laughing-stock; prostitute; *vb.*, to make common and worthless.

STAMP, make valid (by placing a stamp on).

STAND ON OR UPON, insist on; attach value to; have pride in; concern.

STAR, pole-star.

STARVE, die; benumb; paralyze, disable.

STATE, fortune; rank; person or persons of rank and authority, prince, general, etc.; dignity; pomp; a chair of state.

STATION, mode of standing, attitude.

STATUTE, bond, mortgage.

STEAD, benefit, help.

STEALTH, clandestine practice; secret going or coming.

STILL, constant; constantly.

STING, sexual desire.

STINT, stop, cease.

STOCK, *sb.*, stocking; *vb.*, to set in the stocks.

STOMACH, appetite; inclination; anger; courage; pride.

STOOP, swoop, pounce.

STORY, *sb.*, history; *vb.*, relate.

STOUT, proud, overbearing; bold, resolute.

STRAIGHT, immediately, straightway.

STRAIN, *sb.*, impulse, feeling; tendency; disposition; stock, race; *vb.*, constrain; make an effort.

STRAIT, parsimonious; strict.

STRANGE, foreign, reserved, distant; unacquainted.

STRANGELY, distantly, in a reserved manner; extraordinarily.

STRANGENESS, reserve.

STRATAGEM, dreadful deed.

STRAY, straggler.

STRIKE, strike sail; blast.

SUBJECT, subjects.

SUBSCRIBE, become surety for, vouch for; admit, grant; yield.

SUBTLE, deceptive.

SUCCESS, succession; result, outcome, fortune.

SUDDEN, hasty, rash, violent, impetuous.

SUDDENLY, immediately.

SUFFER, to put to death; allow, not to hinder.

SUFFERANCE, pain, distress; connivance, permission.

SUGGEST, prompt, incite; tempt.

SUGGESTION, temptation.

SUIT, clothe, dress; agree, accord.

SULLEN, dismal.

SUPPOSE, supposition.

SURPRISE, seize, take prisoner.

SUSPECT, suspicion.

SWEETING, a kind of sweet apple; a term of endearment.

SWORN BROTHERS, brother-in-arms.

SWOUND, swoon.

'SWOUNDS, see Zounds.

SYMPATHIZE, be of the same disposition; correspond to; express fitly.

SYMPATHY, conformity of disposition, rank, age, etc.; equality.

TABLE, that on which something is painted or written, tablet.

TABOR, a small drum.

TAINT, discredit.

TAKE, charm; blast, bewitch, destroy; take by surprise; learn, understand; think, believe. Take in, subdue; settle; borrow; levy; scold; encounter. Take me with you, let me understand you. Take order, adopt measures.

TARTAR, Tartarus.

TASK, challenge; test; tax.

TASTE, *sb.*, test, trial, specimen; *vb.*, test.

TAX, censure, reproach.

TEEN, pain, grief.

TELL, count.

TEMPER, *sb.*, temperament; *vb.*, bring to a desired state by moisture, warmth, etc.; mould; mix, compound.

TEMPERANCE, moderation; chastity; temperature.

TEMPERATE, chaste.

TEND, attend, wait on.

TENDANCE, attendance.

TENDER, regard.

TENT, search, probe; cure.

THAN, then.

THANE, an old Scotch title, nearly equivalent to Earl.

THICK, quick; quickly.

THIS, such; thus, so.

THOUGHT, sorrow; sorrowful meditation.

THREE-PILE, the best and most costly kind of velvet; hence three-piled, of the best quality, superfine.

THRIFT, profit, gain, success.

THROUGH, thoroughly. Go through, do one's utmost; complete.

THROUGHLY, thoroughly.

THROW, cast (of dice or of a bowl).

TIDE, *sb.*, time; *vb.*, betide.

TIME, the present time, the times.

TIMELESS, untimely.

TINCT, colour; tincture.

TIRE, *sb.*, attire; head-dress; *vb.*, to attire; feed ravenously.

TO, for; compared with; in addition to.

TOP, surpass.

TOUCH, *sb.*, touchstone; affection, feeling; trait, smack; *vb.*, test, try.

TOWARD, willing; in preparation, at hand.

TOWER, soar.

TOY, *sb.*, trifle; fancy; *vb.*, dally.

TRACE, follow; walk over, pace.

TRADE, traffic; resort; business of any kind.

TRAIN, draw; entice.

TRANSLATE, transform.

TRENCH, furrow.

TRICK, *sb.*, knack; habit, custom; peculiarity, trait; toy, trifle; *vb.*, draw in outline (in heraldry).

TRIUMPH, festivity.

TROTH, truth; faith.

TROW, trust; think, believe; wonder.

TRUE, honest.

TRUNCHEON, a short staff, club; a staff of command.

TURK, the Sultan.

TURN, change, transform; return.

TYRANNOUS, cruel, inhuman, pitiless.

TYRANNY, cruelty.

UNADVISED, unintentional; rash, imprudent.

UNAVOIDED, inevitable.

UNDERTAKE, have to do with; guarantee; attempt.

UNFURNISHED, unprepared.

UNGRACIOUS, wanting grace; wicked.

UNHAPPILY, evilly.

UNHAPPY, evil, wicked; disastrous.

UNJUST, dishonest; false faithless.

UNKIND, unnatural.

UNPROVIDED, unprepared.

UP, up in arms.

USE, *sb.*, profit; interest; custom, usage; *vb.*, practise, be accustomed; have, possess.

VAIL, lower; bow.

VALIDITY, strength; value.

VANTAGE, advantage; opportunity; superiority.

VARLET, servant; knave.

VAST, a vast expanse.

VAWARD, vanguard.

VENGEANCE, harm, mischief; used often as a curse.

VIA, interjection of encouragement, forward! on!

VICE, buffoon in the morality plays.

VIE, compete in.

VILLAIN, bondman; wretch, rogue.

VIRTUE, any good or characteristic quality, as bravery, etc.; essence.

VIRTUOUS, efficacious; beneficial.

VISIT, attack, afflict.

VISITATION, visit.

VIZARD, mask.

VOICE, vote.

VOID, emit; quit.

VULGAR, *sb.*, the common people; the vernacular; *adj.*, common, ordinary; public.

WAFT, beckon; turn; carry over the sea.

WAG, move, go.

WAGE, wager, hazard, attempt; pay; be equal to.

WANTON, *sb.*, effeminate person; *adj.*, sportive; loose,

frivolous; luxuriant; lustful; *vb.*, dally.

WANTONNESS, sportiveness; lasciviousness.

WARD, guard; custody; bolt; prison-cell.

WARDER, truncheon (*q.v.*).

WARN, summon.

WATCH, *sb.*, any means by which intervals of time are measured; one or more persons on guard as sentinels; *vb.*, to be awake.

WEALTH, welfare.

WEAR, *sb.*, fashion; *vb.*, use up, wear away; weary.

WEIRD, fatal, belonging to the fates.

WHEN!, exclamation of impatience.

WHENAS, when.

WHERE, whereas; wherever; whence.

WHEREAS, where.

WHILE, till.

WHILES, while.

WHORESON, bastard; frequently used as a vague epithet of contempt (or even affection).

WIDE, far from the mark, astray.

WIGHT, person.

WILD, rash.

WILL, pleasure; sexual impulse.

WISH, ask; recommend.

WIT, mind, intellectual powers; understanding, common sense; wisdom.

WITH, on; by.

WITTY, wise; cunning; clever, ingenious.

WOE, sorry.

WOOD, mad.

WORD, watchword; motto; command.

WORKING, emotion; action, activity.

WORM, any small creeping animal; snake.

WORSHIP, honour.

WOT, know.

WRACK, wreck.

WREAK, revenge.

WRETCHED, hateful.

WRING, writhe.

WRITE, subscribe; claim or assume a title.

YARE, ready, brisk.

YEARN, grieve.

YOUNG, early.

ZOUNDS, God's wounds.